THE COMEDIES OF ARISTOPHANES

VOL. 5

PEACE

edited with translation and notes by

Alan H. Sommerstein

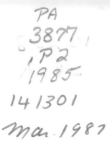

PA
3877
,P2
1985
14 /301
ma. 1987

U.K.   **ISBN 0 85668 262 4** *cloth*
             ISBN 0 85668 263 2 *limp*

U.S.A.   **ISBN 0 86516 090 2** *cloth*
             ISBN 0 86516 065 1 *limp*

Published in England by ARIS & PHILLIPS LTD, Warminster, Wiltshire.
Published in the U.S.A. by BOLCHAZY-CARDUCCI PUBLISHERS, Chicago, Il.
Printed in England by ARIS & PHILLIPS LTD, Warminster, Wilts, England.

CONTENTS

עושה שלום במרומיו הוא יעשה שלום עלינו

May He who makes peace in His heavens make peace also for us

PREFACE

Since the appearance of the last volume in this series, a new era has commenced in the study of Greek comic poetry: the publication has begun of the great collection *Poetae Comici Graeci*, edited by Rudolf Kassel and Colin Austin, who have so far given us the fragments of all the Attic comic dramatists from Aristophanes (in alphabetical order) to Crobylus, in two volumes that will be much welcomed, much admired, and much used. Every Aristophanic scholar is already much in the editors' debt.

I am once again happy to acknowledge with gratitude the assistance of those who have answered my queries and kept me acquainted with the results of their own work: among these special mention must be made, as on previous occasions, of Jeffrey Henderson and Guiseppe Mastromarco. My particular thanks are also due to Nigel Wilson, to whom I owe my information on the readings of the Holkham manuscript (L), and to Colin Austin, who saved me from at least one serious error on the subject of Aristophanes' other play of the same name. Responsibility for all remaining errors is, of course, mine.

The peace which Aristophanes hailed with such delight in 421 B.C. was to prove little better than a mirage. Our own generation in Europe is prone to forget how fortunate it has been to have been free from war for a longer period than Europe has known in all her history. May it have the wisdom to understand how that peace has been preserved, and how it may be preserved for the future.

ALAN H. SOMMERSTEIN,
Nottingham, October 1984.

REFERENCES AND ABBREVIATIONS

(A) COLLECTIONS OF FRAGMENTS

All citations of fragments of Greek authors (other than comic dramatists) made in this volume either are from one of the collections in the following list or are accompanied by the name(s) or initial(s) of the editor(s) in which case particulars will be found in list (C) below. If there is no editor designated and the author is not listed here, it may be assumed that the author is an Attic comic dramatist and the citation is from T. Kock, *Comicorum Atticorum Fragmenta* (Leipzig, 1880-8); unless otherwise stated, such references are also valid for J.M. Edmonds, *The Fragments of Attic Comedy* (Leiden, 1957-61), and in the case of Eubulus for R.L. Hunter, *Eubulus : The Fragments* (Cambridge, 1983).

Achaeus	B. Snell, *TrGF* i (Göttingen, 1971).
Aeschylus	A. Nauck, *Tragicorum Graecorum Fragmenta* ² (Leipzig, 1889) and H.J. Mette, *Die Fragmente der Tragödien des Aischylos* (Berlin, 1959).
Alcaeus	E. Lobel and D.L. Page, *Poetarum Lesbiorum Fragmenta* (Oxford, 1955).
Anacreon	D.L. Page, *Poetae Melici Graeci* (Oxford, 1962).
Archilochus	M.L. West, *Iambi et Elegi Graeci* (Oxford, 1971-2).
Aristotle	V. Rose, *Aristotelis Fragmenta* (Leipzig, 1886).
Callimachus	R.H. Pfeiffer, *Callimachus* (Oxford, 1949-53).
Euripides	Nauck (see Aeschylus).
*Menander	A. Körte (rev. A. Thierfelder), *Menandri quae supersunt : Pars altera* (Leipzig, 1953).
Pindar	B. Snell and H. Maehler, *Pindari Carmina cum Fragmentis : Pars II* (Leipzig, 1975).
Sappho	Lobel and Page (see Alcaeus).
Semonides	West (see Archilochus).
Sophocles	S.L. Radt, *TrGF* iv (Göttingen, 1977); references also valid (unless otherwise stated) for A.C. Pearson, *The Fragments of Sophocles* (Cambridge, 1917).

*Note that references to Menander by play and line, or in the form "Men. *Kolax* F 1", are to the Oxford Classical Text of F.H. Sandbach (Oxford 1972).

(B) ABBREVIATIONS: ANCIENT AUTHORS AND WORKS

Ach.	*Acharnians.*
Ad Att.	*Epistulae ad Atticum* (Cicero).
Aesch.	Aeschylus.
Ag.	*Agamemnon* (Aeschylus).
Alc.	*Alcibiades* (Plato or Plutarch); *Alecestis* (Euripides).
Alex.	*Alexander* (Lucian).
Anab.	*Anabasis* (Xenophon).
Andoc.	Andocides.
Andr.	*Andromache* (Euripides).
Anecd. Bekk.	*Anecdota Graeca* ed. I. Bekker (Berlin, 1814-21).
Ant.	Antiphon.
Ant.	*Antonius* (Plutarch).
Ap.Rh.	Apollonius Rhodius.
Ar.	Aristophanes.
Arist.	Aristotle.
Ath.Pol.	*Athēnaiōn Polīteiā* (pseudo-Xenophon or Aristotle).
Ba.	*Bacchae* (Euripides).
Bacchyl.	Bacchylides.
Carm.	*Carmina* (Odes) (Horace).
Cho.	*Choephoroi* (Aeschylus).
Cim.	*Cimon* (Plutarch).
com. adesp.	*comica adespota* (anonymous fragments of comedy).
Crat.	*Cratylus* (Plato).
Cyneg.	*Cynegeticus* (Xenophon).
Dem.	Demosthenes.
D.S.	Diodorus Siculus.
Dysk.	*Dyskolos* (Menander).
Eccl.	*Ecclesiazusae.*
El.	*Electra* (Sophocles or Euripides).
Ep.	*Epistulae* (Horace).
ep.adesp.	*epica adespota* (anonymous fragments of epic).
Epitr.	*Epitrepontes* (Menander).
Et. Gud.	*Etymologicum Gudianum.*
Et. Mag.	*Etymologicum Magnum.*
Eum.	*Eumenides* (Aeschylus).
Eur.	Euripides.
Fab.	*Fables* (Aesop).
fr.	fragment.
Gorg.	*Gorgias* (Plato).
Hdt.	Herodotus.

Hell.	*Hellenica* (Xenophon).
Hes.	Hesiod.
HF	*Hercules Furens* (*The Madness of Heracles*) (Euripides).
h. Hom. Herm.	*Homeric Hymn to Hermes.*
Hipp.	*Hippolytus* (Euripides).
Hipparch.	*Hipparchicus* (Xenophon).
Hipp. Mi.	*Hippias Minor* (Plato).
Hippocr.	Hippocratic treatises.
HP	*Historia Plantarum* (Theophrastus).
IA	*Iphigeneia at Aulis* (Euripides).
Ichn.	*Ichneutae* (Sophocles).
Isocr.	Isocrates.
La.	*Laches* (Plato).
Lac.	*Lacedaemonian Constitution* (Xenophon).
Lex. Haemod.	Lexicon Αἰμωδεῖν ed. F.W. Sturz (with *Et. Gud.*) (Leipzig, 1818).
Lys.	Lysias.
Lys.	*Lysistrata* (Aristophanes) or *Lysis* (Plato).
Med.	*Medea* (Euripides).
Mem.	*Memorabilia* (Xenophon).
Men.	Menander.
Met.	*Metamorphoses* (Ovid).
Mor.	*Moralia* (Plutarch).
NA	*On the Nature of Animals* (Aelian).
Narr.	*Narrationes* (*Diēgēmata*) (Libanius).
Nem.	*Nemeans* (Pindar).
NH.	*Naturalis Historia* (Pliny the Elder).
Nic.	*Nicias* (Plutarch).
Or.	*Orestes* (Euripides).
OT	*Oedipus Tyrannus* (Sophocles).
Paus.	Pausanias.
Per.	*Pericles* (Plutarch).
Perik.	*Perikeiromene* (Menander).
Pers.	*Persae* (Aeschylus).
Phd.	*Phaedo* (Plato).
Phdr.	*Phaedrus* (Plato).
Phoen.	*Phoenissae* (Euripides).
Phryn.	Phrynichus.
Pind.	Pindar.
Pl.	Plato.
Plut.	Plutarch.
Poet.	*Poetics* (Aristotle).
Probl.	*Problems* (Aristotle).
Prom.	*Prometheus Bound* (ascribed to Aeschylus).

Prot.	*Protagoras* (Plato).
Pyth.	*Pythians* (Pindar).
Rep.	*Republic* (Plato).
schol.	scholium or scholia (ancient and medieval commentaries).
Sik.	*Sikyonios* or *Sikyonioi* (Menander).
Soph.	Sophocles.
Supp.	*Suppliants* (Aeschylus or Euripides).
Symp.	*Symposium* (Plato or Xenophon).
Theocr.	Theocritus.
Thesm.	*Thesmophoriazusae.*
Thg.	*Theogony* (Hesiod).
Thphr.	Theophrastus.
Tht.	*Theaetetus* (Plato).
Thuc.	Thucydides.
Tim.	*Timaeus* (Plato).
Tro.	*Troades* (Euripides).
VH	*Varia Historia* (Aelian).
Xen.	Xenophon.

(C) ABBREVIATIONS: MODERN AUTHORS AND PUBLICATIONS

ABSA	*Annual of the British School at Athens.*
Agora iii	R.E.Wycherley, *Literary and Epigraphical Testimonia* (*The Athenian Agora*, Volume III) (Princeton, 1957).
Agora xiv	H.A. Thompson and R.E. Wycherley, *The Agora of Athens : The History, Shape and Uses of an Acient City Center* (*The Athenian Agora*, Volume XIV) (Princeton, 1972).
AJA	*American Journal of Archaeology.*
AJPh	*American Journal of Philology.*
Allen	T.W. Allen, *Homeri Opera: Tomus V* (Oxford, 1912).
BCH	*Bulletin de Correspondance Hellénique.*
BICS	*Bulletin of the Institute of Classical Studies, University of London.*
Brandt	P. Brandt, *Corpusculum poesis epicae Graecae ludibundae I* (Leipzig, 1888).
CGF	C. Austin, *Comicorum Graecorum fragmenta in papyris reperta* (Berlin, 1973).
Coulon	V. Coulon and H. van Daele, *Aristophane* (Paris, 1923-30).
CQ	*Classical Quarterly.*
CR	*Classical Review.*
Dale[2]	A.M. Dale, *The Lyric Metres of Greek Drama*[2] Cambridge, 1968).
Davies	J.K. Davies, *Athenian Propertied Families 600-300 B.C.* (Oxford, 1971).

Dearden	C.W. Dearden, *The Stage of Aristophanes* (London, 1976).
Degani	[E.] Degani, *Hipponactis testimonia et fragmenta* (Leipzig, 1983).
D-K	H. Diels, *Die Fragmente der Vorsokratiker*[6] (rev. W. Kranz) (Berlin, 1951-2).
Dover	K.J. Dover, *Aristophanic Comedy* (Berkeley, 1972).
Edmonds	see (A).
FGrH	F. Jacoby, *Fragmenta der griechischen Historiker* (Berlin/Leiden, 1923-58).
Förster	R. Förster, *Libanii Opera* (Leipzig, 1903-23).
Friis Johansen and Whittle	H. Friis Johansen and E.W. Whittle, *Aeschylus : The Suppliants* (Copenhagen, 1980).
GHI	M.N. Tod, *A Selection of Greek Historical Inscriptions*[2] (Oxford, 1946-8).
Hall-Geldart	F.W. Hall and W.M. Geldart, *Aristophanis Comoediae*[2] (Oxford, 1906-7).
HCT	A.W. Gomme, A. Andrewes and K.J. Dover, *A Historical Commentary on Thucydides* (Oxford, 1945-81).
Henderson	J.J. Henderson, *The Maculate Muse : Obscene Language in Attic Comedy* (New Haven, 1975).
Holwerda	D. Holwerda, *Scholia in Aristophanem. Pars II. Fasc. II : Scholia vetera et recentiora in Aristophanis Pacem* (Groningen, 1982).
HSCP	*Harvard Studies in Classical Philology.*
ICS	*Illinois Classical Studies*
IG	*Inscriptiones Graecae.*
Inschr. Priene	F. Hiller von Gaertringen, *Inschriften von Priene* (Berlin, 1906).
JHS	*Journal of Hellenic Studies*
K-A	R. Kassel and C. Austin, *Poetae Comici Graeci* (Berlin, 1983-).
Kaibel	G. Kaibel, *Comicorum Graecorum Fragmenta I.1* (Berlin, 1899).
Kannicht	R. Kannicht, *Euripides : Helena* (Heidelberg, 1969).
Kock	see (A).
Koster	W.J.W. Koster, *Scholia in Aristophanem. Pars I, Fasc. IA: Prolegomena de Comoedia* (Gronigen, 1975).
LCM	*Liverpool Classical Monthly.*
M	Mette: see (A), Aeschylus.
MDAI(A)	*Mitteilungen des Deutschen Archäologischen Instituts (Athenische Abteilung).*
Meineke	A. Meineke, *Stephan von Byzanz : Ethnika* (Berlin, 1849).
N	Nauck: see (A), Aeschylus and Euripides.
Oder-Hoppe	E. Oder and C. Hoppe, *Corpus Hippiatricorum Graecorum* (Leipzig, 1924-7).
PA	J. Kirchner, *Prosopographia Attica* (Berlin, 1901-3).
Pack	R.A. Pack, *Artemidori Daldiani Onirocriticon libri V* (Leipzig, 1963).
Page	D.L. Page, *Poetae Melici Graeci* (Oxford, 1962).

Parke	H.W. Parke, *Festivals of the Athenians* (London, 1977).
PCG	R. Kassel and C. Austin, *Poetae Comici Graeci* (Berlin, 1983-).
Perry	B.E. Perry, *Aesopica I* (Urbana, 1952).
Pickard- Cambridge[2]	A.W. Pickard-Cambridge, *The Dramatic Festivals of Athens*[2] (rev. J. Gould and D.M. Lewis) (Oxford, 1968).
Platnauer	M. Platnauer, *Aristophanes : Peace* (Oxtord, 1964).
Powell	J.U. Powell, *Collectanea Alexandrina* (Oxford, 1925).
QUCC	*Quaderni Urbinati di Cultura Classica.*
Rabe	H. Rabe, *Scholia in Lucianum* (Leipzig, 1906).
RFIC	*Rivista di Filologia e di Istruzione Classica.*
RhM	*Rheinisches Museum für Philologie.*
RPh	*Revue de Philologie.*
SEG	*Supplementum Epigraphicum Graecum.*
SIG[3]	W. Dittenberger, *Sylloge Inscriptionum Graecarum*[3] (Leipzig, 1915- 24).
Stone	L.M. Stone, *Costume in Aristophanic Comedy* (New York, 1981).
Taillardat	J. Taillardat, *Les images d'Aristophane*[2] (Paris, 1965).
Theodoridis	C. Theodoridis, *Photii Patriarchae Lexicon* (Berlin, 1982-).
TrGF	*Tragicorum Graecorum Fragmenta* (Gottingen, 1971-); individual tragic dramatists (Carcinus, Morsimus, etc.) are referred to by the serial number they bear in *TrGF* i.
Traill	J.S. Traill, *The Political Organization of Attica* (*Hesperia* Suppl. 14) (Princeton, 1975).
Travlos	J. Travlos, *Pictorial Dictionary of Ancient Athens* (London, 1971).
West	see (A), Archilochus and Semonides.
West (D)	M.L. West, *Delectus ex iambis et elegis Graecis* (Oxford, 1980).
YCS	*Yale Classical Studies.*
Zimmermann	B. Zimmermann, *Untersuchungen zur Form und dramatischen* *Technik der aristophanischen Komödien. Band I: Parodos und* *Amoibaion* (Königstein im Taunus, 1984).
ZPE	*Zeitschrift für Papyrologie und Epigraphik.*

(D) METRICAL SYMBOLS

—	a heavy (long) syllable
ᴗ	a light (short) syllable
x	a position that may be occupied by a syllable of either kind (anceps)

INTRODUCTORY NOTE

Peace was produced at the City Dionysia in spring 421 B.C. It gained second prize; the victory went to Eupolis, Aristophanes' contemporary and greatest rival, for his play *Flatterers* (*Kolakes*), while the obscure Leucon with *The Phratry* (*Phrāteres*) was third, as he had been fourteen months earlier behind *Wasps*.

In one respect *Peace* is unique among Aristophanes' plays. The typical Aristophanic plot takes its start from something that is wrong with the current state of Athenian life and which, while it may be capable in principle of being corrected, stands next to no chance of ever being put right in practice except by the methods of comic fantasy. *Peace* likewise takes its start from something that is wrong with the current situation — namely, as in *Acharnians* and *Lysistrata*, the continuing war against the Peloponnesians; but on this occasion the wrong was one that was actually on the point of being set right in the hard world of reality.

The last major operation of the war had been the Athenian expedition to the northern Aegean coast, commanded by Cleon, in the summer of 422. This had culminated in a battle before Amphipolis in which Cleon fell, as on the other side did Brasidas, the Spartan general who had done so much in the preceding two years to undermine Athenian interests in the north. The battle itself had been a total defeat for the Athenians, and once again, as after their defeat in 424 at Delium, Athenian opinion moved in favour of peace — and now there was no Cleon to oppose the trend. The Spartan authorities also desired peace, not least because they were apprehensive of trouble in the Peloponnese when their treaty with Argos expired, as it was about to do.

The negotiations, however, do not seem to have been easy. They lasted all winter, and towards the end the Spartans went so far as to make it known that they were asking their allies to make preparations to invade Attica and establish a permanent base on Attic territory (Thuc. 5.17.2). This threat must have been largely a bluff (for Athens had long since declared that any Peloponnesian invasion of Attica would be the signal for the execution of nearly 300 Spartan prisoners captured on the island of Sphacteria in 425); but bluff or not, it was effective. Terms of peace were agreed between the Athenian and Spartans, and put to a congress of Sparta's allies, where a majority accepted them (though the most important of the allies, Corinth and Thebes, voted against); and the treaty was finally ratified by mutual oaths on the 25th day of the Athenian month of Elaphebolion (Thuc. 5.19.1), less than a fortnight after the end of the City Dionysia[1].

Aristophanes' play presupposes a situation in which Cleon and Brasidas are dead

(268-284) and peace is therefore attainable but by no means certain: its composition may well have been begun shortly after the battle of Amphipolis and completed while the negotiations were still in progress and their outcome in doubt. Nevertheless, the mood is one of confidence; there is much more of celebration than of apprehension, and irony and cynicism are all but absent. And the confidence proved (at least in the short run) to be justified: there can be little doubt that by the time of the performance the negotiators had agreed the terms of the treaty and the peace-making process had entered its final stages.

Yet even now all could still have been lost, particularly in view of Corinthian and Theban hostility to the draft treaty and the possibility that at Athens opposition to it might be stirred up by politicians like Hyperbolus (see on 681), who was seen by his enemies (and may have seen himself) as a successor to Cleon. Hence in an essential respect the situation was still the same as it had been when Aristophanes had begun work on the play: peace was attainable, but not yet attained. And the theme of the play matches this situation. That theme is that the ending of the war, and a return to the old normality of country life, is now within the grasp of the Greek peoples[2] *if* they will make one final effort to secure it.

At first the obstacles to success seem formidable. Trygaeus has to fly up to heaven and challenge Zeus himself – and when he does so, he discovers that his journey has been in vain, for Zeus has departed to a region yet more remote (195-9); mankind has been abandoned to the doubtful mercies of the terrifying demon War, while the goddess Peace, long absent from earth, has now been imprisoned where there is little hope of her ever seeing the light again.

But as soon as the difficulties and dangers are faced with determination, they evaporate. Neither Zeus nor War does anything effective to hamper the efforts of Trygaeus and the chorus; the only active opposition comes from Hermes, and he is easily won over and is soon actually directing the work of rescuing Peace. And though the political élites of almost every state in Greece seem hostile or indifferent to the cause of peace (464-507), the peasants on their own are strong enough to achieve their goal. And how great are the rewards of success! The play takes us from the smell and taste of manure to the smells and tastes of a wedding feast; from a world in which the Greeks are pounded into a savoury mash to feed voracious War, to a world in which the audience are invited to share a sacrificial meal in honour of Peace; from a world centered upon the anus to a world of exuberant heterosexuality[3] ; and also (counterfactually) from a world of toil (on cam-

---

[1] In 421 the City Dionysia probably ended on the 13th of Elaphebolion; see W.B. Dinsmoor, *Hesperia* 23 (1954) 307-8. It may be that the assembly met on the following day to vote the acceptance of the treaty and elect a delegation to go to Sparta for the exchange of oaths. In 423 the twelve-month truce had been approved by the assembly on the 14th of Elaphebolion (Thuc. 4.118.12).

[2] Trygaeus, unlike Dicaeopolis in *Acharnians*, is seeking peace neither for himself alone nor even for Athens, but for all the Greeks (59, 63, 93, 105-8, 292-8, 406-413, 866, 996-8, 1321).

[3] See Henderson 62-66.

paigns and military exercises: 347-357) to a world of rustic leisure (1127-71). No long-term apprehensions are allowed to darken the horizon. Thebans, Megarians and others may be reluctant to accept peace, but once peace is made they will be powerless to sub-vert it, for they will have against them the combined strength of Sparta and Athens (1082). That Sparta will keep her word is never doubted — except by Hierocles, who has an axe to grind and is treated with contempt. And so far as Athens is concerned, with Cleon dead and Hyperbolus to be discarded (921, 1319), the Athenian people will do as the rejuvenated Demos does at the end of *Knights*: they will take their future in their own hands instead of leaving it to the politicians, and will make sure that they never let Peace go again (705)

Though the play may thus be simpler than some of Aristophanes' other works, and free from the undercurrent of pessimism that flows beneath the brilliant comic surface of many of them, it is a rich as ever in comic idea and incident, and especially in the comic exploitation of many other genres of poetry — tragedy, satyr-play (see on 296-8), choral lyric, epic, elegy; and it is not without its moments of impressive seriousness, above all in the three prayers that accompany three of the major events of the play — the rescue (433-457), the sacrifice (974-1016), and the wedding (1320-8). Trygaeus too has all the determination, resourcefulness and impudence of the typical Aristophanic hero. Aristo-phanes could well have hoped that a play like this, at a time like this, would catch the public mood; and it is quite possible that he only missed the first prize because of his decision to represent the goddess Peace — for much of the play a more central figure even than Trygaeus — by a statue instead of a flesh-and-blood actor, while her attendants Full-fruit and Showtime were played by live performers. At any rate it was for this decision that he was presently ridiculed by two of his professional rivals[4].

The staging of *Peace* raises a number of difficult questions, especially in regard to the representation of the two houses that figure in the action (the house of Trygaeus and the palace of Zeus), of the cave into which Peace has been cast, and of the scene in which she is hauled out[5]. Dover's reconstruction is, on the whole, the best and simplest, and in my stage-directions I have in general followed it. I assume, then, that in this play all three doors to the *skēnē*[6] are put to use. The central door is the entrance to the cave; through this door Peace is hauled on the *ekkyklēma* platform, and there she remains, dominating the stage and the action, for the rest of the play, to be "installed" as a cult-image in the sacrifice-scene. The two flanking doors represent respectively the house of Trygaeus and the palace of Zeus, so that Trygaeus' flight on his beetle takes him, as near-ly as the crane-mechanism will allow, from one end of the *skēnē* to the other.

[4] Eupolis fr. 54; Plato com. fr. 81.

[5] See especially A.M. Dale, *JHS* 77 (1957) 210-1; H.J. Newiger, *RhM* 108 (1965) 235-241 = *Aristophanes und die alte Komödie* (Darmstadt, 1975) 231-8; Dover 134-6; D.W. Olcott, *Aristophanes' Peace : Problems of Staging and Stage Action* (Diss. Stanford 1973); Dearden 62-64, 77-79, 158-162.

[6] On the number of doors in the *skēnē*, see K.J. Dover, *PCPS* 12 (1966) 2-17, and cf. Eupolis fr. 42.

A feature of *Peace* that is at first sight puzzling is that the identity of the chorus seems oddly fluid. Like any Aristophanic chorus, they may at certain moments discard their dramatic identity altogether and·speak or sing simply as Athenians celebrating, and competing at, a dramatic festival (cf. 729-818, the parabasis); but in this play their dramatic identity itself fluctuates. They are introduced, very explicitly, as representatives of the whole Greek people and every class within it (292-8); they call themselves *Panhellēnes* (302). Yet quite early on they speak as if they were all Athenian (349-357). In the hauling scene they are again Panhellenes, classified now, for the most part, politically instead of socially (464-507); then at 508 we are told that only the peasants remain (whether the peasants of Greece or of Attica is not made clear), and from then on, whenever the chorus have a dramatic identity at all, they are Attic peasants. This series of inconsistencies has naturally given rise to the idea that a subsidiary chorus of Panhellenes entered together with the main chorus of Attic peasants and exited before 508 (compare the boys in *Wasps* 230-414), or that the chorus was divided into two groups like the choruses of *Lysistrata, Frogs*[7] and at one moment *Acharnians*[8]. But no such theory can account for all the facts: as we have seen, the chorus have not two but four or five distinguishable identities between 292 and 631. A more helpful view of the problem is that expressed by Sifakis[9]:

> In none of the comedies does the chorus have a consistent and unalterable dramatic character. The boundaries of its character are flexible and . . . can be enlarged, or become narrower, and so its point of view may change. What appears to be a special problem in *Peace* is due to the fact that the fluctuations of the character of the chorus start much earlier than the parabasis, during the most intensive involvement of the chorus in the action. This is unusual but still in keeping with the rules of the chorus' function.

The fact remains, however, that *something* happens to the chorus just before 508. All through the hauling-scene, first one, then another group of those engaged in the work have been accused of idling or even of hindering the efforts of the others; the last two groups, the Megarians and Athenians, are addressed in terms that suggest they are being asked to leave the scene of action ("won't you get to blazes out of here?" 500; "withdraw a little towards the sea" 507). At once the chorus-leader says "Let's us peasants take hold, all by ourselves" (508), and shortly afterwards someone comments "The peasants are pulling the thing off, they and no one else" (511). All this clearly indicates that there has been a reduction in the number of men supposed to be hauling on the ropes: previously there were the peasants together with various groups of non-peasants,

---

[7] In the parodos (316-459) there are semichoruses of male and female initiates, who at certain points sing separately: see Zimmermann 135-6.

[8] *Ach.* 557-571.

[9] G.M. Sifakis, *Parabasis and Animal Choruses* (London, 1971) 32, following a review of the various hypotheses that have been advanced. See also Dover 137-9 and Zimmermann 262-5.

now the peasants are on their own (and getting on much better with the job). It is likely that in this matter the audience's imagination was aided by some change in the stage-picture; the movements within the chorus, which seem to be implicit in the language of 500-7, might well be so managed as to create the impression that their numbers had been reduced even if this had not in fact happened.

It seems likely that at some time Aristophanes wrote another play which also bore the title *Peace*. One of the ancient introductory notes (Hypotheses) to our play[10] preserves the following information:

> Aristophanes appears in the *Didaskaliai* (records of productions) as having likewise produced another[11] *Peace*. Eratosthenes says it is not clear whether he restaged the same play or entered another which is not preserved. Crates, however, is acquainted with two plays, for he writes thus: "at any rate in the *Acharnians* or *Babylonians*, or in one or the other *Peace*"; and from time to time he cites certain passages which are not found in the surviving play.

The implication of this is that Aristophanes had indeed written two plays of the same name (just as he had written two plays called *Thesmophoriazusae*, two plays called *Wealth*, and two versions of *Clouds*), and that while only one of them (our play) was to be found in the library of Alexandria (of which Eratosthenes was curator c.245-195 B.C.), Crates (early second century B.C.) at the rival library of Pergamum had access to both.

Further evidence is provided by the ancient and medieval authors who quote, or appear to quote, words and passages from Aristophanes' *Peace* which are not to be found in the play we possess. At the highest calculation there are seven such quotations. Two of these[12] can almost certainly be discounted, since the quoting sources are not unanimous in ascribing them to *Peace* and in each case we can see how such an ascription could have been made in error; two more may be garbled references to passages in the surviving play[13]; but there remain three quotations[14] which are harder to explain away, and which serve to confirm the evidence of the Hypothesis that a second *Peace* was known in antiquity. The scantiness of the attestation to the play is no doubt due to its not having been available to the scholars of Alexandria.[15]

About the content of the lost play we know only that the goddess Georgia (Agriculture), "faithful nurse, housekeeper, fellow-worker, steward, daughter and sister of Peace", was a character with a speaking part[16], and that someone suggested, in the spirit of *Peace* 1224-64, that with the coming of peace a shield could be used as a cover for a well.[17]

From Eratosthenes' language it is likely, though not certain, that the lost play was later than the surviving one[18]. If so, it cannot have been produced before 412; for it was only in the spring of 413 that war came again to Attica with the Spartan invasion of the country and occupation of Deceleia, and the Attic peasants had again to evacuate their lands. Most probably the lost play belongs to one of the years 410-405[19]. It will have been a completely new play, not a revision of the one we have: our *Peace* is so

---

For footnotes see overleaf.

NOTE ON THE TEXT

Portions of *Peace* are preserved in three papyri, which contain between them all or part of about 130 lines. There are ten medieval manuscripts[1], whose common ancestry is shown by the fact that in the hundred or so lines (most of them fragmentary) preserved in the third-century papyrus Π 11, the medieval tradition is eight times[2] united in erroneous readings from which Π 11 is free.

The medieval manuscripts fall into two families. The two oldest mss., RV, are alone in presenting the text in its entirety; they also share exclusively about fifty errors, showing that they go back to a common ancestor more recent than the archetype of all the medieval mss.

The remaining mss. descend from a copy which had lost lines 948-1011 — a passage that was not restored to the text until the second Juntine edition of 1525[3]. This family in turn consists of two subfamilies. The first subfamily comprises: (i) Γ, which was copied from a seriously defective exemplar and later itself suffered mutilation, so that it now contains little more than half the play; (ii) the close-knit group Vp2CH, here collectively designated *p*; (iii) a lost ms. from which a number of corrections have been introduced into V. The second subfamily represents a recension of the text by the fourteenth century scholar Demetrius Triclinius. There is no trace of his editorial activity after line 1227, and it is likely that the text as known to him ended there: of the mss. descended from his edition, Vv17 still ends at 1227, and so originally did L. The late ms. B, while basically Triclinian, also incorporates readings derived ultimately from Γ, and its text continues as far as 1300 (the point at which Γ ends).

---

[1] Three of these are not listed in the table of sigla following this note: G (Venetus Marcianus 475), a copy of V; H (Hauniensis 1980), which is closely akin to Vp2 and C; and Vv17 (Vaticanus Graecus 2181), which is closely akin to L.

[2] Though in four of these passages Triclinius restored the true reading by conjecture.

[3] But these lines (and also the closing lines of the play) were inserted by Petrus Victorius into his copy of the Aldine edition, from a lost ms. which seems to have been descended from a sibling of R.

The structure of the medieval tradition may be summed up as follows:

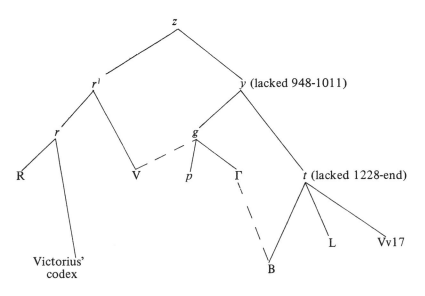

In the apparatus of the present edition, the witnesses regularly cited (where they are available) are the papyri, RVΓ*pt* and (in 948-1011) Victorius.

Collations of RVΓVp2CB may be found in the edition of K. Zacher and O. Bachmann (Leipzig, 1909). I am indebted to the kindness of Mr. N.G. Wilson for a collation of L.

SIGLA

Other Symbols

Σ	scholion
Σ (i, ii, iii)	separate scholia on the same passage in the same ms. or mss.
λ	lemma (words from the text quoted as the heading of a scholion)
Σ+λ	reading found in both the lemma and the body of a scholion
γρ	reading noted in ms. or scholia as a variant
i	implied by or inferable from
ac	before correction
pc	after correction
s	above or below the line
vel sim.	or the like; with unimportant or irrelevant variations
R^1, V^1, etc.	the hand of the original copyist
R^2, V^2, etc.	any later hand
L^r	the hand which added lines 1228-68 in L
[V^{ac}] etc.	the reading referred to is no longer legible
*	an erased letter

EIPHNH

PEACE

TA TOY ΔΡΑΜΑΤΟΣ ΠΡΟΣΩΠΑ

ΟΙΚΕΤΗΣ Α Τρυγαίου.

ΟΙΚΕΤΗΣ Β Τρυγαίου.

ΤΡΥΓΑΙΟΣ 'Αθμονεύς, ἀμπελουργός.

ΘΥΓΑΤΗΡ Τρυγαίου.

ΕΡΜΗΣ.

ΠΟΛΕΜΟΣ.

ΚΥΔΟΙΜΟΣ, θεράπων Πολεμου.

ΧΟΡΟΣ.

ΙΕΡΟΚΛΗΣ.

ΔΡΕΠΑΝΟΥΡΓΟΣ.

ΚΑΠΗΛΟΣ ΟΠΛΩΝ.

ΠΑΙΔΙΟΝ Α, υἱὸς Λαμάχου.

ΠΑΙΔΙΟΝ Β, υἱὸς Κλεωνύμου.

Κωφὰ πρόσωπα

ΘΥΓΑΤΕΡΕΣ Τρυγαίου.

ΕΙΡΗΝΗ.

ΟΠΩΡΑ, ἀκόλουθος Εἰρήνης.

ΘΕΩΡΙΑ, ἀκόλουθος Εἰρήνης.

ΟΙΚΕΤΑΙ Τρυγαίου.

ΚΕΡΑΜΕΥΣ.

ΚΡΑΝΟΠΟΙΟΣ.

ΔΟΡΥΞΟΣ.

2

CHARACTERS OF THE PLAY

FIRST SLAVE *of Trygaeus.*
SECOND SLAVE *of Trygaeus.*
TRYGAEUS *of Athmonum, a vine-grower.*
DAUGHTER *of Trygaeus.*
HERMES.
WAR ·
HURLYBURLY, *servant to War.*
CHORUS*.
HIEROCLES.
SICKLE-MAKER.
ARMS-DEALER.
FIRST BOY, *son of Lamachus.*
SECOND BOY, *son of Cleonymus.*

Silent Characters

DAUGHTERS *of Trygaeus.*
PEACE (a statue).
FULLFRUIT, *handmaid to Peace.*
SHOWTIME, *handmaid to Peace.*
SLAVES *of Trygaeus.*
POTTER.
HELMET-MAKER.
SPEAR-MAKER.

*The chorus assume different identities in different parts
of the play; see Introductory Note, pp. xviii - xix.

3

ΟΙΚΕΤΗΣ Α
 Αἶρ' αἶρε μᾶζαν ὡς τάχος τῷ κανθάρῳ.

ΟΙΚΕΤΗΣ Β
 ἰδού. δὸς αὐτῷ, τῷ κάκιστ' ἀπολουμένῳ·
 καὶ μήποτ' αὐτῆς μᾶζαν ἡδίω φάγοι.

Οι.^α δὸς μᾶζαν ἑτέραν ἐξ ὀνίδων πεπλασμένην.

Οι.^β ἰδοὺ μάλ' αὖθις. ποῦ γὰρ ἦν νυνδὴ 'φερες;   5
 οὐ κατέφαγεν.

Οι.^α   μὰ τὸν Δί', ἀλλ' ἐξαρπάσας
 ὅλην ἐνέκαψε περικυλίσας τοῖν ποδοῖν.
 ἀλλ' ὡς τάχιστα τρῖβε πολλὰς καὶ πυκνάς.

Οι.^β ἄνδρες κοπρολόγοι, προσλάβεσθε πρὸς θεῶν,
 εἰ μή με βούλεσθ' ἀποπνιγέντα περιιδεῖν.   10

Οι.^α ἑτέραν ἑτέραν δός, παιδὸς ἡταιρηκότος·
 τετριμμένης γάρ φησιν ἐπιθυμεῖν.

Οι.^β   ἰδού.
 ἑνὸς μέν, ὦνδρες, ἀπολελύσθαι μοι δοκῶ·
 οὐδεὶς γὰρ ἂν φαίη με μάττοντ' ἐσθίειν.

Οι.^α αἱβοῖ· φέρ' ἄλλην χἁτέραν μοι χἁτέραν,   15
 καὶ τρῖβ' ἔθ' ἑτέρας.

Οι.^β   μὰ τὸν 'Απόλλω 'γὼ μὲν οὔ·
 οὐ γὰρ ἔθ' οἷός τ' εἴμ' ὑπερέχειν τῆς ἀντλίας.

Οι.^α αὐτὴν ἄρ' οἴσω συλλαβὼν τὴν ἀντλίαν.

<hr>

 1 τάχος τῷ Kiehl, cf. Σ^{RVL}: τάχιστα codd. Suda, <u>Anecd. Bekk.</u>
   358.6, Photius, Zonaras, Orion, Eustathius.
 7 περικυλίσας ^λΣ^L i_Σ^{VL}: περικυκλίσας codd. ^λΣ^V.
 16 ἔθ' ἑτέρας Dindorf: ἑτέρας RV: ἑτέρας τε <u>p</u>: ἑτέρας γε <u>t</u>.

[*Outside one of the flanking doors of the stage-house a slave (the second to speak) is kneading cakes of dung in a tub. Presently another slave comes out of the door and hurries across to him, calling out an order as he comes.*]

FIRST SLAVE: Give, give me a cake for the beetle, as fast as you can!

SECOND SLAVE [*handing him one*]: Here you are. [*As the first slave takes it inside*] Give it him, the blasted creature, and may it be the tastiest cake he ever eats!

FIRST SLAVE [*returning*]: Give me another cake, moulded from ass-dung.

SECOND SLAVE: Here you are again. Why, where's the one you just   5
took him? He can't have eaten it!

FIRST SLAVE: Eaten it? Why, he seized it from me, rolled it into place with his feet, and guzzled the whole thing. Anyway, knead them up as fast as possible, lots and lots. [*He goes inside with a dung-cake.*]

SECOND SLAVE [*working feverishly*]: Lend a hand, you dung-collectors, for heaven's sake, unless you want to leave me to suffocate!   10

FIRST SLAVE [*coming out again*]: Another, give us another, from a boy prostitute. He says he wants one that's well pounded.

SECOND SLAVE [*giving him another cake*]: Here you are. [*The first slave goes inside. To the audience*] There's one charge, gentlemen, that I think I'm proved not guilty of: nobody can say I eat the stuff while kneading it!

FIRST SLAVE [*coming out again, his head to one side as if turned from a   15
disgusting smell*]: Ugh! Give me another and another and another, and go on kneading more.

SECOND SLAVE: By Apollo, I won't. I can't get the better of the bilge any longer.

FIRST SLAVE: Then I'll take the bilge itself in with me. [*He picks up the tub and takes it inside.*]

Οι.ᵝ νὴ τὸν Δί' ἐς κόρακάς γε, καὶ σαυτόν γε πρός.

ὑμῶν δέ γ' εἴ τις οἶδέ μοι κατειπάτω   20

πόθεν ἂν πριαίμην ῥῖνα μὴ τετρημένην.

οὐδὲν γὰρ ἔργον ἦν ἄρ' ἀθλιώτερον

ἢ κανθάρῳ μάττοντα παρέχειν ἐσθίειν.

ὗς μὲν γάρ, ὥσπερ ἂν χέσῃ τις, ἢ κύων

φαύλως ἐρείδει· τοῦτο δ' ὑπὸ φρονήματος   25

βρενθύεταί τε καὶ φαγεῖν οὐκ ἀξιοῖ,

ἢν μὴ παραθῶ τρίψας δι' ἡμέρας ὅλης

ὥσπερ γυναικὶ γογγύλην μεμαγμένην.

ἀλλ' εἰ πέπαυται τῆς ἐδωδῆς σκέψομαι

τῃδὶ παροίξας τῆς θύρας, ἵνα μή μ' ἴδῃ.   30

ἔρειδε, μὴ παύσαιο μηδέποτ' ἐσθίων

τέως ἕως σαυτὸν λάθῃς διαρραγείς.

οἷον δὲ κύψας ὁ κατάρατος ἐσθίει

ὥσπερ παλαιστής, παραβαλὼν τοὺς γομφίους,

καὶ ταῦτα τὴν κεφαλήν τε καὶ τὼ χεῖρέ πως   35

ὡδὶ περιάγων, ὥσπερ οἱ τὰ σχοινία

τὰ παχέα συμβάλλοντες εἰς τὰς ὁλκάδας.

Οι.ᵃ μιαρὸν τὸ χρῆμα καὶ κάκοσμον καὶ βορόν,

χὤτου ποτ' ἐστὶ δαιμόνων ἡ προσβολὴ

οὐκ οἶδ'· Ἀφροδίτης μὲν γὰρ οὔ μοι φαίνεται,   40

οὐ μὴν Χαρίτων γε.

Οι.ᵝ   τοῦ γάρ ἐστ';

Οι.ᵃ   οὐκ ἔσθ' ὅπως

τοῦτ' ἐστὶ τὸ τέρας οὐ Διὸς σκαταιβάτου.

---

42 σκαταιβάτου Σ(iii)ᴿ: *καταιβάτου R: καταιβάτου V͟p͟t Σ(i,ii)ᴿ
   Σᵛᶜᴸ λ͟Σ͟RL.

6

SECOND SLAVE [*calling after him*]: Yes, you can take it to blazes, and
yourself as well! [*To the audience*] And whoever of you knows, will he   20
please tell me where I can buy a nose with no openings? Because I've found
there's no more wretched job than to knead and serve food to a beetle. A
pig or a dog stuffs it down any old how, just as it's been shat. But this   25
creature is so conceited, it acts haughty and refuses to eat unless I work
the stuff over all day long and serve it up kneaded into a ball, as if to
a lady. I'll look and see if it's finished its meal, opening the door a   30
crack, like this, so it won't see me. [*Peeping inside*] Go on, stuff yourself!
Never stop eating, not until you burst unawares! [*Withdrawing from the door*]
The way the damned creature eats! — head down, like a wrestler, moving his
jaws sideways, and that while he's circling round with his head and arms   35
something like this [*he tries to imitate the beetle's actions*], like the men
who twist together thick ropes for cargo ships.

    FIRST SLAVE [*coming out of the house*]: It's a vile, smelly, greedy
creature, that one, and I don't know what god this evil visitation comes   39-40
from. I don't think it's from Aphrodite, nor yet from the Graces.

    SECOND SLAVE: Then who's it from?

    FIRST SLAVE: It can only be that this monstrosity comes from Zeus,
the Lord of the Thunder-crap.

Οἰ.^β οὐκοῦν ἂν ἤδη τῶν θεατῶν τις λέγοι
νεανίας δοκησίσοφος· "τὸ δὲ πρᾶγμα τί;
ὁ κάνθαρος δὲ πρὸς τί;"

Οἰ.^α   κᾆτ' αὐτῷ γ' ἀνὴρ   45
Ἰωνικός τίς φησι παρακαθήμενος·
"δοκέω μέν, ἐς Κλέωνα τοῦτ' αἰνίσσεται,
ὡς κεῖνος ἐν Ἅιδεω σπατύλην ἐσθύει."
ἀλλ' εἰσιὼν τῷ κανθάρῳ δώσω πιεῖν.

Οἰ.^β ἐγὼ δὲ τὸν λόγον γε τοῖσι παιδίοις   50
καὶ τοῖσιν ἀνδρίοισι καὶ τοῖς ἀνδράσιν
καὶ τοῖς ὑπερτάτοισιν ἀνδράσιν φράσω
καὶ τοῖς ὑπερηνορέουσιν ἔτι τούτοις μάλα.
ὁ δεσπότης μου μαίνεται καινὸν τρόπον,
οὐχ ὅνπερ ὑμεῖς, ἀλλ' ἕτερον καινὸν πάνυ.   55
δι' ἡμέρας γὰρ εἰς τὸν οὐρανὸν βλέπων
ὡδὶ κεχηνὼς λοιδορεῖται τῷ Διὶ
καί φησιν· "ὦ Ζεῦ, τί ποτε βουλεύει ποιεῖν;
κατάθου τὸ κόρημα· μὴ 'κκόρει τὴν Ἑλλάδα."
ἔα ἔα.   60
σιγήσαθ', ὡς φωνῆς ἀκούειν μοι δοκῶ.

ΤΡΥΓΑΙΟΣ
ὦ Ζεῦ, τί δρασείεις ποθ' ἡμῶν τὸν λεών;
λήσεις σεαυτὸν τὰς πόλεις ἐκκοκκίσας.

Οἰ.^β τοῦτ' ἐστὶ τουτὶ τὸ κακὸν αὖθ' οὑγὼ 'λεγον·

---

47 αἰνίσσεται Dobree: αἰνύττεται codd. Suda.
48 ἐν Ἅιδεω σπατύλην van Leeuwen: ἀναιδέως (ἀναιδῶς pt) τὴν
   σπατύλην codd.
52 ὑπερτάτοισιν B: ὑπερ τούτοισιν vel sim. RVpt.
64 τουτὶ RV: δῆτα pt.

8

SECOND SLAVE: Well, by now some young man in the audience, who fancies himself clever, may be saying "What's all this about? What has the the beetle got to do with?" — 45

FIRST SLAVE: Yes, and then an Ionian fellow sitting beside him says to him: "My opinion is he's using it to allude to Cleon — saying that he's eating muck in Hades." — But I'm going to go inside and give the beetle a drink. [*He goes into the house.*]

SECOND SLAVE: And I'm going to explain the plot to the children and 50 the striplings and the men and the men of high position and yes, even to those proud supermen there. My master is mad in a new kind of way, not the way 55 *you* are, but another way, altogether new. All day long he looks up at the heavens, like this [*throwing back his head to look skywards*], with his mouth open, and rails against Zeus and says "Zeus, what on earth are you aiming to do? Put down your broom; don't sweep Greece away!" — Here, listen! 60 Quiet, now; I think I can hear a voice.

TRYGAEUS [*within*]: Zeus, what on earth are you trying to do to our people? You'll uproot all the cities before you know what you've done!

SECOND SLAVE [*to the audience, as before*]: That's it, that's just the affliction I was talking about! You can hear the pattern that his madness 65

τὸ γὰρ παράδειγμα τῶν μανιῶν ἀκούετε. 65
ἃ δ' εἶπε πρῶτον ἡνίκ' ἤρχεθ' ἡ χολὴ
πεύσεσθ'. ἔφασκε γὰρ πρὸς αὐτὸν αν ταδί·
"πῶς ἄν ποτ' ἀφικοίμην ἂν εὐθὺ τοῦ Διός;"
ἔπειτα λεπτὰ κλιμάκια ποιούμενος
πρὸς ταῦτ' ἀνηρριχᾶτ' ἂν εἰς τὸν οὐρανόν, 70
ἕως ξυνετρίβη τῆς κεφαλῆς καταρρυείς.
ἐχθὲς δὲ μετὰ ταῦτ' ἐκφθαρεὶς οὐκ οἶδ' ὅποι
εἰσήγαγ' Αἰτναῖον μέγιστον κάνθαρον·
κἄπειτα τοῦτον ἱπποκομεῖν μ' ἠνάγκασεν,
καὐτὸς καταψῶν αὐτὸν ὥσπερ πωλίον 75
"ὦ Πηγάσιόν μοί" φησι, "γενναῖον πτερόν,
ὅπως πετήσει μ' εὐθὺ τοῦ Διος λαβών."
ἀλλ' ὅ τι ποιεῖ τηδὶ διακύψας ὄψομαι.
οἴμοι τάλας. ἴτε δεῦρο δεῦρ', ὦ γείτονες·
ὁ δεσπότης γάρ μου μετέωρος αἴρεται 80
ἱππηδὸν εἰς τὸν ἀέρ' ἐπὶ τοῦ κανθάρου.

Τρ. ἥσυχος ἥσυχος, ἠρέμα, κάνθων·
    μή μοι σοβαρῶς χώρει λίαν
    εὐθὺς ἀπ' ἀρχῆς, ῥώμῃ πίσυνος,
    πρὶν ἂν ἱδύσῃς καὶ διαλύσῃς 85
    ἄρθρων ἶνας πτερύγων ῥύμῃ.
    καὶ μὴ πνεῖ μοι κακόν, ἀντιβολῶ σ'·

67 ἂν ταδί Lenting: ἐνθαδί codd.
70 ἀνηρριχᾶτ' Photius: ἀνηριχᾶτ' Phrynichus: ἀνερριχᾶτ' codd.
   $^λΣ^L$ Suda α2313: ἀναρριχᾶτ' vel sim. $^λΣ^R$ Suda α2049, Et.
   Mag., Lex. Haemod. 621.38: ἂν ἀναρριχᾶται Et. Gud.
76 μού φησι (μοι φησὶ) t: φησὶ μοὶ p: φησύ RV.
85 ἱδύσῃς Porson: ἱδύῃς codd. Suda.

10

follows. I'll tell you what he said first when the bile-sickness came
on him. He used to keep saying this to himself: "How could I go all
the way right to Zeus?" Then he'd have light little ladders made and
try to climb up by them to heaven, until he dropped down and broke his   70
head. After that, yesterday, he went out, blast him, I don't know where,
and brought home an enormous Etna beetle; and then he compelled me to be
its groom, and he himself strokes it like a young colt and says: "My little   75
Pegasus, my thoroughbred flier, you must take me and fly straight to Zeus."
I'm going to peep through here and see what he's doing. [*He peeps through
the door for a moment, then starts back in horrified amazement.*] Help,
help! Come here, come here, neighbours! My master is rising aloft into   80
the air, mounted on the beetle as if on a horse!

    [*As he speaks, Trygaeus is raised into view by the theatrical crane from
behind the façade of his house, mounted astride his giant dung-beetle.*]
    TRYGAEUS: Softly, softly; gently, little moke;
                do not go too violently, please,
                right from the start, trusting in your strength,
                until you have got up a sweat and loosened up   85
                the sinews of your limbs with the impetus of your wings.
                And don't breathe foul breath at me, I beg you:

εἰ δὲ ποιήσεις τοῦτο, κατ' οἴκους
αὐτοῦ μεῖνον τοὺς ἡμετέρους.

Οἰ.^β ὦ δέσποτ' ἄναξ, ὡς παραπαίεις.   90

Τρ. σίγα σίγα.

Οἰ.^β ποῖ δῆτ' ἄλλως μετεωροκοπεῖς;

Τρ. ὑπὲρ Ἑλλήνων πάντων πέτομαι
τόλμημα νέον παλαμησάμενος.

Οἰ.^β τί πέτει; τί μάτην οὐχ ὑγιαίνεις;   95

Τρ. εὐφημεῖν χρὴ καὶ μὴ φλαῦρον
μηδὲν γρύζειν, ἀλλ' ὀλολύζειν·
τοῖς τ' ἀνθρώποισι φράσον σιγᾶν,
τούς τε κοπρῶνας καὶ τὰς λαύρας
καιναῖς πλίνθοισιν ἀποικοδομεῖν   100
καὶ τοὺς πρωκτοὺς ἐπικλῄειν.

Οἰ.^β οὐκ ἔσθ' ὅπως σιγήσομ', ἢν μή μοι φράσῃς
ὅποι πέτεσθαι διανοεῖ.

Τρ.   τί δ' ἄλλο γ' ἢ
ὡς τὸν Δί' εἰς τὸν οὐρανόν;

Οἰ.^β   τίνα νοῦν ἔχων;

Τρ. ἐρησόμενος ἐκεῖνον Ἑλλήνων πέρι   105
ἁπαξαπάντων ὅ τι ποιεῖν βουλεύεται.

Οἰ.^β ἐὰν δὲ μή σοι καταγορεύσῃ;

Τρ.   γράψομαι
Μήδοισιν αὐτὸν προδιδόναι τὴν Ἑλλάδα.

100 ἀποικοδομεῖν Florent Chrestien, cf. Σ^{RVL}: ἀνοικοδομεῖν codd.

                if you're going to do that, you can stay
                right here in our house.

SECOND SLAVE [*calling up to Trygaeus*]:   90
                O lord and master, how really crazy you are!

TRYGAEUS: Be silent, be silent!

SECOND SLAVE:
                Then why are you senselessly beating the air?

TRYGAEUS: I am making a flight on behalf of all the Greeks;
                I have planned a venture without precedent.

SECOND SLAVE: 95
                Why are you flying? Why are you sick with mad folly?

TRYGAEUS: You should speak fair and not utter
                the least ill-omened sound, but shout for joy;
                and bid all men keep silence,
                and shut off with new brickwork   99-100
                the privies and the alleys,
                and close up their arses.

SECOND SLAVE: There's no way I'll keep silent, unless you tell me
where you mean to fly.

TRYGAEUS: Why, to Zeus in heaven, of course.

SECOND SLAVE: Having what in mind?

TRYGAEUS: To ask him about the Greeks, the whole lot of them, what   105
he's aiming to do with them.

SECOND SLAVE: And if he doesn't tell you?

TRYGAEUS: I'll indict him for betraying Greece to the Medes!

Οι.^β   μὰ τὸν Διόνυσον οὐδέποτε ζῶντός γ' ἐμοῦ.

Τρ.   οὐκ ἔστι παρὰ ταῦτ' ἄλλ'.

Οι.^β   ἰοὺ ἰοὺ ἰού.   110
      ὦ παιδί', ὁ πατὴρ ἀπολιπὼν ἀπέρχεται
      ὑμᾶς ἐρήμους εἰς τὸν οὐρανὸν λάθρᾳ.
      ἀλλ' ἀντιβολεῖτε τὸν πατέρ', ὦ κακοδαίμονα.

ΘΥΓΑΤΗΡ
      ὦ πάτερ, ὦ πάτερ, ἆρ' ἔτυμός γε
      δώμασιν ἡμετέροις φάτις ἥκει,   115
      ὡς σὺ μετ' ὀρνίθων προλιπὼν ἐμὲ
         ἐς κόρακας βαδιεῖ μεταμώνιος;
      ἔστι τι τῶνδ' ἐτύμως; εἴπ', ὦ πάτερ, εἴ τι φιλεῖς με.

Τρ.   δοξάσαι ἐστί, κόραι· τὸ δ' ἐτήτυμον, ἄχθομαι ὑμῖν,
      ἡνίκ' ἂν αἰτίζητ' ἄρτον πάππαν με καλοῦσαι,   120
      ἔνδον δ' ἀργυρίου μηδὲ φακᾶς ᾖ πάνυ πάμπαν.
      ἢν δ' ἐγὼ εὖ πράξας ἔλθω πάλιν, ἕξετ' ἐν ὥρᾳ
      κολλύραν μεγάλην καὶ κόνδυλον ὄψον ἐπ' αὐτῇ.

Θυ.   καὶ τίς πόρος σοι τῆς ὁδοῦ γενήσεται;
      ναῦς μὲν γὰρ οὐκ ἄξει σε ταύτην τὴν ὁδόν.   125

Τρ.   πτηνὸς πορεύσει πῶλος· οὐ ναυσθλώσομαι.

Θυ.   τίς δ' ἡπίνοιά σούστὶν ὥστε κάνθαρον
      ζεύξαντ' ἐλαύνειν εἰς θεούς, ὦ παππία;

Τρ.   ἐν τοῖσιν Αἰσώπου λόγοις ἐξηυρέθη
      μόνος πετηνῶν εἰς θεοὺς ἀφιγμένος.   130

Θυ.   ἄπιστον εἶπας μῦθον, ὦ πάτερ πάτερ,
      ὅπως κάκοσμον ζῷον ἦλθεν εἰς θεούς.

Τρ.   ἦλθεν κατ' ἔχθραν αἰετοῦ πάλαι ποτέ,

14

SECOND SLAVE: By Dionysus, never, while I live!

TRYGAEUS: There is no alternative. 110

SECOND SLAVE: [*calling into the house*]: Help, help, help! Children, your father is going away secretly to heaven, and leaving you all on your own! [*Trygaeus' three daughters come out of the house.*] Come, poor wretched things, beg and beseech your father.

[*All the girls stretch out their hands in supplication to Trygaeus, while one of them sings.*]

DAUGHTER: O father, O father, is it really true,
    the tale that has come to our house, 115
    that you are among the birds, have abandoned me,
    and mean to go airborne to the dogs above?
    Is any of this really so? Tell me, father, if you love me
      at all.

TRYGAEUS: "You may guess, maidens; but the truth"...is, I'm fed up with you,
    when you keep asking me for bread and calling me daddy 120
    and there absolutely isn't even a drop of money in the house at all.
    If I come back successful, you will speedily have
    a large bun, and as savoury to go with it — a bunch of fives.

DAUGHTER: And what means will you have of making the journey? For a ship will not take you on this voyage. 125

TRYGAEUS: A winged colt will convey me; I shall not go by sea.

DAUGHTER: But what idea have you, daddy, that has made you harness a beetle and ride up to the gods?

TRYGAEUS: In the fables of Aesop it was the only winged creature 129-
that I found had reached the gods' realm. 130

DAUGHTER: O father, father, it is an incredible tale you tell, how an evil-smelling animal could come among the gods.

TRYGAEUS: It went once, long ago, because it was at feud with an eagle,

15

ῷ' ἐκκυλίνδων κἀντιτιμωρούμενος.

Θυ. οὔκουν ἐχρῆν σε Πηγάσου ζεῦξαι πτερόν,   135
    ὅπως ἐφαίνου τοῖς θεοῖς τραγικώτερος;

Τρ. ἀλλ', ὦ μέλ', ἂν μοι σιτίων διπλῶν ἔδει·
    νῦν δ' ἅττ' ἂν αὐτὸς καταφάγω τὰ σιτία,
    τούτοισι τοῖς αὐτοῖσι τοῦτον χορτάσω.

Θυ. τί δ', ἢν ἐς ὑγρὸν πόντιον πέσῃ βάθος;   140
    πῶς ἐξολισθεῖν πτηνὸς ὢν δυνήσεται;

Τρ. ἐπίτηδες εἶχον πηδάλιον, ᾧ χρήσομαι·
    τὸ δὲ πλοῖον ἔσται Ναξιουργὴς κάνθαρος.

Θυ. λιμὴν δὲ τίς σε δέξεται φορούμενον;

Τρ. ἐν Πειραιεῖ δήπου 'στὶ Κανθάρου λιμήν.   145

Θυ. ἐκεῖνο τήρει, μὴ σφαλεὶς καταρρυῇς
    ἐντεῦθεν, εἶτα χωλὸς ὢν Εὐριπίδῃ
    λόγον παράσχῃς καὶ τραγῳδία γένῃ.

Τρ. ἐμοὶ μελήσει ταῦτά γ'· ἀλλὰ χαίρετε.
    ὑμεῖς δέ γ', ὑπὲρ ὧν τοὺς πόνους ἐγὼ πονῶ,   150
    μὴ βδεῖτε μηδὲ χέζεθ' ἡμερῶν τριῶν·
    ὡς εἰ μετέωρος οὗτος ὢν ὀσφρήσεται,
    κατωκάρα ῥίψας με βουκολήσεται.

    ἀλλ' ἄγε, Πήγασε, χώρει χαίρων,
    χρυσοχάλινον πάταγον ψαλίων   155
    διακινήσας φαιδροῖς ὠσίν.
    τί ποιεῖς, τί ποιεῖς; ποῖ παρακλίνεις
    τοὺς μυκτῆρας πρὸς τὰς λαύρας;
    ἵει σαυτὸν θαρρῶν ἀπὸ γῆς,
    κᾆτα δρομαίαν πτέρυγ' ἐκτείνων   160

16

on whom it was taking revenge by rolling eggs out of its nests.

DAUGHTER: Should you not then have harnessed the wings of Pegasus, 135
so as to appear more like a tragic hero in the eyes of the gods?

TRYGAEUS: But, my dear girl, I'd have needed double rations. As it
is, whatever food I eat I can use again to feed this creature.

DAUGHTER: What if it falls into the watery depths of the sea? How 140
will it be able to escape, winged as it is?

TRYGAEUS: I brought for that very purpose an oar [*indicating his
phallus*], which I will use; and my vessel will be a beetle-boat, made
in Naxos.

DAUGHTER: And as you drift, what harbour will receive you?

TRYGAEUS: There's a Beetle Harbour at Peiraeus, isn't there? 145

DAUGHTER: Watch out for one thing, that you don't slip off and drop
from up there, and then be lamed and provide Euripides with a plot and
get turned into a tragedy.

TRYGAEUS: I'll take care I don't. Farewell! [*The girls and the
slave go inside. To the audience*] And you, on whose behalf I am performing 150
these labours, pray do not fart or crap for three days; for if this creature
smells it while in the air, he'll throw me off, head first, and go off to
graze.

[*The beetle, which until now has been more or less stationary in the air,
now begins to carry Trygaeus upwards and away from the house. Its motion is,
however, rather jerky, and from time to time an abrupt downward lurch nearly
throws the rider off.*]

TRYGAEUS: Come now, Pegasus, get going, and good luck to you,
        with bright ears pricked, setting in motion 155-6
        the rattle of cavesson and golden bit. —
        What are you doing, what are you doing? Why are you
        bending your nostrils towards the alleyways?
        Let yourself confidently go, away from earth,
        and then stretch out your racing wings 160

ὀρθὸς χώρει Διὸς εἰς αὐλάς,
ἀπὸ μὲν κάκκης τὴν ῥῖν' ἀπέχων,
ἀπό θ' ἡμερίων σίτων πάντων.
ἄνθρωπε, τί δρᾷς, οὗτος ὁ χέζων
ἐν Πειραιεῖ παρὰ ταῖς πόρναις;   165
ἀπολεῖς μ', ἀπολεῖς. οὐ κατορύξεις
κἀπιφορήσεις τῆς γῆς πολλὴν
κἀπιφυτεύσεις ἕρπυλλον ἄνω
καὶ μύρον ἐπιχεῖς; ὡς ἤν τι πεσὼν
ἐνθένδε πάθω, τοὐμοῦ θανάτου   170
πέντε τάλανθ' ἡ πόλις ἡ Χίων
διὰ τὸν σὸν πρωκτὸν ὀφλήσει.

οἴμ', ὡς δέδοικα· κοὐκέτι σκώπτων λέγω.
ὦ μηχανοποιέ, πρόσεχε τὸν νοῦν, ὡς ἐμὲ
ἤδη στρέφει τι πνεῦμα περὶ τὸν ὀμφαλόν,   175
κεἰ μὴ φυλάξει, χορτάσω τὸν κάνθαρον.
ἀτὰρ ἐγγὺς εἶναι τῶν θεῶν ἐμοὶ δοκῶ·
καὶ δὴ καθορῶ τὴν οἰκίαν τὴν τοῦ Διός.
τίς ἐν Διὸς θύραισιν; οὐκ ἀνοίξετε;
ΕΡΜΗΣ
    πόθεν βροτοῦ με προσέβαλ'—; ὦναξ Ἡράκλεις·   180

161 ὀρθὸς V: ὀρθῶς Rpt.
163 ἡμερίων ᶦΣ^RV: ἡμεριῶν (altered to -ινῶν, then altered back)
        λΣ^R: ἡμερινῶν codd. λSuda.
163 σίτων Brunck: σιτίων codd. λSuda: σκατίων Bentley.
175 στρέφει Dindorf: στροφεῖ codd.
176 φυλάξει Reiske: φυλάξεις codd.

18

and make straight for the halls of Zeus,
keeping your nose far from shit
and from all mortal foods. —
You, man, what are you doing, you that's shitting
in Peiraeus, in the whores' quarter?   165
You'll kill me, you'll kill me! Will you please bury the stuff
and heap lots of earth on top
and plant thyme over it
and pour on perfume? Because if I fall from up here
and anything happens to me, the state of Chios   170
will be fined five talents on account of my death,
and all thanks to your arsehole!

[*The beetle is now at the highest point of its flight; with the crane
moving it somewhat jerkily, Trygaeus finds himself being rocked uncomfortably
backwards and forwards.*]

TRYGAEUS: Help! I'm terrified! And I'm not joking now! Mr. Crane
Operator, pay attention! There's already a sort of wind that's doubling   175
me up round about the navel, and if you don't take care, I'll be giving the
beetle a meal! [*The beetle, now moving more smoothly, begins to descend.*]
Ah, I think I'm near the gods now; in fact I can see the house of Zeus, [*The
beetle lands in front of the door at the far end of the stage-house from that
at which its flight began. Trygaeus dismounts, goes to the door and knocks.*]
Who is within Zeus's doors? Open up, will you?

HERMES [*within, coming to the door*] : Whence came that mortal voice   180
that — [*He opens the door and sees Trygaeus and the beetle.*] Lord Heracles!

```
                τουτὶ τί ἐστι τὸ κακόν;

Τρ.                              ἱπποκάνθαρος.

Ερ.  ὦ βδελυρὲ καὶ τολμηρὲ κάναίσχυντε σὺ
     καὶ μιαρὲ καὶ παμμίαρε καὶ μιαρώτατε.
     πῶς δεῦρ' ἀνῆλθες, ὦ μιαρῶν μιαρώτατε;
     τί σού ποτ' ἔστ' ὄνομ'; οὐκ ἐρεῖς;

Τρ.                              Μιαρώτατος.            185

Ερ.  ποδαπὸς τὸ γένος δ' εἶ; φράζε μοι.

Τρ.                              Μιαρώτατος.

Ερ.  πατὴρ δέ σοι τίς ἐστ';

Τρ.                    ἐμοί; Μιαρώτατος.

Ερ.  οὗτοι μὰ τὴν Γῆν ἐσθ' ὅπως οὐκ ἀποθανεῖ,
     εἰ μὴ κατερεῖς μοι τοὔνομ' ὅ τί ποτ' ἐστί σοι.

Τρ.  Τρυγαῖος Ἀθμονεύς, ἀμπελουργὸς δεξιός,        190
     οὐ συκοφάντης οὐδ' ἐραστὴς πραγμάτων.

Ερ.  ἥκεις δὲ κατὰ τί;

Τρ.              τὰ κρέα ταυτί σοι φέρων.

Ερ.  ὦ δειλακρίων, πῶς ἦλθες;

Τρ.                    ὦ γλίσχρων, ὁρᾷς
     ὡς οὐκέτ' εἶναί σοι δοκῶ μιαρώτατος;
     ἴθι νυν κάλεσόν μοι τὸν Δί'.

Ερ.                    ἰὴ ἰὴ ἰή,            195
     ὅτ' οὐδὲ μέλλεις ἐγγὺς εἶναι τῶν θεῶν·
     φροῦδοι γάρ· ἐχθές εἰσιν ἐξῳκισμένοι.


   182  βδελυρὲ Dindorf, cf. Frogs 465: μιαρὲ codd. Suda.

                              20
```

what is this awful thing?

TRYGAEUS: It's a hippobeetle.

[*During the ensuing dialogue the beetle is swung offstage by the crane.*]

HERMES [*passing from shock to rage*]: You loathsome, audacious, shameless creature! You villain, you arch-villain, you utter villain! How did you come up here, you arch-villain of all villains? What may your name be? 185
Say it, won't you?

TRYGAEUS: Archvillain.

HERMES: And where are you from by birth, tell me?

TRYGAEUS: I'm an Archvillain.

HERMES: And who is your father?

TRYGAEUS: Archvillain.

HERMES: By holy Earth, you shall most certainly die if you don't tell me just what your name is.

TRYGAEUS: I'm Trygaeus of Athmonum, a skilled vine-grower, not a 190
bringer of malicious accusations and not a lover of disputes.

HERMES: And what have you come for?

TRYGAEUS: To give you this meat [*presenting it to him*].

HERMES: [*eagerly taking the meat, and with a complete change of tone*]:
You poor little thing! you really came here for that?

TRYGAEUS: You old cadger! do you see, you don't think I'm an arch-
villain any more! Now please go and call Zeus for me. 195

HERMES: Ha-ha-ha-ha! When you haven't even a chance of getting
near the gods! They're gone. They moved out yesterday.

Τρ. ποῖ γῆς;

Ερ.   ἰδοὺ γῆς.

Τρ.   ἀλλὰ ποῖ;

Ερ.   πόρρω πάνυ·
ὑπ' αὐτὸν ἀτεχνῶς τοὐρανοῦ τὸν κύτταρον.

Τρ. πῶς οὖν σὺ δῆτ' ἐνταῦθα κατελείφθης μόνος;   200

Ερ. τὰ λοιπὰ τηρῶ σκευάρια τὰ τῶν θεῶν,
χυτρίδια καὶ σανίδια καμφορείδια.

Τρ. ἐξῳκίσαντο δ' οἱ θεοὶ τίνος οὕνεκα;

Ερ. Ἕλλησιν ὀργισθέντες. εἶτ' ἐνταῦθα μέν,
ἵν' ἦσαν αὐτοί, τὸν Πόλεμον κατῴκισαν,   205
ὑμᾶς παραδόντες δρᾶν ἀτεχνῶς ὅ τι βούλεται·
αὐτοὶ δ' ἀνῳκίσανθ' ὅπως ἀνωτάτω,
ἵνα μὴ βλέποιεν μαχομένους ὑμᾶς ἔτι
μηδ' ἀντιβολούντων μηδὲν αἰσθανοίατο.

Τρ. τοῦ δ' οὕνεχ' ἡμᾶς ταῦτ' ἔδρασαν; εἰπέ μοι.   210

Ερ. ὁτιὴ πολεμεῖν ᾑρεῖσθ', ἐκείνων πολλάκις
σπονδὰς ποιούντων· κεἰ μὲν οἱ Λακωνικοὶ
ὑπερβάλοιντο μικρόν, ἔλεγον ἂν ταδί·
"ναὶ τὼ σιώ, νῦν ἀττικίων δωσεῖ δίκαν."
εἰ δ' αὖ τι πράξαιτ' ἀγαθὸν ἀττικωνικοὶ   215
κἄλθοιεν οἱ Λάκωνες εἰρήνης πέρι,
ἐλέγετ' ἂν ὑμεῖς εὐθύς· "ἐξαπατώμεθα,

211 ὁτιὴ Bentley: ὅτι codd.
214 δίκαν Hirschig: δίκην codd.
215 πράξαιτ' Bekker: πράξαιντ' codd.

22

TRYGAEUS: Where on earth to?

HERMES [*scornfully*] : On earth indeed!

TRYGAEUS: Well, where?

HERMES: Far, far away, right under the very cupola of heaven.

TRYGAEUS: So how come, then, you were left behind here on your own?   200

HERMES: I'm keeping an eye on the bits of equipment the gods left here
— the odd pots and boards and jars.

TRYGAEUS: And what was the reason for the gods' moving house?

HERMES: They were angry with the Greeks. So here, where they used to   205
live, they installed War in residence, handing you over to him to do exactly
as he liked with; while for themselves they took new quarters as high up
as they could get, so that they couldn't see you fighting any more or hear
your entreaties at all.

TRYGAEUS: But tell me, why did they do that to us?   210

HERMES: Because when they repeatedly tried to make peace, you
preferred to wage war. If the Laconians gained a small advantage, this is what
they'd say: "Ah, by the Twin Gods, now the Attic boys will get what's coming
to them!" And on the other hand if you Atticonians gained some success and   215
the Laconians came to discuss peace, at once you'd say "We're being tricked,

νὴ τὴν ᾿Αθηνᾶν." — "νὴ Δί᾿, οὐχὶ πειστέον·
ἥξουσι καὖθις, ἢν ἔχωμεν τὴν Πύλον."

Τρ. ὁ γοῦν χαρακτὴρ ἡμεδαπὸς τῶν ῥημάτων.   220

Ερ. ὧν οὔνεκ᾿ οὐκ οἶδ᾿ εἴ ποτ᾿ Εἰρήνην ἔτι
τὸ λοιπὸν ὄψεσθ᾿.

Τρ.   ἀλλὰ ποῖ γὰρ οἴχεται;

Ερ. ὁ Πόλεμος αὐτὴν ἐνέβαλ᾿ εἰς ἄντρον βαθύ.

Τρ. εἰς ποῖον;

Ερ.   εἰς τουτὶ τὸ κάτω. κἄπειθ᾿ ὁρᾷς
ὅσους ἄνωθεν ἐπεφόρησε τῶν λίθων,   225
ἵνα μὴ λάβητε μηδέποτ᾿ αὐτήν;

Τρ.   εἰπέ μοι,
ἡμᾶς δὲ δὴ τί δρᾶν παρασκευάζεται;

Ερ. οὐκ οἶδα πλὴν ἕν, ὅτι θυείαν ἑσπέρας
ὑπερφυᾶ τὸ μέγεθος εἰσηνέγκατο.

Τρ. τί δῆτα ταύτῃ τῇ θυείᾳ χρήσεται;   230

Ερ. τρίβειν ἐν αὐτῇ τὰς πόλεις βουλεύεται.
ἀλλ᾿ εἶμι· καὶ γὰρ ἐξιέναι, γνώμην ἐμήν,
μέλλει· θορυβεῖ γοῦν ἔνδον.

Τρ.   οἴμοι δείλαιος.
φέρ᾿ αὐτὸν ἀποδρῶ· καὶ γὰρ ὥσπερ ᾐσθόμην
καὐτὸς θυείας φθέγμα πολεμιστηρίας.   235
ΠΟΛΕΜΟΣ
ἰὼ βροτοὶ βροτοὶ βροτοὶ πολυτλήμονες,
ὡς αὐτίκα μάλα τὰς γνάθους ἀλγήσετε.

219   Πύλον pt: πόλιν RV: Σ^{RV} discuss both readings.

24

by Athena!" — "By Zeus, yes, we mustn't be persuaded; they'll come again,
if we hold on to Pylos."

TRYGAEUS: Certainly those words bear the stamp of our people. 220

HERMES: And therefore I don't know whether in the future you'll ever
see Peace again.

TRYGAEUS: Why, where has she gone?

HERMES: War has cast her into a deep cavern.

TRYGAEUS: What cavern?

HERMES [*taking Trygaeus to the central portal of the stage-house, and
pointing into it at a downward angle*]: That one down there. And then do
you see how many stones he's heaped on top, so that you'll never be able 225
to get her?

TRYGAEUS: And tell me, what's he getting ready to do to *us*?

HERMES: I only know one thing, that last evening he brought home a
mortar of enormous size.

TRYGAEUS: So what's he going to do with this mortar? 230

HERMES: He's planning to pound up the Greek states in it. But I'm
off. He's just going to come outside, if you ask me — at any rate he's
making some noise in there.

[*Hermes goes off by a side passage. The noise within grows louder.*]

TRYGAEUS: Heaven help us! Here, let me escape from him; I've also
sort of become aware of the voice of a martial mortar. 235

[*Trygaeus conceals himself. War comes out of the house of Zeus, carrying
a gigantic mortar and a basket of foodstuffs.*]

WAR: Oho, mortals, mortals, most wretched mortals, how sore you're
going to be in the jaws very shortly!

Τρ. ὦναξ Ἄπολλον, τῆς θυείας τοῦ πλάτους.
     ὅσον κακὸν καὶ τοῦ Πολέμου τοῦ βλέμματος.
     ἆρ' οὗτός ἐστ' ἐκεῖνος ὃν καὶ φεύγομεν,   240
     ὁ δεινός, ὁ ταλαύρινος, ὁ κατὰ τοῖν σκελοῖν;

Πο. ἰὼ Πρασιαὶ τρὶς ἄθλιαι καὶ πεντάκις
     καὶ πολλοδεκάκις, ὡς ἀπολεῖσθε τήμερον.

Τρ. τουτὶ μέν, ἄνδρες, οὐδὲν ἡμῖν πρᾶγμά πω·
     τὸ γὰρ κακὸν τοῦτ' ἐστὶ τῆς Λακωνικῆς.   245

Πο. ὦ Μέγαρα Μέγαρ', ὡς ἐπιτετρίψεσθ' αὐτίκα
     ἀπαξάπαντα καταμεμυττωτευμένα.

Τρ. βαβαὶ βαβαιάξ, ὡς μεγάλα καὶ δριμέα
     τοῖσι Μεγαρεῦσιν ἐνέβαλεν τὰ κλαύματα.

Πο. ἰὼ Σικελία, καὶ σὺ δ' ὡς ἀπόλλυσαι.   250

Τρ. οἵα πόλις τάλαινα διακναισθήσεται.

Πο. φέρ' ἐπιχέω καὶ τὸ μέλι τουτὶ τἀττικόν.

Τρ. οὗτος, παραινῶ σοι μέλιτι χρῆσθαι 'τέρῳ.
     τετρώβολον τοῦτ' ἐστί· φείδου τἀττικοῦ.

Πο. παῖ παῖ Κυδοιμέ.
ΚΥΔΟΙΜΟΣ
               τί με καλεῖς;

Πο.   κλαύσει μακρά.   255
     ἕστηκας ἀργός; οὑτοσί σοι κόνδυλος.

246 ὦ ... ἐπιτετρίψεσθ' Elmsley: ὦ ... ἐπιτρίψεσθ' (ἐπιτρίβεσθ'
     V^{ac}) RV: ἰὼ ... ἐπιτρίψεσθ' pt: ἐπιτρίψεσθ' also ^λΣ^R and
     (-σθαι) Σ^V 252.
253 χρῆσθαι 'τέρῳ Brunck: χρῆσθαι θἀτέρῳ codd.

26

TRYGAEUS [*peeping out of his hiding place*]: Lord Apollo, the size of
that mortar! And how much evil there is, too, in War's expression! Is   240
he the same god that we all shun, the fearsome one, the redoubtable one,
the one that gets into your legs?

WAR [*taking leeks from the basket and throwing them into the mortar*]:
Oho, Prasiae, thrice wretched, five times wretched, umpteen times wretched,
how you'll be murdered today!

TRYGAEUS [*aside to the audience*]: Well, gentlemen, that doesn't bother
us as yet; that's Laconia's headache.   245

WAR [*adding garlic*]: Ho, Megara, Megara, how you will be crushed
presently, every bit of you, and made a savoury mash of!

TRYGAEUS [*aside*]: Whew, whewee! What big and bitter wailings he's
thrown in there for the Megarians!

WAR [*adding cheese*]: Oho, Sicily, what a doom is yours too!   250

TRYGAEUS [*aside*]: What a fine country is to be miserably grated up!

WAR [*adding honey*]: Here, let me also pour on this Attic honey.

TRYGAEUS [*aside*]: Hey, you, I recommend you to use different honey.
Be sparing with the Attic; it costs four obols!

WAR [*calling into the house*]: Boy, boy! Hurlyburly!   255

HURLYBURLY [*coming out*]: What did you call for?

WAR: I'll make you really howl! Standing idle, are you? Here's a
fist for you! [*He cuffs Hurlyburly in the face.*]

Κυ. ὡς δριμύς. οἴμοι μοι τάλας, ὦ δέσποτα.

Τρ. μῶν τῶν σκορόδων ἐνέβαλες εἰς τὸν κόνδυλον;

Πο. οἴσεις ἀλετρίβανον τρέχων;

Κυ.   ἀλλ', ὦ μέλε,
οὐκ ἔστιν ἡμῖν· ἐχθὲς εἰσῳκίσμεθα.   260

Πο. οὔκουν παρ' Ἀθηναίων †μεταθρέξει ταχύ†;

Κυ. ἔγωγε νὴ Δί'· εἰ δὲ μή γε, κλαύσομαι.

Τρ. ἄγε δή, τί δρῶμεν, ὦ πόνηρ' ἀνθρώπια;
ὁρᾶτε τὸν κίνδυνον ἡμῖν ὡς μέγας·
εἴπερ γὰρ ἥξει τὸν ἀλετρίβανον φέρων,   265
τούτῳ ταράξει τὰς πόλεις καθήμενος.
ἀλλ', ὦ Διόνυσ', ἀπόλοιτο καὶ μὴ 'λθοι φέρων.

Κυ. οὗτος.

Πο.   τί ἐστιν; οὐ φέρεις;

Κυ.   τὸ δεῖνα γάρ,
ἀπόλωλ' Ἀθηναίοισιν ἀλετρίβανος,
ὁ βυρσοπώλης, ὃς ἐκύκα τὴν Ἑλλάδα.   270

Τρ. εὖ γ', ὦ πότνια δέσποιν' Ἀθηναία, ποιῶν
ἀπόλωλ' ἐκεῖνος κἂν δέοντι τῇ πόλει.   272

Πο. οὔκουν ἕτερον δῆτ' ἐκ Λακεδαίμονος μέτει   274

257 οἴμοι μοι t: οἴμοι RVp.
261 †μεταθρέξει ταχύ† codd.: <σὺ> μ. ταχύ Brunck: μ. ταχὺ
      <πάνυ> Dobree.
271 πότνια δέσποιν' Bᵖᶜ: δέσποινα πότνι' RVpt: [Bᵃᶜ].
[273] ἢ (εἰ ¹ΣRVL 271) πρίν γε τὸν μυττωτὸν ἡμῖν ἐγχέαι codd.
      Suda: del. Dindorf.

28

HURLYBURLY [*in pain*] : What a sting! Aah, poor me! Master!

TRYGAEUS [*aside*] : You didn't put some of the garlic into that blow, did you?

WAR [*to Hurlyburly*] : Will you run and fetch a pestle?

HURLYBURLY: But, sir, we haven't got one. We only moved in yesterday.   260

WAR: So won't you run and get one from Athens, fast?

HURLYBURLY: I certainly will; [*aside*] if I *don't*, I'll be made to howl for it. [*He runs off.*]

TRYGAEUS [*to the audience*] : Come on now, poor unhappy folk, what are we to do? You see what great danger we're in: if the boy does come back   265
with that pestle, he'll sit down and make a pulp of the Greek states with
it. Please, Dionysus, may he perish and not come back with it!

HURLYBURLY [*returning*] : I say!

WAR: What's the matter? Haven't you brought it?

HURLYBURLY: Well, er, the thing is — the Athenians have lost their pestle, the leather-seller who churned up all Greece.   270

TRYGAEUS [*aside*] : Sovereign Lady Athena! he did well to get lost, just when the city needed to lose him!

WAR [*to Hurlyburly*] : Then you'd better hurry up and go and get another   274-5
from Sparta.

ἀνύσας τι;

Κυ.   ταῦτ', ὦ δέσποθ'.

Πο.   ἧκέ νυν ταχύ.   275

Τρ. ὦνδρες, τί πεισόμεσθα; νῦν ἀγὼν μέγας.
    ἀλλ' εἴ τις ὑμῶν ἐν Σαμοθρᾴκῃ τυγχάνει
    μεμυημένος, νῦν ἐστιν εὔξασθαι καλὸν
    ἀποστραφῆναι τοῦ μετιόντος τὼ πόδε.

Κυ. οἴμοι τάλας· οἴμοι γε κᾆτ' οἴμοι μάλα.   280

Πο. τί ἐστι; μῶν οὐκ αὖ φέρεις;

Κυ.   ἀπόλωλε γὰρ
    καὶ τοῖς Λακεδαιμονίοισιν ἀλετρίβανος.

Πο. πῶς, ὦ πανοῦργ';

Κυ.   εἰς τἀπὶ Θρᾴκης χωρία
    χρήσαντες ἑτέροις αὐτὸν εἶτ' ἀπώλεσαν.

Τρ. εὖ γ' εὖ γε ποιήσαντες, ὦ Διοσκόρω.   285
    ἴσως ἂν εὖ γένοιτο· θαρρεῖτ', ὦ βροτοί.

Πο. ἀπόφερε τὰ σκεύη λαβὼν ταυτὶ πάλιν·
    ἐγὼ δὲ δοίδυκ' εἰσιὼν ποιήσομαι.

Τρ. νῦν τοῦτ' ἐκεῖν'· ἧκει τὸ Δάτιδος μέλος,
    ὃ δεφόμενός ποτ' ᾖδε τῆς μεσημβρίας·   290
    "ὡς ἥδομαι καὶ χαίρομαι κεὐφραίνομαι."
    νῦν ἐστιν ἡμῖν, ὦνδρες Ἕλληνες, καλὸν
    ἀπαλλαγεῖσι πραγμάτων τε καὶ μαχῶν
    ἐξελκύσαι τὴν πᾶσιν Εἰρήνην φίλην,
    πρὶν ἕτερον αὖ δοίδυκα κωλῦσαί τινα.   295

292 ἡμῖν t: ὑμῖν RVp.

30

HURLYBURLY: Yes, master. [*He runs off.*]

WAR [*calling after him*]: Come back quickly now.

TRYGAEUS [*To the audience*]: What's going to happen to us, men? This is the crunch now! If any of you happens to have been initiated at Samothrace, now's a fine chance for you to pray that the errand-boy may safely — get two twisted feet!

HURLYBURLY [*returning*]: Woe is me! Oh woe! And woe once more!   280

WAR: What is it? You don't mean to say you still haven't brought one?

HURLYBURLY: Yes, the Spartans have lost their pestle too!

WAR: What do you mean, you rogue?

HURLYBURLY: They lent it to some other people to use in the Thracian Coast area, and lost it there.

TRYGAEUS [*aside*]: Oh, Sons of Zeus, well done, well done of them!   285
Things may perhaps be all right. Take heart, mortals!

WAR [*to Hurlyburly*]: Pick up this stuff and take it back inside. I'll go in and make myself a pestle. [*The two go into the house, Hurlyburly carrying mortar and basket.*]

TRYGAEUS [*coming forward*]: This is it now! Here comes the old song of Datis, which he used to sing when he was wanking of a noonday: "How   290 I'm delighted, how I'm rejoiced, how I'm elated!" Now, men of Greece, now's a fine chance for us to be rid of broils and battles and to haul out Peace, so dear to us all, before some other pestle can interfere! You peasants and   295

ἀλλ', ὦ γεωργοὶ κἄμποροι καὶ τέκτονες
καὶ δημιουργοὶ καὶ μέτοικοι καὶ ξένοι
καὶ νησιῶται, δεῦρ' ἴτ', ὦ πάντες λεῴ,
ὡς τάχιστ', ἅμας λαβόντες καὶ μοχλοὺς καὶ σχοινία.
νῦν γὰρ †ἡμῖν ἁρπάσαι† πάρεστιν ἀγαθοῦ δαίμονος.   300

ΧΟΡΟΣ
   δεῦρο πᾶς χώρει προθύμως εὐθὺ τῆς σωτηρίας.
ὦ Πανέλληνες, βοηθήσωμεν, εἴπερ πώποτε,
τάξεων ἀπαλλαγέντες καὶ κακῶν φοινικίδων·
ἡμέρα γὰρ ἐξέλαμψεν ἥδε μισολάμαχος.
πρὸς τάδ' ἡμῖν, εἴ τι χρὴ δρᾶν, φράζε κἀρχιτεκτόνει·   305
οὐ γάρ ἐσθ' ὅπως ἀπειπεῖν ἂν δοκῶ μοι τήμερον,
πρὶν μοχλοῖς καὶ μηχαναῖσιν εἰς τὸ φῶς ἀνελκύσαι
τὴν θεῶν πασῶν μεγίστην καὶ φιλαμπελωτάτην.

Τρ. οὐ σιωπήσεσθ'; ὅπως μὴ περιχαρεῖς τῷ πράγματι
τὸν Πόλεμον ἐκζωπυρήσετ' ἔνδοθεν κεκραγότες.   310

Χο. ἀλλ' ἀκούσαντες τοιούτου χαίρομεν κηρύγματος·
οὐ γὰρ ἦν ἔχοντας ἥκειν σιτί' ἡμερῶν τριῶν.

Τρ. εὐλαβεῖσθέ νυν ἐκεῖνον τὸν κάτωθεν Κέρβερον,
μὴ παφλάζων καὶ κεκραγώς, ὥσπερ ἡνίκ' ἐνθάδ' ἦν,
ἐμποδὼν ἡμῖν γένηται τὴν θεὸν μὴ 'ξελκύσαι.   315

Χο. †οὔτι καὶ νῦν† ἐστιν αὐτὴν ὅστις ἐξαιρήσεται,
ἢν ἅπαξ εἰς χεῖρας ἔλθῃ τὰς ἐμάς. ἰοὺ ἰού.

300 †ἡμῖν ἁρπάσαι† codd.: ἡμῖν αὖ σπάσαι van Herwerden.
303 καλῶν Sommerstein, φοινικίδων (cf. Σ^RVL) Meineke: κακῶν
     φοινικικῶν (φοινικίων V^ac) codd. Suda ^λΣ^L.
314 καὶ κεκραγὼς t: καὶ κραγὼς V^ac: κεκραγὼς RV^pc p.
316 †οὔτι καὶ νῦν† codd.: οὔτι χαίρων Meineke: οὐδ'
     ἐκεῖθεν Richter.

merchants and carpenters and craftsmen and immigrants and foreigners and   islanders, come hither, all ye people, as quickly as you can, bringing shovels and crowbars and ropes; for now is our chance to have a pull at the Good Spirit's cup!   300

[*The chorus enter, with quick and enthusiastic step, by one of the side passages, carrying ropes, shovels, etc.*]

CHORUS-LEADER: Come this way, everyone eagerly, straight to our liberation! All you Greeks, let us come and help — now or never — and be rid of military formations and smart scarlet cloaks; for now has brightly dawned the day that Lamachus abhors! [*To Trygaeus*] So you   305 tell us whatever has to be done, and be our director; there's no way I can see myself getting tired today, until with levers and every kind of contrivance we have hauled up to the light the greatest and most vine-loving of all goddesses.

TRYGAEUS: *Will* you be quiet? Take care that in your joy at what has happened you don't rekindle War in there by your shouting.   310

CHORUS-LEADER: The thing is, we're delighted to have heard *that* kind of proclamation, because it wasn't an order to "come with three days' rations".

TRYGAEUS: Beware now of that Cerberus in the underworld, in case he starts spluttering and screaming as he did when he was up here, and makes   315 himself an obstacle to our rescuing the goddess.

CHORUS-LEADER: There is no one who will take her away from us if once she comes into our possession! [*The chorus give two loud cheers.*]

33

Τρ. ἐξολεῖτε μ', ὦνδρες, εἰ μὴ τῆς βοῆς ἀνήσετε·
     ἐκδραμὼν γὰρ πάντα ταυτὶ συνταράξει τοῖν ποδοῖν.

Χο. ὡς κυκάτω καὶ πατείτω πάντα καὶ ταραττέτω·   320
     οὐ γὰρ ἂν χαίροντες ἡμεῖς τήμερον παυσαίμεθ' ἄν.

Τρ. τί τὸ κακόν; τί πάσχετ', ὦνδρες; μηδαμῶς, πρὸς τῶν θεῶν,
     πρᾶγμα κάλλιστον διαφθείρητε διὰ τὰ σχήματα.

Χο. ἀλλ' ἔγωγ' οὐ σχηματίζειν βούλομ', ἀλλ' ὑφ' ἡδονῆς
     οὐκ ἐμοῦ κινοῦντος αὐτὼ τὼ σκέλει χορεύετον.   325

Τρ. μή τί μοι νυνί γ' ἔτ', ἀλλὰ παῦε παῦ' ὀρχούμενος.

Χο. ἤν, ἰδού· καὶ δὴ πέπαυμαι.

Τρ.   φής γε, παύει δ' οὐδέπω.

Χο. ἓν μὲν οὖν τουτί μ' ἔασον ἑλκύσαι, καὶ μηκέτι.

Τρ. τοῦτό νυν, καὶ μηκέτ' ἄλλο· μηδὲν ὀρχήσησθ' ἔτι.

Χο. οὐκ ἂν ὀρχησαίμεθ', εἴπερ ὠφελήσομέν τί σε.   330

Τρ. ἀλλ', ὁρᾶτ', οὔπω πέπαυσθε.

Χο.   τουτογὶ νὴ τὸν Δία
     τὸ σκέλος ῥίψαντες ἤδη λήγομεν τὸ δεξιόν.

Τρ. ἐπιδίδωμι τοῦτό γ' ὑμῖν, ὥστε μὴ λυπεῖν ἔτι.

Χο. ἀλλὰ καὶ τἀριστερόν τού μ' ἔστ' ἀναγκαίως ἔχον.
     ἥδομαι γὰρ καὶ γέγηθα καὶ πέπορδα καὶ γελῶ   335
     μᾶλλον ἢ τὸ γῆρας ἐκδὺς ἐκφυγὼν τὴν ἀσπίδα.

326 τί μοι Blaydes: τι καὶ codd.
329 ὀρχήσησθ' Bekker: ὀρχήσεσθ' codd.
330 ὠφελήσομέν Blaydes: ὠφελήσαιμέν codd.

34

TRYGAEUS: You'll be the ruin of me, men, if you don't ease up on your shouting. He'll rush out and trample the whole place into chaos.

CHORUS-LEADER: I tell you — let him make chaos, let him make confusion, let him trample everything — today we're not going to stop rejoicing! 320

[*The chorus begin a dance of joy.*]

TRYGAEUS: What's wrong with you? What's got into you, men? In the gods' name, don't ruin a splendid situation with your dances.

CHORUS-LEADER: *I* don't actually *want* to dance — it's just that from sheer delight my legs are dancing by themselves without my moving them. 325

TRYGAEUS: Well, no more now, please. Stop, stop dancing!

CHORUS-LEADER: There, look; there you are; I've stopped. [*But they dance on.*]

TRYGAEUS: That's what you *say*, but you still *don't* stop!

CHORUS-LEADER: No, let me tread this one figure, and then no more.

TRYGAEUS [*when they have completed the figure*]: That's it then; nothing else now. [*The chorus still continue dancing.*] Don't dance *any* more!

CHORUS-LEADER: If it'll really help you, we won't dance. [*But they dance on.*] 330

TRYGAEUS: But look, you still haven't stopped!

CHORUS-LEADER: Yes, I swear; we kick out this right leg here, and then we're finished.

TRYGAEUS: I make you a gift of that, so long as you don't go on making a nuisance of yourselves.

CHORUS-LEADER: But I can't avoid doing the same with the left as well, you know! [*And after this second high kick the chorus still continue their dance.*] I'm glad, I'm happy, I fart, I laugh, at having escaped from my 335 shield, more than if I'd cast off my old age!

Τρ. μή τί μοι νυνί γε χαίρετ'· οὐ γὰρ ἴστε πω σαφῶς·
ἀλλ' ὅταν λάβωμεν αὐτήν, τηνικαῦτα χαίρετε
καὶ βοᾶτε καὶ γελᾶτ'· ἤ-
    δη γὰρ ἐξέσται τόθ' ὑμῖν   340
    πλεῖν, μένειν, κινεῖν, καθεύδειν,
    εἰς πανηγύρεις θεωρεῖν,
    ἑστιᾶσθαι, κοτταβίζειν,
    συβαριάζειν,
    "ἰοὺ ἰοὺ" κεκραγέναι.   345

Χο. εἰ γὰρ ἐκγένοιτ' ἰδεῖν ταύτην μέ ποτε τὴν ἡμέραν.   (στρ.
πολλὰ γὰρ ἀνεσχόμην
    πράγματά τε καὶ στιβάδας,
    ἃς ἔλαχε Φορμίων.
κοὐκέτ' ἄν μ' εὕροις δικαστὴν δριμὺν οὐδὲ δύσκολον,
οὐδὲ τοὺς τρόπους γε δήπου σκληρόν, ὥσπερ καὶ πρὸ τοῦ, 350
ἀλλ' ἁπαλὸν ἄν μ' ἴδοις
    καὶ πολὺ νεώτερον ἀπ-
    αλλαγέντα πραγμάτων.
καὶ γὰρ ἱκανὸν χρόνον ἀπ-
    ολλύμεθα, καὶ κατατε-
    τρίμμεθα πλανώμενοι   355
εἰς Λύκειον κἀκ Λυκείου ξὺν δορὶ ξὺν ἀσπίδι.
ἀλλ' ὅ τι μάλιστα χαρι-
    ούμεθα ποιοῦντες, ἄγε

337 μή τί μοι Blaydes: μή τι (μήτε C) καὶ RVp: μηκέτ' οὖν t.
344 συβαριάζειν Meineke: συβαρίζειν codd. Apostolius.
346 ποτε τὴν ἡμέραν Dindorf (following the metrical analysis of
     Σ^V): τὴν ἡμέραν ποτέ codd.: τὴν ἡμέραν Bergk.
347 ἀνεσχόμην Brunck (cf. Σ^V 346): ἠνεσχόμην codd.

TRYGAEUS: Please don't rejoice just now. You don't know for certain
yet. But when we've got her, then you can rejoice and shout and laugh,
for then at last you'll be able to travel or stay at home, to screw or   340
sleep, to attend international festivals, to feast, to play cottabus,
to be a regular Sybarite, and to cry "hurrah, hurrah!"   345
CHORUS: Ah, may it be granted me to see that day at last!
                 I have endured many tribulations
                 and many palliasses,
                 of which Phormio is patron saint.
                 And you will no longer find me a fierce or ill-tempered juryman
                 nor, I fancy, hard in character, as I was hitherto,   350
                 but you will see me tender
                 and far more youthful
                 when I am released from troubles.
                 For long enough we've
                 been killing ourselves, and we're   355
                 worn out with traipsing
                 to the Lyceum and from the Lyceum "with spear, with shield".
                 But what can we do
                 to please you most? Come,

φράζε· σὲ γὰρ αὐτοκράτορ'
εὔλετ' ἀγαθή τις ἡμῖν τύχη.   360

Τρ. φέρε δὴ κατίδω πῇ τοὺς λίθους ἀφέλξομεν.

Ερ. ὦ μιαρὲ καὶ τολμηρέ, τί ποιεῖν διανοεῖ;

Τρ. οὐδὲν πονηρόν, ἀλλ' ὅπερ καὶ Κιλλικῶν.

Ερ. ἀπόλωλας, ὦ κακόδαιμον.

Τρ.   οὐκοῦν, ἢν λάχω.   364

Ερ. ἀπόλωλας, ἐξόλωλας.

Τρ.   εἰς τίν' ἡμέραν;   366

Ερ. εἰς αὐτίκα μάλ'.

Τρ.   ἀλλ' οὐδὲν ἠμπόληκά πω,
οὔτ' ἄλφιτ' οὔτε τυρόν, ὡς ἀπολούμενος.

Ερ. καὶ μὴν ἐπιτέτριψαί γε.

Τρ.   κᾆτα τῷ τρόπῳ
οὐκ ᾐσθόμην ἀγαθὸν τοσουτονὶ λαβών;   370

Ερ. ἆρ' οἶσθα θάνατον ὅτι προεῖφ' ὁ Ζεύς, ὃς ἂν
ταύτην ἀνορύττων εὑρεθῇ;

Τρ.   νῦν ἄρά με
ἅπασ' ἀνάγκη 'στ' ἀποθανεῖν;

Ερ.   εὖ ἴσθ' ὅτι.

Τρ. εἰς χοιρίδιόν μού νυν δάνεισον τρεῖς δραχμάς·
δεῖ γὰρ μυηθῆναί με πρὶν τεθνηκέναι.   375

361 πῇ Boissonade: ποῖ codd.
[365] Ἑρμῆς γὰρ ὢν κλήρῳ ποιήσεις οἶδ' ὅτι codd.: del. van Leeuwen

38

tell us; for a happy chance has chosen   359-
you to be our supreme commander.   360

TRYGAEUS [*going towards the central portal*]: Here now, let me see how we can pull the stones away.

[*He is about to go inside when he is stopped short by the voice of Hermes, who has re-entered by a side passage.*]

HERMES: You audacious villain! what are you meaning to do?

TRYGAEUS: Nothing wrong; the same as Cillicon.

HERMES: You are doomed to perish, you miserable wretch!   364

TRYGAEUS: Very well, I will, if the lot falls on me.

HERMES: You are doomed to perish, you are doomed to extinction!   366

TRYGAEUS: On what date?

HERMES: Immediately!

TRYGAEUS: But I haven't yet bought any groats or cheese for when I go to my death!

HERMES: And moreover you are utterly ruined and crushed!

TRYGAEUS: Then how come I didn't notice receiving so great a boon?   370

HERMES: Do you know that Zeus has proclaimed death to whoever is found digging that goddess up?

TRYGAEUS: So it's absolutely inevitable that I must die now?

HERMES: Be assured that it is.

TRYGAEUS: Then please lend me three drachmas for a sucking-pig; I   375 must get initiated before I die.

Ερ. ὦ Ζεῦ κεραυνοβρόντα—

Τρ.   μή, πρὸς τῶν θεῶν,
ἡμῶν κατείπῃς, ἀντιβολῶ σε, δέσποτα.

Ερ. οὐκ ἂν σιωπήσαιμι.

Τρ.   ναί, πρὸς τῶν κρεῶν,
ἁγὼ προθύμως σοι φέρων ἀφικόμην.

Ερ. ἀλλ', ὦ μέλ', ὑπὸ τοῦ Διὸς ἀμαλδυνθήσομαι,   380
εἰ μὴ τετορήσω ταῦτα καὶ λακήσομαι.

Τρ. μή νυν λακήσῃς, λίσσομαί σ', ὡρμήδιον.
εἰπέ μοι, τί πάσχετ', ὦνδρες; ἕστατ' ἐκπεπληγμένοι.
ὦ πόνηροι, μὴ σιωπᾶτ'· εἰ δὲ μή, λακήσεται.

Χο. μηδαμῶς, ὦ δέσποθ' Ἑρμῆ, μηδαμῶς, μή, μηδαμῶς,   (ἀντ.
εἴ τι κεχαρισμένον   386
    χοιρίδιον οἶσθα παρ' ἐ-
    μοῦ γε κατεδηδοκώς,
τοῦτο μὴ φαῦλον νόμιζ' ἐν τῇδε τῷ πράγματι.

Γρ. οὐκ ἀκούεις οἷα θωπεύουσί σ', ὦναξ δέσποτα;

Χο. μὴ γένῃ παλίγκοτος
    †ἀντιβολοῦσιν ἡμῖν,†   390
    ὥστε τήνδε μὴ λαβεῖν·
    ἀλλὰ χάρισ', ὦ φιλαν-

382 ὡρμήδιον Schwabe: ὡρμίδιον vel sim. codd.
385 μηδαμῶς μὴ μηδαμῶς t: μὴ μηδαμῶς μηδαμῶς RVp2: μὴ μηδαμῶς
     μὴ μηδαμῶς ΓC: μηδαμῶς μηδαμῶς V.
387 γε t: om. RVΓp.
388 νόμιζ' Bentley: νομίζων codd.
390 †ἀντιβολοῦσιν ἡμῖν† codd. Suda: σ' ἀντιάζουσιν ἡμῖν White.

40

HERMES [*raising his eyes and arms towards the upper heavens*]: O Zeus,
lord of thunder and the lightning-bolt —

TRYGAEUS: Don't, in the name of the gods, don't denounce us, Lord, I
beseech you.

HERMES: I refuse to remain silent.

TRYGAEUS: Do, in the name of the meat, which I eagerly came here to
bring you!

HERMES: But, my good man, I'll be annihilated by Zeus if I fail to   380
shrill this out and cry it aloud.

TRYGAEUS: Don't cry aloud, I implore you, my sweet little Hermes.
[*To the chorus*] I say, men, what's happened to you? You're standing stupefied.
Don't keep quiet, you silly fools; if you do, he'll cry aloud.

CHORUS: Do not, Lord Hermes, do not, no do not,   385
      if you remember ever
      having eaten with pleasure
      a young pig given by me,
      think that a slight thing at this present juncture.

TRYGAEUS: Do you not hear, O sovereign Lord, how they blandish you?

CHORUS: Do not be hostile   390
      to our entreaties
      so that we cannot get Peace;
      but be gracious, O most

θρωπότατε καὶ μεγαλο-
δωρότατε δαιμόνων,
εἴ τι Πεισάνδρου βδελύττει τοὺς λόφους καὶ τὰς ὀφρῦς, 395
καί σε θυσίαισιν ἱε-
ραῖσι προσόδοις τε μεγά-
λαισι διὰ παντός, ὦ
δέσποτ', ἀγαλοῦμεν ἡμεῖς ἀεί.

Τρ. ἴθ', ἀντιβολῶ σ', ἐλέησον αὐτῶν τὴν ὄπα, 400
ἐπεί σε καὶ τιμῶσι μᾶλλον ἢ πρὸ τοῦ,—

Ερ. κλέπται γάρ εἰσι νῦν γε μᾶλλον ἢ πρὸ τοῦ.

Τρ. καί σοι φράσω τι πρᾶγμα δεινὸν καὶ μέγα,
ὃ τοῖς θεοῖς ἅπασιν ἐπιβουλεύεται.

Ερ. ἴθι δὴ κάτειπ'· ἴσως γὰρ ἂν πείσαις ἐμέ. 405

Τρ. ἡ γὰρ Σελήνη χὠ πανοῦργος Ἥλιος
ὑμῖν ἐπιβουλεύοντε πολὺν ἤδη χρόνον
τοῖς βαρβάροισι προδίδοτον τὴν Ἑλλάδα.

Ερ. ἵνα δὴ τί τοῦτο δρᾶτον;

Τρ.   ὁτιὴ νὴ Δία
ἡμεῖς μὲν ὑμῖν θύομεν, τούτοισι δὲ 410
οἱ βάρβαροι θύουσι· διὰ τοῦτ' εἰκότως
βούλοιντ' ἂν ἡμᾶς πάντας ἐξολωλέναι,
ἵνα τὰς τελετὰς λάβοιεν αὐτοὶ τῶν θεῶν.

402 εἰσι νῦν γε μᾶλλον t: εἰσι νῦν μᾶλλον Γ: νῦν εἰσι μᾶλλον p
     (cf. νῦν εἰσιν ^λΣΓ): νῦν μᾶλλον εἰσὶν RV.
409 δὴ τί Bentley: τί δὴ RVΓp: τί δὲ t.
412 ἡμᾶς RV: ὑμᾶς Γpt.

42

      friendly to men and most generous

      in your gifts of all the gods,

      if you are at all sickened by Peisander's crests and brows,   395

      and we will always, Lord,

      glorify you continually

      with holy sacrifices

      and with great processions.

TRYGAEUS: Come, I beg you, take pity on their cry, even as they now   400
honour you more than ever before —

HERMES: Because they're bigger thieves than ever before.

TRYGAEUS: And I will tell you of something important and terrible, a
plot that has been made against all the gods.

HERMES: Come then, tell me; perchance you may persuade me.   405

TRYGAEUS: Well, the Moon and that villain the Sun have been plotting
against you for a long time now and trying to betray Greece to the barbarians.

HERMES: And for what purpose are they doing that?

TRYGAEUS: It's because, you see, we sacrifice to you and the barbarians   410
sacrifice to *them*; because of that it's natural that they should want us
all to be utterly destroyed, so that they could take over the cults of the
gods for themselves.

Ερ. ταῦτ' ἄρα πάλαι τῶν ἡμερῶν παρεκλεπτέτην
     καὶ τοῦ κύκλου παρέτρωγον ὑφ' ἁμαρτωλίας.   415

Τρ. ναὶ μὰ Δία. πρὸς ταῦτ', ὦ φίλ' Ἑρμῆ, ξύλλαβε
     ἡμῖν προθύμως †τήνδε καὶ† ξυνανέλκυσον,
     καὶ σοὶ τὰ μεγάλ' ἡμεῖς Παναθήναι' ἄξομεν
     πάσας τε τὰς ἄλλας τελετὰς τὰς τῶν θεῶν,
     μυστήρι' Ἑρμῆ, Διπολύει', Ἀδώνια·   420
     ἄλλαι τέ σοι πόλεις πεπαυμέναι κακῶν
     ἀλεξικάκῳ θύσουσιν Ἑρμῆ πανταχοῦ,
     χἄτερ' ἔτι πόλλ' ἕξεις ἀγαθά. πρῶτον δέ σοι
     δῶρον δίδωμι τήνδ', ἵνα σπένδειν ἔχῃς.

Ερ. οἴμ', ὡς ἐλεήμων εἴμ' ἀεὶ τῶν χρυσίδων.   425

Τρ. ὑμέτερον ἐντεῦθεν ἔργον, ὦνδρες. ἀλλὰ ταῖς ἅμαις
     εἰσιόντες ὡς τάχιστα τοὺς λίθους ἀφέλκετε.

Χο. ταῦτα δράσομεν· σὺ δ' ἡμῖν, ὦ θεῶν σοφώτατε,
     ἄττα χρὴ ποιεῖν ἐφεστὼς φράζε δημιουργικῶς·
     τἄλλα δ' εὑρήσεις ὑπουργεῖν ὄντας ἡμᾶς οὐ κακούς.   430

Τρ. ἄγε δὴ σὺ ταχέως ὕπεχε τὴν φιάλην, ὅπως
     ἔργῳ 'φιαλοῦμεν εὐξάμενοι τοῖσιν θεοῖς.

Ερ. σπονδὴ σπονδή·

414 παρεκλεπτέτην Brunck: παρεκλέπτετον RV^s: παρακλέπτετον V:
     παρέκλεπτον Γpt.
415 ἁμαρτωλίας ^{i}Anecd.Bekk. 79.10, ^{i}Photius: ἁρματωλίας codd. Sude
     Phrynichus in Σ^{VΓL}.
417 †τήνδε καὶ† codd.: τῶνδε καὶ or τήνδε τε Meineke.
417 ξυνανέλκυσον Dobree: ξυνέλκυσον codd.
420 Διπολύει' Wackernagel: Διιπόλει' codd. Σ^Γ+λ Σ^L: Διιπόλια Σ^V.

44

HERMES: Ah, that's why for a long time they've been quietly stealing some of the days and nibbling at the cycle of the year, wicked ones that they are! 415

TRYGAEUS: Yes, indeed. Therefore, dear Hermes, help us wholeheartedly in this task and join in hauling up Peace, and we will hold the great Panathenaea in *your* honour and also all the other cults of the gods — the Mysteries, the Dipolieia, the Adonia, in honour of Hermes: and the other states everywhere, released from their troubles, will sacrifice to you as Hermes the Averter of Evil, and you will have many other benefits as well. To begin with, I give you this as a present [*offering Hermes a gold-libation-bowl*], so that you'll have something to pour libations from. 420

HERMES [*taking the bowl*]: Dear me, what a soft spot I've always had for gold plate! 425

TRYGAEUS [*to the chorus*]: Now then, men, it's over to you. Go inside, and move away the stones with your shovels as quickly as possible.

CHORUS-LEADER: We'll do that. [*Some members of the chorus go in through the central portal, with shovels and ropes. The chorus-leader turns to Hermes.*] And you, cleverest of gods, you be in charge of us and tell us, like a master-builder, what we need to do; you'll find that for the rest we won't be slack in serving you. 430

[*By now those who went inside have come out and rejoined the chorus, having attached ropes to the trolley within. One of them brings out a flask of wine, which he gives to Trygaeus.*]

TRYGAEUS [*to Hermes*]: Come on, hurry up and hold out the bowl, so we can get boldly on with the job after praying to the gods. [*Hermes holds out the libation-bowl, and Trygaeus fills it.*]

HERMES: Libation, libation! Speak fair, speak fair! As we pour 435

εὐφημεῖτε εὐφημεῖτε.

σπένδοντες εὐχώμεσθα τὴν νῦν ἡμέραν   435
Ἕλλησιν ἄρξαι πᾶσι πολλῶν κἀγαθῶν,
χὤστις προθύμως ξυλλάβοι τῶν σχοινίων,
τοῦτον τὸν ἄνδρα μὴ λαβεῖν ποτ' ἀσπίδα.

Τρ. μὰ Δί', ἀλλ' ἐν εἰρήνῃ γε διάγειν τὸν βίον,
ἔχονθ' ἑταίραν καὶ σκαλεύοντ' ἄνθρακας.   440

Ἑρ. ὅστις δὲ πόλεμον μᾶλλον εἶναι βούλεται,—

Τρ. μηδέποτε παύσασθ' αὐτόν, ὦ Διόνυσ' ἄναξ,
ἐκ τῶν ὀλεκράνων ἀκίδας ἐξαιρούμενον.

Ἑρ. κεἴ τις ἐπιθυμῶν ταξιαρχεῖν σοι φθονεῖ
εἰς φῶς ἀνελθεῖν, ὦ πότνι', ἐν ταῖσιν μάχαις—   445

Τρ. πάσχοι γε τοιαῦθ' οἷάπερ Κλεώνυμος.

Ἑρ. κεἴ τις δορυξὸς ἢ κάπηλος ἀσπίδων,
ἵν' ἐμπολᾷ βέλτιον, ἐπιθυμεῖ μαχῶν,—

Τρ. ληφθείς γ' ὑπὸ λῃστῶν ἐσθίοι κριθὰς μόνας.

Ἑρ. κεἴ τις στρατηγεῖν βουλόμενος μὴ ξυλλάβῃ   450
ἢ δοῦλος αὐτομολεῖν παρεσκευασμένος,—

Τρ. ἐπὶ τοῦ τροχοῦ γ' ἕλκοιτο μαστιγούμενος.

Ἑρ. ἡμῖν δ' ἀγαθὰ γένοιτ'. ἰὴ Παιών, ἰή.

Τρ. ἄφελε τὸ παίειν, ἀλλ' ἰὴ μόνον λέγε.

439   γε διάγειν Rogers: διάγειν RVΓp Suda: διάγειν με t:
       διαπλέκειν Kock.
449   γ' Neil: om. codd. Suda.
450   ξυλλάβῃ codd. Suda: cf. Knights 698, 700, 805, Lys.
       580: ξυλλάβοι Meineke.

46

libation, let us pray that this day may be the beginning of many blessings
for all the Greeks, and that every man who zealously assists with the ropes
may never again take up a shield.

TRYGAEUS: No, indeed; rather may he spend his life in peace, keeping   440
a mistress and poking the coals.

HERMES: And whoever prefers there to be war —

TRYGAEUS: May he, Lord Dionysus, never-endingly be extracting
arrowheads from his funny-bones!

HERMES: And if anyone, out of desire to be a taxiarch, grudges to let
thee, O Lady, rise again into the light, then in his battles —   445

TRYGAEUS: May he suffer the same fate as Cleonymus!

HERMES: And if any maker of spears or seller of shields desires battles
in order to do better business —

TRYGAEUS: May he be captured by brigands, and eat nothing but barley!

HERMES: And if any man fail to assist because he wishes to be a general,   450
or is a slave ready to run away —

TRYGAEUS: May he be stretched out on the wheel and whipped at the
same time!

HERMES: But for us may there be blessings. Strike up the paean: hail!

TRYGAEUS: Leave out the striking: just say "hail".

Ερ.　ἰὴ ἰὴ τοίνυν, ἰὴ μόνον λέγω.　　　　　　　　　455
　　　Ἑρμῇ, Χάρισιν, Ὥραισιν, Ἀφροδίτῃ, Πόθῳ.

Τρ.　Ἄρει δὲ μή.

Ερ.　　　　　μή.

Τρ.　　　　　　　μηδ' Ἐνυαλίῳ γε.

Ερ.　　　　　　　　　　　　μή.
　　　ὑπότεινε δὴ πᾶς, καὶ κάταγε τοῖσιν κάλῳς.

Χο.　ὦ εἶα.　　　　　　　　　　　　　　　　(στρ.
—　εἶα μάλα.　　　　　　　　　　　　　　　460
—　ὦ εἶα.
—　εἶα ἔτι μάλα.
—　ὦ εἶα, ὦ εἶα.

Τρ.　ἀλλ' οὐχ ἕλκουσ' ἄνδρες ὁμοίως.
　　　οὐ ξυλλήψεσθ'; οἷ' ὀγκύλλεσθ'.　　　　　465
　　　οἰμώξεσθ', οἱ Βοιωτοί.

Χο.　εἶά νυν.
—　εἶα ὤ.
—　ἄγετε ξυνανέλκετε καὶ σφώ.

Τρ.　οὔκουν ἕλκω κἀξαρτῶμαι　　　　　　　470
　　　κἀπεμπίπτω καὶ σπουδάζω;

Χο.　　πῶς οὖν οὐ χωρεῖ τοὔργον;

Τρ.　ὦ Λάμαχ', ἀδικεῖς ἐμποδὼν καθήμενος.

455　ἰὴ μόνον t: ἰὴ ἰὴ μόνον RVΓp.
458　κάλῳς L^s: κάλοις RVΓpt Suda.
462　εἶα t (cf. Σ^VΓ 459): om. RVΓp.
469　ἄγετε ξυνανέλκετε Dobree: ἄγετον ξυνάλκετον V: ἄγετον
　　　ξυνέλκετον RΓpt.

HERMES: All right, I simply say: hail, hail, hail! [*Raising the bowl*]   455
To Hermes [*drinks some of the wine*] − to the Graces [*pours a libation*] −
to the Seasons [*pours*] − to Aphrodite [*pours*] − to Desire [*pours*]!
    TRYGAEUS: But *not* to Ares.
    HERMES: No!
    TRYGAEUS: Nor to Enyalius either.
    HERMES: No!
    [*The chorus take their places at the ropes, ready to haul.*]
    HERMES: Now put your backs into it, everyone, and bring her in with
the ropes.
    CHORUS-LEADER: Heave-ho!
    CHORUS [*hauling, the ropes over their shoulders*]:   460
            Heave it is!
    CHORUS-LEADER: Heave-ho!
    CHORUS: Heave it is again!
    CHORUS-LEADER AND CHORUS:
            Heave-ho! Heave ho!
    TRYGAEUS: Here, the men aren't hauling equally.
        [*To a group in the chorus*]
          Will you do your share? What airs you give yourselves!   465
          You'll howl for this, you Boeotians!
    CHORUS-LEADER: Heave now!
    CHORUS: Heave-ho!
    CHORUS-LEADER [*to Hermes and Trygaeus*]:
          Come along, you two as well, help to haul her up.
    TRYGAEUS [*taking hold of one of the ropes*]:   470
          I'm pulling, aren't I, and hanging on to the rope,
          and getting stuck in, and taking it seriously?
    CHORUS-LEADER: Then why isn't the job getting anywhere?
    TRYGAEUS [*to a member of one of the hauling teams*]: Lamachus,
you've no right to obstruct the work like that. We can do without that bogy of

οὐδὲν δεόμεθ', ὦνθρωπε, τῆς σῆς μορμόνος.

Ερ. οὐδ' οὗδε γ' εἷλκον οὐδὲν ἀργεῖοι πάλαι   475
    ἀλλ' ἢ κατεγέλων τῶν ταλαιπωρουμένων,
    καὶ ταῦτα διχόθεν μισθοφοροῦντες ἄλφιτα.

Τρ. ἀλλ' οἱ Λάκωνες, ὦγαθ', ἕλκουσ' ἀνδρικῶς.

Ερ. ἆρ' οἶσθ'; ὅσοι γ' αὐτῶν ἔχοντ' ἐν τῷ ξύλῳ
    μόνοι προθυμοῦντ'· ἀλλ' ὁ χαλκεὺς οὐκ ἐᾷ.   480

Τρ. οὐδ' οἱ Μεγαρῆς δρῶσ' οὐδέν.

Ερ.   ἕλκουσιν δ' ὅμως
    γλισχρότατα, σαρκάζοντες ὥσπερ κυνίδια—

Τρ. ὑπὸ τοῦ γε λιμοῦ νὴ Δί' ἐξολωλότες.

Χο. οὐδὲν ποιοῦμεν, ἄνδρες. ἀλλ' ὁμοθυμαδὸν
    ἅπασιν ἡμῖν αὖθις ἀντιληπτέον.   485

    ὢ εἶα.   (ἀντ.
— εἶα μάλα.
— ὢ εἶα.
— εἶα νὴ Δία.
— μικρόν γε κινοῦμεν.   490

Τρ. οὔκουν δεινὸν τοὺς μὲν τείνειν,
    τοὺς δ' ἀντισπᾶν;
    πληγὰς λήψεσθ', ἀργεῖοι.

Χο. εἶά νυν.

479 ἔχοντ' (ἔχονται) ἐν τῷ ξύλῳ van Leeuwen, cf. Σ^R: ἔχονται τοῦ
     ξύλου codd.
491 after δεινὸν Dindorf posited a lacuna and Merry added κάτοπον
     ὑμῶν (cf. Σ^V): but cf. Ach. 216/231, Wasps 297/309, 544/64
493 ἀργεῖοι Meineke: ὦργεῖοι codd.

50

yours, mister!

HERMES [*who is inspecting the work of the other team*]: And these 475
Argives too, they haven't been hauling at all for a long time, just laughing at
others in distress, and that while they get their daily groats by drawing
pay from both sides.

TRYGAEUS: But the Laconians, my dear fellow, they're pulling manfully.

HERMES: Do you know the truth? It's only those of them who are 479-
gripped tight by stocks and gyves: they're eager to help, but the smith won't 480
let them.

TRYGAEUS: The Megarians aren't managing to do anything either.

HERMES: And yet they're pulling with great determination, showing their
teeth like puppy-dogs.

TRYGAEUS: Because they're perishing with hunger, of course!

CHORUS-LEADER: We're getting nowhere, men. [*The chorus relax.*]
Now we must take hold again, all of us, with one accord. 485

          Heave-ho!

CHORUS: Heave it is!

CHORUS-LEADER: Heave-ho!

CHORUS: Heave it is, by Zeus!

CHORUS-LEADER AND CHORUS: 490

          We're not shifting it much!

TRYGAEUS: Well, isn't it dreadful that some are straining
          while others are pulling the other way?

    [*To a group in the chorus*]

          You'll be getting some thumps, you Argives!

CHORUS-LEADER: Heave now!

— εἷα ὤ.   495
— κακόνοι τινές εἰσιν ἐν ἡμῖν.

Τρ. ὑμεῖς μὲν γοῦν οἱ κιττῶντες
       τῆς εἰρήνης σπᾶτ' ἀνδρείως.

Χο.   ἀλλ' εἷσ' οἳ κωλύουσιν.

Ερ. ἄνδρες Μεγαρῆς, οὐκ ἐς κόρακας ἐρρήσετε;   500
       μισεῖ γὰρ ὑμᾶς ἡ θεὸς μεμνημένη·
       πρῶτοι γὰρ αὐτὴν τοῖς σκορόδοις ἠλείψατε.
       καὶ τοῖς Ἀθηναίοισι παύσασθαι λέγω
       ἐντεῦθεν ἐχομένοις ὅθεν νῦν ἕλκετε·
       οὐδὲν γὰρ ἄλλο δρᾶτε πλὴν δικάζετε.   505
       ἀλλ' εἴπερ ἐπιθυμεῖτε τήνδ' ἐξελκύσαι,
       πρὸς τὴν θάλατταν ὀλίγον ὑποχωρήσατε.

Χο. ἄγ', ὦνδρες, αὐτοὶ δὴ μόνοι λαβώμεθ' οἱ γεωργοί.

Ερ. χωρεῖ γέ τοι τὸ πρᾶγμα πολλῷ μᾶλλον, ὦνδρες, ὑμῖν.

Χο. χωρεῖν τὸ πρᾶγμά φησιν· ἀλλὰ πᾶς ἀνὴρ προθυμοῦ. 510

Τρ. οὔ τοι γεωργοὶ τοὔργον ἐξέλκουσι, κἄλλος οὐδείς.

Χο. ἄγε νυν, ἄγε πᾶς.

Ερ.   καὶ μὴν ὁμοῦ 'στιν ἤδη.

Χο. μή νυν ἀνῶμεν, ἀλλ' ἐπέν-
       τείνωμεν ἀνδρικώτερον.   515

Ερ.   ἤδη 'στὶ τοῦτ' ἐκεῖνο.

496 κακόνοι White: ὡς κακόνοι vel sim. codd. Suda.
496 ἡμῖν Suda: ὑμῖν codd.
497 γοῦν (γ' οὖν) Bentley: οὖν codd.
498 ἀνδρείως Bentley: ἀνδρικῶς codd.

CHORUS: Heave-ho!   495

CHORUS-LEADER [*finding that still no progress is being made*]:

                    There are some traitors to the cause among us.

TRYGAEUS: At least you who are craving

                    for peace are hauling away bravely.

CHORUS-LEADER: But there are some who are hindering us.

HERMES: You Megarians, won't you get to blazes out of here? The   500
goddess remembers you, and hates you: you were the first to smear her
with your garlic. And I tell you Athenians to stop holding on at the
place from which you're pulling at present. You're doing nothing but   505
. . . judge in the courts! If you really want to haul out this goddess,
then withdraw a little towards the sea.

    [*During Hermes' speech there is much confused scurrying to and fro
by members of the chorus. At its end they regroup by the ropes, more
closely bunched than before.*]

CHORUS-LEADER: Come on, men, let's us peasants take hold, all by
ourselves. [*The chorus resume hauling.*]

HERMES: You know, you've got the job *moving*, men, much better now.

CHORUS-LEADER: He says the job's moving! With a will, now, everyone! 510

TRYGAEUS: You see, the peasants are pulling the thing off, they and
no one else.

CHORUS-LEADER: Come on now, come on, everyone!

HERMES: Yes, look, we're nearly there now.

CHORUS-LEADER: Then don't let's ease up; rather

                    let's strain more manfully still.   515

HERMES: That's it now!

*The trolley begins to emerge through the door, though the figures on
cannot yet be seen.*]

Χο. ὣ εἶά νυν, ὣ εἶα πᾶς·
     ὣ εἶα εἶα εἶά νυν·
     ὣ εἶα εἶα εἶα πᾶς.

Τρ. ὣ πότνια βοτρυόδωρε, τί προσείπω σ' ἔπος;   520
     πόθεν ἂν λάβοιμι ῥῆμα μυριάμφορον
     ὅτῳ προσείπω σ'; οὐ γὰρ εἶχον οἴκοθεν.
     ὣ χαῖρ', Ὀπώρα, καὶ σὺ δ', ὣ Θεωρία.
     οἷον δ' ἔχεις τὸ πρόσωπον, ὣ Θεωρία.
     οἷον δὲ πνεῖς· ὡς ἡδὺ κατὰ τῆς καρδίας·   525
     γλυκύτατον, ὥσπερ ἀστρατείας καὶ μύρου.

Ερ. μῶν οὖν ὅμοιον καὶ γυλιοῦ στρατιωτικοῦ;

Τρ. ἀπέπτυσ' ἐχθροῦ φωτὸς ἔχθιστον πλέκος.
     τοῦ μὲν γὰρ ὄζει κρομμυοξυρεγμίας,
     ταύτης δ' ὀπώρας, ὑποδοχῆς, Διονυσίων,   530
     αὐλῶν, τραγῳδῶν, Σοφοκλέους μελῶν, κιχλῶν,
     ἐπυλλίων Εὐριπίδου—

Ερ.   κλαύσἄρα σὺ
     ταύτης καταψευδόμενος· οὐ γὰρ ἥδεται
     αὕτη ποιητῇ ῥηματίων δικανικῶν.

Τρ. —κιττοῦ, τρυγοίπου, προβατίων βληχωμένων,   535
     κόλπου γυναικῶν διατρεχουσῶν εἰς ἀγρόν,
     δούλης μεθυούσης, ἀνατετραμμένου χοῶς,

518 νυν (νῦν) Richter, cf. Σ^R 512: εἶα εἶα R: εἶα εἶα εἶα vel
     sim. Vpt.
519 εἶα three times Richter: five times RVp: εἶα ὣ εἶα t.
524 ὣ Θεωρία codd.: Εἰρήνη φίλη Meineke.
536 ἀγρόν codd.: ἱπνόν $^{γρ}Σ^V$.

CHORUS: Heave now, heave all!
                              Heave, heave, heave now!
                              Heave, heave, heave all!

[*The trolley is now completely out of the door; on it stands the statue
of Peace, flanked by her two live attendants, Opora (Fullfruit) and Theoria
(Showtime).*]

TRYGAEUS [*to Peace*]: O my Lady Grape-giver, with what words shall   520
I greet you? Where can I find a million-gallon word with which to address
you? I didn't have one I could bring from home. — Welcome, Fullfruit,
and you too, Showtime! What a face you've got, Showtime! And what a   525
fragrance! how its sweetness goes to my heart! Delicious, like perfume
and demobilization!

HERMES: Then it's not the same smell you get from a soldier's ration-
bag?

TRYGAEUS: "I spurn that odious man's most odious pouch!" That
smells of onions and indigestion. *She* smells of fruit-harvest, entertaining, the   530
Dionysia, the pipes, performances of tragedy, songs by Sophocles, thrush,
neat little lines by Euripides —

HERMES: You'll be for it, slandering her like that. She doesn't take
pleasure in a composer of little phrases from the lawcourts.

TRYGAEUS [*ignoring the interruption*]: — ivy, wine-strainers, bleating   535
flocks, the bosoms of women running errands to the fields, a drunken slave-
girl, an overturned jug, and many other good things.

ἄλλων τε πολλῶν κἀγαθῶν.

Ερ.   ἴθι νυν ἄθρει
οἷον πρὸς ἀλλήλας λαλοῦσιν αἱ πόλεις
διαλλαγεῖσαι καὶ γελῶσιν ἄσμεναι—   540

Τρ. καὶ ταῦτα δαιμονίως ὑπωπιασμέναι
ἁπαξάπασαι καὶ κυάθους προσκείμεναι.

Ερ. καὶ τῶνδε τοίνυν τῶν θεωμένων σκόπει
τὰ πρόσωφ', ἵνα γνῷς τὰς τέχνας.

Τρ.   αἰβοῖ τάλας.

Ερ. ἐκεινονὶ γοῦν τὸν λοφοποιὸν οὐχ ὁρᾷς   545
τίλλονθ' ἑαυτόν;

Τρ.   ὁ δέ γε τὰς σμινύας ποιῶν
κατέπαρδεν ἄρτι τοῦ ξιφουργοῦ 'κεινουί.

Ερ. ὁ δὲ δρεπανουργὸς οὐχ ὁρᾷς ὡς ἥδεται,
καὶ τὸν δορυξὸν οἷον ἐσκιμάλισεν;
ἴθι νυν ἄνειπε τοὺς γεωργοὺς ἀπιέναι.   550

Τρ. ἀκούετε λεῴ· τοὺς γεωργοὺς ἀπιέναι
τὰ γεωργικὰ σκεύη λαβόντας εἰς ἀγρὸν
ὡς τάχιστ', ἄνευ δορατίου καὶ ξίφους κἀκοντίου·
ὡς ἅπαντ' ἤδη 'στὶ μεστὰ τἀνθάδ' εἰρήνης σαπρᾶς.
ἀλλὰ πᾶς χώρει πρὸς ἔργον εἰς ἀγρὸν παιωνίσας.   555

Χο. ὦ ποθεινὴ τοῖς δικαίοις καὶ γεωργοῖς ἡμέρα,
ἄσμενός σ' ἰδὼν προσειπεῖν βούλομαι τὰς ἀμπέλους,
τάς τε συκᾶς ἃς ἐγὼ 'φύτευον ὢν νεώτερος
ἀσπάσασθαι θυμὸς ἡμῖν ἐστι πολλοστῷ χρόνῳ.

549 καὶ ... οἷον codd. Suda: perh. (Τρ.) καὶ ... γ' οἷον.
557 σ' B, Stobaeus: γ' t: om. RVΓp.

56

HERMES [*inviting Trygaeus by gesture to view the face of the earth, imagined as spread out before and below him*]: Come now, look and see how all the states have been reconciled, how they're talking to one another and laughing in gladness —

539-540

TRYGAEUS: And that though they've got incredible black eyes, the whole lot of them, and have cupping-vessels applied to them.

HERMES: Then also look at the faces of the people in the audience here, so that you can recognize their occupations.

TRYGAEUS: Good grief, what an idea!

HERMES [*pointing into the audience*]: Well, at least you see that crest-maker, don't you, tearing his hair?

545

TRYGAEUS: Yes, and the man who makes mattocks has just let off a fart at that swordsmith.

HERMES: And don't you see how delighted the sickle-maker is, and how he gave the spear-maker the long finger? Come on now, make proclamation for the peasants to go off home.

550

TRYGAEUS: Hear ye, O people! The peasants may go off home to the country, taking their agricultural tools, as quickly as may be, without spear and sword and javelin; for this whole place is now awash with mellowed old peace! Now raise the paean, everyone, and off to your work in the country!

555

CHORUS-LEADER: O day long yearned for by peasants and honest men, I rejoice to see you; now I wish to greet my vines, and it is my eager desire, after a long, long time, to re-salute the fig trees that I planted when I was a young man.

Τρ. νῦν μὲν οὖν, ἄνδρες, προσευξώμεσθα πρῶτον τῇ θεῷ,   560
     ἥπερ ἡμῶν τοὺς λόφους ἀφεῖλε καὶ τὰς Γοργόνας·
     εἶθ' ὅπως λιταργιοῦμεν οἴκαδ' εἰς τὰ χωρία,
     ἐμπολήσαντές τι χρηστὸν εἰς αγρὸν ταρίχιον.

Ερ. ὦ Πόσειδον, ὡς καλὸν τὸ στῖφος αὐτῶν φαίνεται
     καὶ πυκνὸν καὶ γοργόν, ὥσπερ μᾶζα καὶ πανδαισία.   565

Τρ. νὴ Δί' ἡ γοῦν σφῦρα λαμπρὸν ἦν ἄρ' ἐξωπλισμένη,
     αἵ τε θρίνακες διαστίλβουσι πρὸς τὸν ἥλιον.
     ἦ καλῶς αὐτῶν ἀπαλλάξειεν ἂν μετόρχιον.
     ὥστ' ἔγωγ' ἤδη 'πιθυμῶ καὐτὸς ἐλθεῖν εἰς αγρον
     καὶ τριαινοῦν τῇ δικέλλῃ διὰ χρόνου τὸ γῄδιον.   570
     ἀλλ' ἀναμνησθέντες, ἄνδρες,
           τῆς διαίτης τῆς παλαιᾶς,
           ἣν παρεῖχ' αὕτη ποθ' ἡμῖν,
           τῶν τε παλασίων ἐκείνων,
           τῶν τε σύκων, τῶν τε μύρτων,   575
           τῆς τρυγός τε τῆς γλυκείας,
           τῆς ἰωνιᾶς τε τῆς πρὸς
           τῷ φρέατι, τῶν τ' ἐλαῶν
           ὧν ποθοῦμεν,
           ἀντὶ τούτων τήνδε νυνὶ   580
           τὴν θεὸν προσείπατε.

Χο. χαῖρε χαῖρ'· ὡς ἀσμένοισιν ἦλθες ἡμῖν, φιλτάτη·

566 νὴ Δί' t: νὴ τὸν Δί' RVΓp.
566 γοῦν Sommerstein: cf. Clouds 408, Lys. 561, Frogs 980: γὰρ
     codd.: γε Blaydes.
582-3 ὡς ἀσμένοισιν ἦλθες ἡμῖν, φιλτάτη Enger: ὦ φίλταθ' ὡς ἀσμέ-
     νοισιν ἡμῖν ἦλθες codd.: ὡς ἀσμένοισιν ἦλθες, ὦ φιλτάτη
     Bergk: cf. 346 and 385.

58

TRYGAEUS: Then, men, let us now first address our prayers to the   560
goddess who has rid us of crests and Gorgons; and then let us scoot off home to
our farms, after buying some good salt-fish to take to the country!

[*During this speech agricultural implements have been brought out by
attendants and distributed to the chorus, who now form ranks like soldiers
ready for a march.*]

HERMES: Poseidon! how fine their serried ranks look, how compact and   565
spirited — like barley cake or a feast of plenty!

TRYGAEUS: Certainly, by Zeus, I see that beetle-maul's a splendid thing
when it's ready for action, and the three-pronged forks gleam brightly in
the sun. For sure, the lanes of a vineyard would benefit from an encounter
with them! It makes *me* now eager to go back to the country myself too,
and at long last to break up the earth of my dear old farm with my mattock!   570

[*To the chorus*] Now, men, call to mind the old way of life that Peace
once made possible for us, the pressed figs, the fresh figs, the myrtle-berries,   575
the sweet new wine, the bed of violets by the well, the olive-trees that
we yearn for — and in thanks for these address this goddess now.   580

CHORUS [*to Peace*]:

Welcome, welcome! how glad we are, beloved one, that you have
come to us!

59

σῷ γὰρ ἐδάμην πόθῳ,

δαιμόνια βουλόμενος   585

εἰς ἀγρὸν ἀνερπύσαι.

ἦσθα γὰρ μέγιστον ἡμῖν κέρδος, ὦ ποθουμένη,

πᾶσιν ὁπόσοι γεωρ-

γὸν βίον ἐτρίβομεν· μό-   590

νη γὰρ ἡμᾶς ὠφέλεις.

πολλὰ γὰρ ἐπάσχομεν

πρίν ποτ' ἐπὶ σοῦ γλυκέα

κἀδάπανα καὶ φίλα·

τοῖς ἀγροίκοισιν γὰρ ἦσθα χῖδρα καὶ σωτηρία.   595

ὥστε σε τά τ' ἀμπέλια

καὶ τὰ νέα συκίδια

τἄλλα θ' ὁπόσ' ἐστὶ φυτα

προσγελάσεται λαβόντ' ἄσμενα.   600

ἀλλὰ ποῦ ποτ' ἦν ἀφ' ἡμῶν τὸν πολὺν τοῦτον χρόνον

ἥδε; τοῦθ' ἡμᾶς δίδαξον, ὦ θεῶν εὐνούστατε.

Ερ.   ὦ λιπερνῆτες γεωργοί, τἀμὰ δὴ ξυνίετε

ῥήματ', εἰ βούλεσθ' ἀκοῦσαι τήνδ' ὅπως ἀπώλετο.

πρῶτα μὲν γὰρ †ταύτης ἦρξε† Φειδίας πράξας κακῶς.   605

εἶτα Περικλέης φοβηθεὶς μὴ μετάσχοι τῆς τύχης,

---

584 ἐδάμην $^i\Sigma^{VГ}$ 584 $^i\Sigma^V$ 582: ἐδάμημεν codd. $^{Υρ}\Sigma^V$ 582.

585 βουλόμενος $^i\Sigma^{VГ}$ 584: βουλόμενοι codd.

589-590 γεωργὸν Bothe, cf. Σ^V 585: γεωργικὸν codd.

599 ὁπόσ' Bentley: ὅσσ' V: ὅσ' RГpt.

603 λιπερνῆτες Diodorus Siculus 12.40.6, Aristodemus FGrH 104
     F 16: cf. $\Sigma^{VГ}$ and Archilochus fr. 109: σοφώτατοι codd.

605 †ταύτης ἦρξε† codd.: αὐτῆς ἦρχε Diodorus: ἦρξατ' αὐτῆς
     Aristodemus: ἦρξεν αὐτοῦ Blaydes.

For I am overcome with longing for you,
and my desire is marvellously strong   585
to go back to the countryside.
For you, goddess of our yearning, were the greatest
    benefit to us,
to all of us who spent
our life in working the land, for   590
you alone were a help to us;
for many things came to us
in former days, in your time, that were sweet
and without cost and to be cherished.
For to the country folk you meant boiled grits and security.   595
And therefore the vines
and the young fig-trees
and all the other plants there are
will receive you with smiles of delight.   600
    CHORUS-LEADER [*to Hermes*]: But where can this goddess have been,
to be away from us all this long time? Friendliest of gods, do explain this to us.
    HERMES: "O indigent peasants, mark well my words," if you want to hear   605
how it was that she vanished. What started it all in the first place was
Pheidias getting into trouble. Then Pericles became frightened he might
share Pheidias' fate — for he was afraid of your character and your hard-

τὰς φύσεις ὑμῶν δεδοικὼς καὶ τὸν αὐτοδὰξ τρόπον,
πρὶν παθεῖν τι δεινὸν αὐτός, ἐξέφλεξε τὴν πόλιν,
ἐμβαλὼν σπινθῆρα μικρὸν Μεγαρικοῦ ψηφίσματος·
κἀξεφύσησεν τοσοῦτον πόλεμον ὥστε τῷ καπνῷ   610
πάντας Ἕλληνας δακρῦσαι, τούς τ' ἐκεῖ τούς τ' ἐνθάδε·
ὡς δ' ἅπαξ τὸ πρῶτον ἄκουσ' ἐφύφησεν ἄμπελος
καὶ πίθος πληγεὶς ὑπ' ὀργῆς ἀντελάκτισεν πίθῳ,
οὐκέτ' ἦν οὐδεὶς ὁ παύσων, ἥδε δ' ἠφανίζετο.

Τρ. ταῦτα τοίνυν μὰ τὸν Ἀπόλλω 'γὼ 'πεπύσμην οὐδενός,   615
    οὐδ' ὅπως αὐτῇ προσήκοι Φειδίας ἠκηκόη.

Χο. οὐδ' ἔγωγε, πλήν γε νυνί. ταῦτ' ἄρ' εὐπρόσωπος ἦν,
    οὖσα συγγενὴς ἐκείνου. πολλά γ' ἡμᾶς λανθάνει.

Ερ. κᾆτ' ἐπειδὴ 'γνωσαν ὑμᾶς αἱ πόλεις ὧν ἤρχετε
    ἠγριωμένους ἐπ' ἀλλήλοισι καὶ σεσηρότας,   620
    πάντ' ἐμηχανῶντ' ἐφ' ὑμῖν τοὺς φόρους φοβούμεναι,
    κἀνέπειθον τῶν Λακώνων τοὺς μεγίστους χρήμασιν.
    οἱ δ', ἅτ' ὄντες αἰσχροκερδεῖς καὶ διειρωνόξενοι,
    τήνδ' ἀπορρίψαντες αἰσχρῶς τὸν Πόλεμον ἀνήρπασαν.
    κᾆτα τἀκείνων γε κέρδη τοῖς γεωργοῖς ἦν κακά·   625
    αἱ γὰρ ἐνθένδ' αὖ τριήρεις ἀντιτιμωρούμεναι
    οὐδὲν αἰτίων ἂν ἀνδρῶν τὰς κράδας κατήσθιον.

Τρ. ἐν δίκῃ μὲν οὖν, ἐπεί τοι τὴν κορώνεών γέ μου
    ἐξέκοψαν, ἣν ἐγὼ 'φύτευσα κἀξεθρεψάμην.

610 κἀξεφύσησεν Bentley: ἐξεφύσησε(ν) RVΓp Suda, Diodorus,
     Aristodemus: ἐξεφύσησε γὰρ t.
616 ἠκηκόη Brunck: ἠκηκόειν codd.:]ηκοειν Π61.
629 'φύτευσα κἀξεθρεψάμην Bentley: φυτεύσας ἐξεθρεψάμην codd.

62

biting temper — and before anything terrible could happen to *him*, he set
the city ablaze by dropping into it a tiny spark of a Megarian decree: and he   610
fanned up so great a war that all the Greeks were in tears with the smoke,
both those over there and those over here; and as soon as the first vine
had reluctantly begun to crackle, and the first wine-jar received a knock
and kicked out in vengeful anger at another jar, there was no longer anyone
who could put a stop to it, and Peace was disappearing.

TRYGAEUS: Well, by Apollo, I'd never been told that by anyone before,   615
nor had I heard how she was connected with Pheidias.

CHORUS-LEADER: No more had I, not till now. So that's why she's so
fair of face — because she's a relation of his! There's a lot of things
we don't realize!

HERMES: And then the states which you ruled over, when they became
aware that you were enraged and showing your teeth at one another, schemed in   620
every way against you because they were afraid of the tribute, and sought to win
over by bribes the greatest men among the Laconians. And these latter, being
avaricious and treacherous towards outsiders, threw this goddess out in
a disgraceful fashion and seized on War instead. And then the profit they   625
made proved harmful to the peasants; for the warships kept coming from here
to retaliate in their turn and devouring the fig-sprays belonging to totally
innocent men.

TRYGAEUS: On the contrary, they deserved it. They cut down my
raven-fig tree, you know, which I'd planted and nurtured.

Χο. νὴ Δί', ὦ μέλ', ἐν δίκῃ γε δῆτ', ἐπεὶ κάμοῦ λίθον   630
    ἐμβαλόντες ἐξμέδιμνον κυφέλην ἀπώλεσαν.

Ερ. κἀνθάδ', ὡς ἐκ τῶν ἀγρῶν ξυνῆλθεν οὐργάτης λεώς,
    τὸν τρόπον πωλούμενος τὸν αὐτὸν οὐκ ἐμάνθανεν,
    ἀλλ' ἅτ' ὢν ἄνευ γιγάρτων καὶ φιλῶν τὰς ἰσχάδας
    ἔβλεπεν πρὸς τοὺς λέγοντας· οἱ δὲ γιγνώσκοντες εὖ   635
    τοὺς πένητας ἀσθενοῦντας κἀποροῦντας ἀλφίτων
    τήνδε μὲν δικροῖς ἐώθουν τὴν θεὸν κεκράγμασιν
    πολλάκις φανεῖσαν αὐτὴν τῆσδε τῆς χώρας πόθῳ,
    τῶν δὲ συμμάχων ἔσειον τοὺς παχεῖς καὶ πλουσίους,
    αἰτίας ἂν προστιθέντες ὡς "φρονεῖ τὰ Βρασίδου".   640
    εἶτ' ἂν ὑμεῖς τοῦτον ὥσπερ κυνίδι' ἐσπαράττετε·
    ἡ πόλις γὰρ ὠχριῶσα κἂν φόβῳ καθημένη,
    ἄττα διαβάλοι τις αὐτῇ, ταῦτ' ἂν ἥδιστ' ἤσθιεν.
    οἱ δὲ τὰς πληγὰς ὁρῶντες ἃς ἐτύπτονθ', οἱ ξένοι,
    χρυσίῳ τῶν ταῦτα ποιούντων ἐβύνουν τὸ στόμα,   645
    ὥστ' ἐκείνους μὲν ποιῆσαι πλουσίους, ἡ δ' Ἑλλας ἂν
    ἐξερημωθεῖσ' ἂν ὑμᾶς ἔλαθε. ταῦτα δ' ἦν ὁ δρῶν
    βυρσοπώλης—

Τρ.   παῦε παῦ', ὦ δέσποθ' Ἑρμῆ, μὴ λέγε,
    ἀλλ' ἔα τὸν ἄνδρ' ἐκεῖνον οὗπέρ ἐστ' εἶναι κάτω·
    οὐ γὰρ ἡμέτερος ἔτ' ἔστ' ἐκεῖνος ἀνήρ, ἀλλὰ σός.   650
    ἄττ' ἂν οὖν λέγῃς ἐκεῖνον,

630 ἐν δίκῃ Porson: ἐνδίκως codd.
630 γε Bentley: om. codd.
632 κἀνθάδ' Dobree: κᾶτα δ' codd.
640 φρονεῖ t Suda: φρονοῖ RVΓp.
643 ἄττα Florent Chrestien: ἄττ' ἂν codd.
648 βυρσοπώλης t: ὁ βυρσοπώλης RVΓp.

CHORUS-LEADER: Yes, by Zeus, my good sir, they did deserve it, because 630 they destroyed something of mine too — a six-bushel corn-bin, by dropping a stone on it.

HERMES [*resuming*]: And back here, when the working folk flocked in from the countryside, they didn't understand that they were being sold out in just the same way; because they were without raisins and were fond of their dried figs, they looked for aid to the orators. The orators, knowing well 635 that the poor people were weak and were short of groats, thrust this goddess away with two-pronged bawlings when she repeatedly appeared of her own accord because she pined for this land, and they took to shaking up the rich fat cats among the allies, pinning charges on them and saying "he's a supporter of 640 Brasidas". Then you'd tear the man apart like puppy-dogs; for the city was all pale, it sat in fear, and would eat up with great pleasure any scraps of slander that were thrown to it. The foreigners, seeing the blows that were being struck at them, began to stuff shut with gold the mouths of those who 645 were doing it; so they made *them* rich, and meanwhile Greece could have been depopulated without your noticing. And the man who brought all this about was a leather-seller —

TRYGAEUS: Stop, stop, Lord Hermes, say no more! Just let that man stay where he is, down below. That man isn't ours any more, he's yours! So 650 whatever you say about him — even if he was a villain while he lived and

65

κεἰ πανοῦργος ἦν, ὅτ' ἔζη,
καὶ λάλος καὶ συκοφάντης
καὶ κύκηθρον καὶ τάρακτρον,
ταῦθ' ἀπαξάπαντα νυνὶ   655
τοὺς σεαυτοῦ λοιδορεῖς.

ἀλλ' ὅ τι σιωπᾷς, ὦ πότνια, κάτειπέ μοι.

Ερ.   ἀλλ' οὐκ ἂν εἴποι πρός γε τοὺς θεωμένους·
      ὀργὴν γὰρ αὐτοῖς ὧν ἔπαθε πολλὴν ἔχει.

Τρ.   ἡ δ' ἀλλὰ πρὸς σὲ μικρὸν εἰπάτω μόνον.   660

Ερ.   εὔφ' ὅ τι νοεῖς αὐτοῖσι πρὸς ἔμ', ὦ φιλτάτη.
      ἴθ', ὦ γυναικῶν μισοπορπακιστάτη.
      εἶέν· ἀκούω. ταῦτ' ἐπικαλεῖς; μανθάνω.
      ἀκούσαθ' ὑμεῖς ὧν ἕνεκα μομφὴν ἔχει.
      ἐλθοῦσά φησιν αὐτομάτη μετὰ τὰν Πύλῳ   665
      σπονδῶν φέρουσα τῇ πόλει κίστην πλέαν
      ἀποχειροτονηθῆναι τρὶς ἐν τἠκκλησίᾳ.

Τρ.   ἡμάρτομεν ταῦτ'. ἀλλὰ συγγνώμην ἔχε·
      ὁ νοῦς γὰρ ἡμῶν ἦν τότ' ἐν τοῖς σκύτεσιν.

Ερ.   ἴθι νυν ἄκουσον οἷον ἄρτι μ' ἤρετο·   670
      ὅστις κακόνους αὐτῇ μάλιστ' ἦν ἐνθάδε,
      χὦστις φίλος κἄσπευδεν εἶναι μὴ μάχας.

Τρ.   εὐνούστατος μὲν ἦν μακρῷ Κλεώνυμος.

Ερ.   ποῖός τις οὖν εἶναι 'δόκει τὰ πολεμικὰ

664 ὑμεῖς VΓpt: ἡμεῖς R: ...ν Π61 (Carlini doubtfully reads υμιν)
674 'δόκει Richards: δοκεῖ codd.

66

a windbag and a trumper-up of accusations and an agitator and a trouble-
maker — *now* in saying each and every one of these things you're reviling   655
one of your own! [*To Peace*] But tell me, my Lady, why do you keep silent?

HERMES: She doesn't want to speak, not to the spectators; she's very
angry with them because of what was done to her.

TRYGAEUS: Well, let her at least just say a little to *you*.   660

HERMES [*approaching Peace*]: Say to me, beloved one, what your feelings
are towards them. [*He pauses for a reply.*] Come on, you most shield-band-
hating of all women. [*He puts his ear to Peace's lips, pretending to hear
her speak.*] All right, I hear you. [*He listens again.*] Is that your
complaint? [*He listens briefly.*] I understand. [*To the audience*] Listen,
all of you, to what she blames you for. She says that after the events at   665
Pylos she came here of her own accord, offering to the city a hamper full
of treaties, but was voted down three times in the Assembly.

TRYGAEUS: We were wrong to do that. But pardon us: at that time our
brains were in our shoe-leather.

HERMES [*after listening to Peace again*]; Now please listen to   670
the question she's just asked me: who was most hostile to her here, and
who was her friend and was eager for there not to be any battles?

TRYGAEUS: Well, her most loyal friend, by a long way, was Cleonymus.

HERMES: Oh, what sort of person did Cleonymus give the impression   674-5
of being, as regards warfare?

ὁ Κλεώνυμος;

Τρ.　　　　　　ψυχήν γ' ἄριστος, πλήν γ' ὅτι　　　　675
οὐκ ἦν ἄρ' οὗπέρ φησιν εἶναι τοῦ πατρός.
εἰ γάρ ποτ' ἐξέλθοι στρατιώτης, εὐθέως
ἀποβολιμαῖος τῶν ὅπλων ἐγίγνετο.

Ερ.　ἔτι νυν ἄκουσον οἷον ἄρτι μ' ἤρετο·
ὅστις κρατεῖ νῦν τοῦ λίθου τοῦ 'ν τῇ Πυκνί.　　680

Τρ.　Ὑπέρβολος νῦν τοῦτ' ἔχει τὸ χωρίον.
αὕτη, τί ποιεῖς; τὴν κεφαλὴν ποῖ περιάγεις;

Ερ.　ἀποστρέφεται τὸν δῆμον ἀχθεσθεῖσ', ὅτι
οὕτω πονηρὸν προστάτην ἐπεγράψατο.

Τρ.　ἀλλ' οὐκέτ' αὐτῷ χρησόμεθ' οὐδέν, ἀλλὰ νῦν　　685
ἀπορῶν ὁ δῆμος ἐπιτρόπου καὶ γυμνὸς ὢν
τοῦτον τέως τὸν ἄνδρα περιεζώσατο.

Ερ.　πῶς οὖν ξυνοίσει ταῦτ' ἐρωτᾷ τῇ πόλει.

Τρ.　εὐβουλότεροι γενησόμεθα.

Ερ.　　　　　　　　τρόπῳ τίνι;

Τρ.　ὅτι τυγχάνει λυχνοποιὸς ὤν. πρὸ τοῦ μὲν οὖν　　690
ἐψηλαφῶμεν ἐν σκότῳ τὰ πράγματα,
νυνὶ δ' ἅπαντα πρὸς λύχνον βουλεύσομεν.

Ερ.　ὦ ὦ·
οἷά μ' ἐκέλευσεν ἀναπυθέσθαι σου.

Τρ.　　　　　　　　　τὰ τί;

676　οὗπερ Bentley: ὅπερ RVΓp: ὥσπερ t.
684　οὕτω Cobet: αὐτῷ RVΓ: αὑτῷ pt.

68

TRYGAEUS: Oh, very stout-hearted — except that it turned out he wasn't the son of the man he claims is his father; because whenever he marched out on a military expedition, he showed himself *deposititious* of his equipment!

HERMES [*after listening again to Peace*]: Listen now again to the question she's just asked me: who is now master of the rock on the Pnyx? 680

TRYGAEUS: Hyperbolus now occupies that position. [*The head of Peace suddenly turns away from the audience.*] Here, you, what are you doing? Where are you turning your head?

HERMES: She's turning away from the people in annoyance, because they've chosen such a rotten patron.

TRYGAEUS: Oh, we're not going to have any more to do with him in 685 future. [*Peace turns back to face the audience.*] It's just that at present, the people, being in want of a guardian and feeling naked, have wrapped themselves in this man for the time being.

HERMES [*after listening again*]: She asks how this will benefit the city.

TRYGAEUS: We shall be better judges of policy.

HERMES: How will that be?

TRYGAEUS: Because he happens to be a lamp-maker. So whereas 690 previously we were groping in the dark at our problems, we'll now do all our planning by lamplight!

HERMES [*after listening again*]: Oh, oh, the things she's told me to find out from you!

TRYGAEUS: What things?

Ερ. πάμπολλα, καὶ τἀρχαῖ' ἃ κατέλιπεν τότε.
πρῶτον δ' ὅ τι πράττει Σοφοκλῆς ἀνήρετο.　　　　695

Τρ. εὐδαιμονεῖ· πάσχει δὲ θαυμαστόν.

Ερ. 　　　　　　　　　　　　　τὸ τί;

Τρ. ἐκ τοῦ Σοφοκλέους γίγνεται Σιμωνίδης.

Ερ. Σιμωνίδης; πῶς;

Τρ. 　　　　　　　ὅτι γέρων ὢν καὶ σαπρὸς
κέρδους ἕκατι κἂν ἐπὶ ῥιπὸς πλέοι.

Ερ. τί δαὶ Κρατῖνος ὁ σοφός; ἔστιν;

Τρ. 　　　　　　　　　　　　ἀπέθανεν,　　　　700
ὅθ' οἱ Λάκωνες ἐνέβαλον.

Ερ. 　　　　　　　　　τί παθών;

Τρ. 　　　　　　　　　　　　ὅ τι;
ὠρακιάσας· οὐ γὰρ ἐξηνέσχετο
ἰδὼν πίθον καταγνύμενον οἴνου πλέων.
χἄτερα πόσ' ἄττ' οἴει γεγενῆσθ' ἐν τῇ πόλει;
ὥστ' οὐδέποτ', ὦ δέσποιν', ἀφησόμεσθά σου.　　　　705

Ερ. ἴθι νυν, ἐπὶ τούτοις τὴν Ὀπώραν λάμβανε
γυναῖκα σαυτῷ τήνδε, κᾆτ' ἐν τοῖς ἀγροῖς
ταύτῃ ξυνοικῶν ἐκποιοῦ σαυτῷ βότρυς.

Τρ. ὦ φιλτάτη, δεῦρ' ἐλθὲ καὶ δός μοι κύσαι.
ἆρ' ἂν βλαβῆναι διὰ χρόνου τί σοι δοκῶ,　　　　710
ὦ δέσποθ' Ἑρμῆ, τῆς Ὀπώρας κατελάσας;

Ερ. οὔκ, εἴ γε κυκεῶν' ἐπιπίοις βληχωνίαν.
ἀλλ' ὡς τάχιστα τήνδε τὴν Θεωρίαν
ἀπάγαγε τῇ βουλῇ λαβών, ἥσπέρ ποτ' ἦν.

70

HERMES: Many, many things, and in particular the things from long ago, the things she left behind her then. First of all she has asked how Sophocles is doing. 695

TRYGAEUS: He's prospering; but an extraordinary thing is happening to him.

HERMES: What is it?

TRYGAEUS: He's turning from Sophocles into Simonides.

HERMES: Simonides? How do you mean?

TRYGAEUS: Because although he's old and decayed, "for profit's sake he'd go to sea upon a mat"!

HERMES: And how about that fine artist Cratinus? Is he alive? 700

TRYGAEUS: He died when the Laconians invaded.

HERMES: What happened to him?

TRYGAEUS: What happened? He just passed out; he couldn't endure the sight of a jar full of wine being smashed. And how many other such things do you imagine have happened in the city? After that experience, my Lady, 705 we'll never let go of you again.

HERMES: Well then, on that understanding you can take Fullfruit here to be your wife; live with her in the countryside and produce . . . grapes for yourself.

TRYGAEUS [*to Fullfruit*]: Come here, darling, and give us a kiss. [*She does so.*] Do you think, Lord Hermes, that it would harm me at all, if I were 710 to indulge in Fullfruit after such a long interval?

HERMES: No, not if you took an infusion of pennyroyal afterwards. But now take Showtime here, and bring her as quickly as possible to the Council, whom she used to belong to. [*He leads Showtime over to Trygaeus.*]

Τρ. ὦ μακαρία βουλὴ σὺ τῆς θεωρίας·   715
     ὅσον ῥοφήσει ζωμὸν ἡμερῶν τριῶν,
     ὅσας δὲ κατέδει χόλικας ἐφθὰς καὶ κρέα.
     ἀλλ', ὦ φίλ' Ἑρμῆ, χαῖρε πολλά.

Ερ.   καὶ σύ γε,
     ὤνθρωπε, χαίρων ἄπιθι καὶ μέμνησό μου.

Τρ. ὦ κάνθαρ', οἴκαδ' οἴκαδ' ἀποπετώμεθα.   720

Ερ. οὐκ ἐνθάδ', ὦ τᾶν, ἐστι.

Τρ.   ποῖ γὰρ οἴχεται;

Ερ. ὑφ' ἅρματ' ἐλθὼν Ζηνὸς ἀστραπηφορεῖ.

Τρ. πόθεν οὖν ὁ τλήμων ἐνθάδ' ἕξει σιτία;

Ερ. τὴν τοῦ Γανυμήδους ἀμβροσίαν σιτήσεται.

Τρ. πῶς δῆτ' ἐγὼ καταβήσομαι;

Ερ.   θάρρει, καλῶς·   725
     τηδὶ παρ' αὐτὴν τὴν θεόν.

Τρ.   δεῦρ', ὦ κόραι,
     ἔπεσθον ἅμ' ἐμοὶ θᾶττον, ὡς πολλοὶ πάνυ
     ποθοῦντες ὑμᾶς ἀναμένουσ' ἐστυκότες.

Χο. ἀλλ' ἴθι χαίρων· ἡμεῖς δὲ τέως τάδε τὰ σκεύη παραδόντες
     τοῖς ἀκολούθοις δῶμεν σῴζειν, ὡς εἰώθασι μάλιστα   730
     περὶ τὰς σκηνὰς πλεῖστοι κλέπται κυπτάζειν καὶ κακοποιεῖν.
     ἀλλὰ φυλάττετε ταῦτ' ἀνδρείως· ἡμεῖς δ' αὖ τοῖσι θεαταῖς
     ἣν ἔχομεν ὁδὸν λόγων εἴπωμεν ὅσα τε νοῦς ἔχει.

715 βουλὴ σὺ $^i\Sigma^{VΓ}$: σὺ βουλὴ codd.
716 ῥοφήσει Elmsley: ῥοφήσεις codd.

TRYGAEUS: Oh, you happy councillors, to have Showtime! How much   715
soup you'll be slurping down over three days, and how much boiled sausage and
meat you'll be eating! And now, dear Hermes, farewell to you.

HERMES: And you too, mortal, go from here in peace, and remember me.

TRYGAEUS [*turning to where he had left his beetle*]: O beetle, homeward,   720
homeward let us fly! [*But he finds the beetle gone.*]

HERMES: It's not here, my dear fellow.

TRYGAEUS: Why, where's it gone?

HERMES: "Yoked to the car of Zeus, it bears the lightning."

TRYGAEUS: Then where's the poor creature going to get food from, up
here?

HERMES: It will be fed on Ganymede's . . . ambrosia.

TRYGAEUS: So how am I going to get back down?   725

HERMES: You will all right, don't worry. This way, right past the
goddess.

[*Taking the route indicated by Hermes, Trygaeus moves towards the central
portal of the stage-house, and beckons to Fullfruit and Showtime.*]

TRYGAEUS: Follow with me this way, girls, nice and fast, because an
awful lot of folk are waiting for you longingly — and they're horny!

[*Trygaeus, Fullfruit and Showtime disappear into the stage-house; Hermes
goes out by a side passage.*]

CHORUS-LEADER: Go, and good luck to you. As for us, meanwhile, let us
hand over this gear to the attendants and give it them to keep safe, because   730
there are a great many thieves who are very much in the habit of skulking
around the stage-building and doing their dirty work there. [*As the chorus
give their agricultural tools to the attendants*] Now guard these bravely;
and let us for our part tell the spectators "the path of words that is ours,
and all that is in our minds".

χρῆν μὲν τύπτειν τοὺς ῥαβδούχους, εἴ τις κωμῳδοποιητης
αὐτὸν ἐπῄνει πρὸς τὸ θέατρον παραβὰς ἐν τοῖς ἀναπαύστοις.   735
εἰ δ' οὖν εἰκός τινα τιμῆσαι, θύγατερ Διός, ὅστις ἄριστος
κωμῳδοδιδάσκαλος ἀνθρώπων καὶ κλεινότατος γεγένηται,
ἄξιος εἶναί φησ' εὐλογίας μεγάλης ὁ διδάσκαλος ἡμῶν.
πρῶτον μὲν γὰρ τοὺς ἀντιπάλους μόνος ἀνθρώπων κατέπαυσεν
εἰς τὰ ῥάκια σκώπτοντας ἀεὶ καὶ τοῖς φθειρσὶν πολεμοῦντας·   740
τούς θ' Ἡρακλέας τοὺς μάττοντας καὶ τοὺς πεινῶντας ἐκείνους
                                                                741
ἐξήλασ' ἀτιμώσας πρῶτος, καὶ τοὺς δούλους παρέλυσεν   743
τοὺς φεύγοντας κἀξαπατῶντας καὶ τυπτομένους, ἐπίτηδες   742
ἵν' ὁ σύνδουλος σκώψας αὐτοῦ τὰς πληγας εἶτ' ἀνέροιτο·   745
"ὦ κακόδαιμον, τί τὸ δέρμ' ἔπαθες; μῶν ὑστριχὶς εἰσέβαλέν σοι
εἰς τὰς πλευρὰς πολλῇ στρατιᾷ κἀδενδροτόμησε τὸ νῶτον;"
τοιαῦτ' ἀφελὼν κακὰ καὶ φόρτον καὶ βωμολοχεύματ' ἀγεννῆ
ἐποίησε τέχνην μεγάλην ἡμῖν κἀπύργωσ' οἰκοδομήσας
ἔπεσιν μεγάλοις καὶ διανοίαις καὶ σκώμμασιν οὐκ ἀγοραίοις,   750
οὐκ ἰδιώτας ἀνθρωπίσκους κωμῳδῶν οὐδὲ γυναῖκας,
ἀλλ' Ἡρακλέους ὀργήν τιν' ἔχων τοῖσι μεγίστοις ἐπεχείρει,
διαβὰς βυρσῶν ὀσμὰς δεινὰς κἀπειλὰς βορβοροθύμους.
καὶ πρῶτον μὲν μάχομαι πάντων αὐτῷ τῷ καρχαρόδοντι,
οὗ δεινόταται μὲν ἀπ' ὀφθαλμῶν Κύννης ἀκτῖνες ἔλαμπον,   755
ἑκατὸν δὲ κύκλῳ κεφαλαὶ κολάκων οἰμωξομένων ἐλιχμῶντο
περὶ τὴν κεφαλήν, φωνὴν δ' εἶχεν χαράδρας ὄλεθρον τετοκυίας,

742 follows 743 in Π11 codd.: transposed by Bergk.
[744] οὓς ἐξῆγον (εξηγαγον Π11) κλάοντας ἀεὶ καὶ τούτους οὕνεκα
       τουδί vel sim. Π11 codd.: del. Bergk: possibly an
       author's variant for 742.
745 εἶτ' ἀνέροιτο Bentley: ἐπανέροιτο codd. Suda: ε̣π̣[....]ο̣ι̣το Π11.
749 ἡμῖν codd.: ὑμῖν Blaydes.
753 βορβοροθύμους codd.: βαρβαροθύμους Σ^R: βαρβαρομύθους Meineke.

74

Really the stewards ought to beat any comic poet who
comes forward and extols himself before the audience in the anapaests.   735
However, if it is proper, O daughter of Zeus, to honour one who has been
and is the best and most renowned comic producer in the world, then our
producer says that he is worthy of great praise. First of all, he, alone
of all men, stopped his rivals always making fun of rags and waging war   740
on lice; then he was the first to outlaw and expel from the stage those   741/3
Heracleses who kneaded dough or went hungry; and he got rid of the slaves
who were always running away from someone, or deceiving someone, or getting   742
beaten just in order that a fellow-slave might make fun of his bruises and   745
ask him: "Poor devil, what have you had done to your skin? It's not a
bristle-whip, is it, that's invaded your sides in great strength and laid
waste your back?" Such poor stuff, such rubbish, such ignoble buffoonery,
he has removed; he has created a great art for us, and built it up to
towering dimensions with mighty words and ideas and with jokes that are   750
not vulgar. Nor has he satirized the little man or woman in private life;
rather, with a spirit like that of Heracles, he tackled the greatest monsters,
striding through terrible smells of leather and the menaces of a muckraker's
rage. And first of all these I fought with the Jag-toothed One himself,
from whose eyes shone terrible rays like those of the Bitch-star, while   755
all around his head licked serpent-like a hundred head of accursed flatterers;
he had the voice of a torrent in destructive spate, the smell of a seal,

φώκης δ' ὀσμήν, Λαμίας δ' ὄρχεις ἀπλύτους, πρωκτὸν δὲ καμήλου.
τοιοῦτον ἰδὼν τέρας οὐ κατέδεισ', ἀλλ' ὑπὲρ ὑμῶν πολεμίζων
ἀντεῖχον ἀεὶ καὶ τῶν ἄλλων νήσων. ὦν οὕνεκα νυνὶ   760
ἀποδοῦναί μοι τὴν χάριν ὑμᾶς εἰκὸς καὶ μνήμονας εἶναι.
καὶ γὰρ πρότερον πράξας κατὰ νοῦν οὐχὶ παλαίστρας περινοστῶν
παῖδας ἐπείρων, ἀλλ' ἀράμενος τὴν σκευὴν εὐθὺς ἐχώρουν,
παῦρ' ἀνιάσας, πόλλ' εὐφράνας, πάντα παρασχὼν τὰ δέοντα.
πρὸς ταῦτα χρεὼν εἶναι μετ' ἐμοῦ   765
    καὶ τοὺς ἄνδρας καὶ τοὺς παῖδας.
    καὶ τοῖς φαλακροῖσι παραινοῦμεν
    ξυσπουδάζειν περὶ τῆς νίκης·
    πᾶς γάρ τις ἐρεῖ νικῶντος ἐμοῦ
    κἀπὶ τραπέζῃ καὶ ξυμποσίοις·   770
    "φέρε τῷ φαλακρῷ, δὸς τῷ φαλακρῷ
    τῶν τρωγαλίων, καὶ μὴ 'φαίρει
    γενναιοτάτου τῶν ποιητῶν
    ἀνδρὸς τὸ μέτωπον ἔχοντος."   774

Μοῦσα, σὺ μὲν πολέμους ἀπωσαμένη μετ' ἐμοῦ   (στρ.
    τοῦ φίλου χόρευσον,
κλείουσα θεῶν τε γάμους ἀνδρῶν τε δαῖτας
    καὶ θαλίας μακάρων· σοὶ γὰρ τάδ' ἐξ ἀρχῆς μέλει.   780
ἢν δέ σε Καρκίνος ἐλθὼν
    ἀντιβολῇ μετὰ τῶν παίδων χορεῦσαι,
    μήθ' ὑπάκουε μήτ' ἔλ-   785
    θῃς συνέριθος αὐτοῖς·
    ἀλλὰ νόμιζε πάντας
ὄρτυγας οἰκογενεῖς, γυλιαύχενας ὀρχηστὰς
    νανοφυεῖς, σφυράδων ἀποκνίσματα, μηχανοδίφας.   790

785 ὑπάκουε Bentley: ὑπακουση[Π11: ὑπακούσης RVΓp: ὑπάσης t.

the unwashed balls of a Lamia, and the arse of a camel. On seeing such
a monstrosity I did not take fright; no, I stood my ground all the time,   760
fighting for you and also for the islands. Because of this is it fair now
that you should remember me and pay me your debt of gratitude. After
all, when I was successful before, I didn't tour round the wrestling-schools
and make passes at boys; rather I immediately packed up my gear and went
on my way, having caused little pain and much delight and given you everything the way it should be.

	In view of this, both the men	765-6
	and the boys ought to be on my side.	
	And we advise all bald men	
	to join in striving for my victory;	
	for if I win, everyone will say	
	both at table and at drinking parties:	770
	"Offer the baldhead, give the baldhead	
	some of the dessert, and don't withhold it	
	from a man who has the same forehead	
	as the noblest of poets."	
CHORUS:	O Muse, thrust wars aside and dance	775
	with me, thy friend,	
	celebrating the weddings of gods, the banquets of men,	
	and the festivities of the blest; for these have been thy	780
	chosen themes from the first.	
	But if Carcinus comes	
	and begs you to dance with his children,	
	do not listen to them nor go	785
	to aid them in their work,	
	but regard them all as	
	home-bred quails, dwarfish dancers	789-
	with hedgehogs' necks, snippets of dung-balls, hunters	790
	after gimmicks.	

καὶ γὰρ ἔφασχ' ὁ πατὴρ ὃ παρ' ἐλπίδας
    εἶχε τὸ δρᾶμα γαλῆν τῆς   795
    ἑσπέρας ἀπάγξαι.

τοιάδε χρὴ Χαρίτων δαμώματα καλλικόμων   (ἀντ.
    τὸν σοφὸν ποιητὴν
ὑμνεῖν, ὅταν ἠρινὰ μὲν φωνῇ χελιδὼν   800
    ἑζομένη κελαδῇ, χορὸν δὲ μὴ 'χῃ Μόρσιμος
μηδὲ Μελάνθιος, οὗ δὴ
    πικροτάτην ὄπα γηρύσαντος ἤκουσ',   805
    ἡνίκα τῶν τραγῳδῶν
    τὸν χορὸν εἶχον ἀδελ-
    φός τε καὶ αὐτός, ἄμφω
Γοργόνες ὀψοφάγοι, βατιδοσκόποι Ἅρπυιαι,   810
    γραοσόβαι μιαροί, τραγομάσχαλοι ἰχθυολῦμαι·
ὧν καταχρεμψαμένη μέγα καὶ πλατύ,   815
    Μοῦσα θεά, μετ' ἐμοῦ ξύμ-
    παιζε τὴν ἑορτήν.

Τρ. ὡς χαλεπὸν ἐλθεῖν ἦν ἄρ' εὐθὺ τῶν θεῶν.
     ἔγωγέ τοι πεπόνηκα κομιδῇ τὼ σκέλει.   820
     μικροὶ δ' ὁρᾶν ἄνωθεν ἦστ'· ἐμοιγέ τοι
     ἀπὸ τοὐρανοῦ 'φαίνεσθε κακοήθεις πάνυ,
     ἐντευθενὶ δὲ πολύ τι κακοηθέστεροι.

Οι. ὦ δέσποθ', ἥκεις;

Τρ.   ὥς γ' ἐγὼ 'πυθόμην τινός.

802 ἑζομένη codd.: [.].[ο]μενη Π11: ἡδομένη Bergk.
824 ὥς γ' ἐγὼ 'πυθ- Dindorf: ὡς ἐγὼ πυθ- Π11 t: ὡς ἔγωγ' ἐπυθ-
     RVΓp.

78

For their father once claimed that the play   793-5
which he'd unexpectedly got a booking for
had been throttled one evening by a ferret!

Such songs as these, songs of the lovely-haired Graces,
it is right for the skilful poet to sing
to the people, when the perching swallow sounds out with her voice   800-2
her songs of spring, and when Morsimus does *not* get a chorus,
nor does Melanthius, he whose
most piercing voice I once heard shrilling out,   805
that time when his brother
and he had a chorus
for a tragedy, that pair of
gastronomic Gorgons, skate-eyeing Harpies,   810
villainous scarecrones, fish-destroyers with goat-scented armpits.
Loose at them, divine Muse, a big fat glob   815
of spittle, and come sport
with me throughout this festival.

[*Trygaeus re-enters by a side passage, leading Fullfruit and Showtime.*]
TRYGAEUS [*to the audience*]: How hard it was indeed to go all the way to
the gods! *I'm* thoroughly sore in the legs, at any rate. You were small to   820
look at from up there. To my eyes, looking from heaven, you seemed a right
wicked lot; looking from *here*, you seem a good deal wickeder!
[*A slave comes out of Trygaeus' house.*]
SLAVE: Master, you've really come home?
TRYGAEUS: Well, so someone's told me!

79

Οι. τί δ' ἔπαθες;

Τρ.   ἤλγουν τὼ σκέλει μακρὰν ὁδὸν   825
διεληλυθώς.

Οι.   ἴθι νυν κάτειπέ μοι—

Τρ.   τὸ τί;

Οι. ἄλλον τιν' εἶδες ἄνδρα κατὰ τὸν ἀέρα
πλανώμενον πλὴν σαυτόν;

Τρ.   οὔκ, εἰ μή γέ που
ψυχὰς δύ' ἢ τρεῖς διθυραμβοδιδασκάλων.

Οι. τί δ' ἔδρων;

Τρ.   ξυνελέγοντ' ἀναβολὰς ποτώμεναι   830
τὰς ἐνδιαεριαυρινηχέτους τινάς.

Οι. οὐκ ἦν ἄρ' οὐδ' ἃ λέγουσι, κατὰ τὸν ἀέρα
ὡς ἀστέρες γιγνόμεθ', ὅταν τις ἀποθάνῃ;

Τρ. μάλιστα.

Οι.   καὶ τίς ἐστιν ἀστὴρ νῦν ἐκεῖ;

Τρ. Ἴων ὁ Χῖος, ὅσπερ ἐποίησεν πάλαι   835
ἐνθάδε τὸν Ἀοῖόν ποθ'· ὡς δ' ἦλθ', εὐθέως
Ἀοῖον αὐτὸν πάντες ἐκάλουν ἀστέρα.

Οι. τίνες γάρ εἰσ' οἱ διατρέχοντες ἀστέρες,
οἳ καόμενοι θέουσιν;

Τρ.   ἀπὸ δείπνου τινὲς

_____

831 -αυρι- Dindorf: -αερι- RV, Didymus in Σ^V (where he is
     criticized for accepting this un-Attic form): -αιερι-
     Suda δ1029: -ανερι- Γpt Suda ε1174: -αυστρι- Σ^Γ.

80

SLAVE: What happened to you?   825
TRYGAEUS: I got sore legs from travelling such a long way.
SLAVE: Well now, tell me —
TRYGAEUS: What?
SLAVE: Did you see any other man wandering through the air, except
yourself?
TRYGAEUS: No — except, I suppose, two or three souls of dithyrambic
composers.
SLAVE: What were they doing?   830
TRYGAEUS: They were flitting about collecting ideas for some preludes
of the air-haunting-swiftly-soaring kind.
SLAVE: So also it isn't true after all what they say, that when we
die we become stars in the sky?
TRYGAEUS: It's very true indeed.
SLAVE: And who's a star up there now?
TRYGAEUS: Ion of Chios, the man who years ago, down here, composed   835
The Star of Dawning. When he came up there, right away everyone called
him the Star of Dawning!
SLAVE: And who are the shooting stars that rush blazing through the sky?
TRYGAEUS: They're some of the wealthy stars walking home after dinner,   840

81

τῶν πλουσίων οὗτοι βαδίζουσ' ἀστέρων   840
ἱπνοὺς ἔχοντες, ἐν δὲ τοῖς ἱπνοῖσι πῦρ.
ἀλλ' εἴσαγ' ὡς τάχιστα ταυτηνὶ λαβών,
καὶ τὴν πύελον κατάκλυζε καὶ θέρμαιν' ὕδωρ,
στόρνυ τ' ἐμοὶ καὶ τῇδε κουρίδιον λέχος·
καὶ ταῦτα δράσας ἧκε δεῦρ' αὖθις πάλιν.   845
ἐγὼ δ' ἀποδώσω τήνδε τῇ βουλῇ τέως.

Οι.   πόθεν δ' ἔλαβες ταύτας σύ;

Τρ.   πόθεν; ἐκ τοὐρανοῦ.

Οι.   οὐκ ἂν ἔτι δοίην τῶν θεῶν τριώβολον,
      εἰ πορνοβοσκοῦσ' ὥσπερ ἡμεῖς οἱ βροτοί.

Τρ.   οὔκ, ἀλλὰ κἀκεῖ ζῶσιν ἀπὸ τούτων τινές.   850

Οι.   ἄγε νυν ἴωμεν. εἰπέ μοι, δῶ καταφαγεῖν
      ταύτῃ τι;

Τρ.   μηδέν· οὐ γὰρ ἐθελήσει φαγεῖν
      οὔτ' ἄρτον οὔτε μᾶζαν, εἰωθυῖ' ἀεὶ
      παρὰ τοῖς θεοῖσιν ἀμβροσίαν λείχειν ἄνω.

Οι.   λείχειν ἄρ' αὐτῇ κἀνθάδε σκευαστέον.   855

Χο.   εὐδαιμονικῶς γ' ὁ πρε-   (στρ.
         σβύτης, ὅσα γ' ὧδ' ἰδεῖν,
         τὰ νῦν τάδε πράττει.

Τρ.   τί δῆτ', ἐπειδὰν νυμφίον μ' ὁρᾶτε λαμπρὸν ὄντα;

Χο.   ζηλωτὸς ἔσει, γέρων   860
         αὖθις νέος ὢν πάλιν,

844   τ' ἐμοὶ Brunck: τέ μοι codd.
860   γέρων B: γέρον RVpt.

82

carrying lanterns with fire in them. But now [*bringing Fullfruit forward*]
take this girl and take her inside right away, rinse the bathtub and heat
water, and spread the nuptial couch for her and me; and when you've done   845
that, come back here again. Meanwhile I'll give this other girl back to
the Council.

  SLAVE: Where did you get them from?

  TRYGAEUS: Where from? From heaven.

  SLAVE: I wouldn't give three obols for the gods after this, if they
go in for pimping just like us mortals.

  TRYGAEUS: It's not like that — though up there too there are some   850
who live off these girls.

  SLAVE [*to Fullfruit*]: Come on now, let's go. [*To Trygaeus*] Tell me,
should I give her anything to eat?

  TRYGAEUS: Nothing. She won't be willing to eat either bread or barley
cake, when she's always been used to licking up ambrosia with the gods above.

  SLAVE: Then we'll have to prepare something for her to *lick* down here   855
too. [*He takes Fullfruit inside.*]

  CHORUS: The old man is doing,
       as far as one can see at the moment,
       very happily right now.

  TRYGAEUS: What about when you see me as a resplendent bridegroom?

  CHORUS: You will be enviable, an old man   860
       turned young once again,

μύρῳ κατάλειπτος.

Τρ. οἶμαι. τί δῆθ', ὅταν ξυνὼν τῶν τιτθίων ἔχωμαι;

Χο. εὐδαιμονέστερος φανεῖ τῶν Καρκίνου στροβίλων.

Τρ. οὔκουν δικαίως; ὅστις εἰς
    ὄχημα κανθάρου 'πιβὰς   865
    ἔσωσα τοὺς Ἕλληνας, ὥστ'
    ἐν τοῖς ἀγροῖς
    ἅπαντας ὄντας ἀσφαλῶς
    κινεῖν τε καὶ καθεύδειν.

Οι. ἡ παῖς λέλουται καὶ τὰ τῆς πυγῆς καλά·
    ὁ πλακοῦς πέπεπται, σησαμῆ ξυμπλάττεται,
    καὶ τἄλλ' ἀπαξάπαντα· τοῦ πέους δὲ δεῖ.   870

Τρ. ἴθι νυν ἀποδῶμεν τήνδε τὴν θεωρίαν
    ἀνύσαντε τῇ βουλῇ.

Οι.   τί; ταυτηνί; τί φής;
    αὕτη θεωρία 'στίν, ἣν ἡμεῖς ποτε
    ἐπαίομεν Βραυρωνάδ' ὑποπεπωκότες;

Τρ. σάφ' ἴσθι· κἀλήφθη γε μόλις.

Οι.   ὦ δέσποτα,   875
    ὅσην ἔχει τὴν πρωκτοπεντετηρίδα.

Τρ. εἶέν· τίς ἐσθ' ὑμῶν δίκαιος; τίς ποτε;
    τίς διαφυλάξει τήνδε τῇ βουλῇ λαβών;

865 εἷς Nenci: εἰς codd. Suda.
866 ἀγροῖς RV<u>p</u>: ἀγροῖσιν αὐτοὺς <u>t</u>: cf. 920.
874 ὑποπεπωκότες B, cf. Σ^{RV}: ὑποπεπτωκότες RV<u>pt</u>.

anointed with perfume.

TRYGAEUS: I think I will. What about when I'm in bed with her, holding those titties close?

CHORUS-LEADER: You will be seen to be happier than . . .Carcinus' young spinning-tops.

TRYGAEUS: And do I not deserve it? I who all alone   865
mounted my beetle-steed
and saved the Greeks, so that now
they can all live
in the countryside
and screw and sleep in security.

[*The slave comes out of the house.*]

SLAVE: The girl's been bathed, and her bottom part's in order. The flat-cake has been baked, sesame-balls are being shaped, and absolutely   870 everything else is ready. Only the prick's missing!

TRYGAEUS: Come on then, let's hurry up and give Showtime here back to the Council.

SLAVE [*surprised to hear the name Showtime*]: What? This girl here? What did you say? Is this the Showtime we used to have when we'd screw our way to Brauron after a few drinks?

TRYGAEUS: I assure you it is; and it was a hard job catching her.   875

SLAVE: Oh, master, what a big quadrennial bum she's got!

[*Trygaeus and the slave now bring Showtime forward to show her to the audience.*]

TRYGAEUS: All right then, who is an honest man among you? who now? Who will take this girl and keep her safe for the Council? [*Turning*

85

οὗτος, τί περιγράφεις;

Οι.   τὸ δεῖν', εἰς Ἴσθμια

σκηνὴν ἐμαυτοῦ τῷ πέει καταλαμβάνω.   880

Τρ. οὔπω λέγεθ' ὑμεῖς τίς ὁ φυλάξων; δεῦρο σύ·

κατᾱθήσομαι γὰρ αὐτὸς εἰς μέσους σ' ἄγων.

Οι. ἐκεινοσὶ νεύει.

Τρ.   τίς;

Οι.   ὅστις; Ἀριφράδης,

ἄγειν παρ' αὐτὸν ἀντιβολῶν.

Τρ.   ἀλλ', ὦ μέλε,

τὸν ζωμὸν αὐτῆς προσπεσὼν ἐκλάψεται.   885

ἄγε δὴ σὺ κατάθου πρῶτα τὴν σκευὴν χαμαί.

βουλή, πρυτάνεις, ὁρᾶτε τὴν θεωρίαν.

σκέψασθ' ὅσ' ὑμῖν ἀγαθὰ παραδώσω φέρων,

ὥστ' εὐθέως ἄραντας ὑμᾶς τὼ σκέλει

ταύτης μετεώρω κᾆτ' ἀγαγεῖν ἀνάρρυσιν.   890

τουτὶ δ' ὁρᾶτε τοὐπτάνιον.

Οι.   οὔμ', ὡς καλόν.

διὰ ταῦτα καὶ κεκάπνικεν ἄρ'· ἐνταῦθα γὰρ

πρὸ τοῦ πολέμου τὰ λάσανα τῇ βουλῇ ποτ' ἦν.

---

882 αὐτὸς εἰς μέσους Seidler: αὐτοὺς ἐς μέσους V: εἰς μέσους
     αὐτοὺς vel sim. R p t.

882 σ' Rogers: om. codd.

886 τὴν σκευὴν Meineke: τὰ σκεύη codd.

890 μετεώρω Blaydes: μετέωρα codd.

890 κᾆτ' ἀγαγεῖν van Herwerden: καταγαγεῖν codd.

891 οὔμ', ὡς καλόν Zacher: ἡμῖν ὡς καλόν R: ὡς καλὸν ἡμῖν V:
     ὑμῖν ὡς καλόν p t: all mss. continue these words to Trygaeι

abruptly to the slave, who is running his hands over Showtime's person]
Here, you, what's that zone you're marking out?

SLAVE: Well — er — actually — I'm staking a claim to camping space   880
for my prick for the Isthmian games.

TRYGAEUS [*taking Showtime firmly away from him and again addressing
tha audience*]: Will you still not tell me who's going to take care of her?
[*Coming further down towards the audience, leading Showtime and speaking
to her*] Come this way; I'm going to take you and deposit you in the middle
of them.

SLAVE [*pointing into the audience*]: There's someonc nodding!
TRYGAEUS: Who is it?
SLAVE: Who is it? It's Ariphrades, begging you to take her to him.
TRYGAEUS: Why, man, he'll fall upon her and lap up her broth! [*To   885
Showtime, who is now in front of the seats reserved for the councillors*]
Come on now, first of all put down your things on the ground. [*Showtime
removes her clothes.*] Councillors, Prytaneis, behold Showtime. Look what
a bundle of blessings I'm bringing to hand over to you — you can raise
up her legs in the air straight away, and then have a feast of a time!   890
And look at this oven of hers.

SLAVE: My, how beautiful! Ah, *that's* why it's got all smoky black
— because the Council used to keep their trivet there before the war.

Τρ. κἄπειτ' ἀγῶνά γ' εὐθὺς ἐξέσται ποιεῖν

ταύτην ἔχουσιν αὔριον καλὸν πάνυ,   895

ἐπὶ γῆς παλαίειν, τετραποδηδὸν ἱστάναι,   896a

καὶ παγκράτιόν γ' ὑπαλειφαμένοις νεανικῶς   897

παύειν, ὀρύττειν, πὺξ ὁμοῦ καὶ τῷ πέει.

τρίτῃ δὲ μετὰ ταῦθ' ἱπποδρομίαν ἄξετε,

ἵνα δὴ κέλης κέλητα παρακελητιεῖ,   900

ἅρματα δ' ἐπ' ἀλλήλοισιν ἀνατετραμμένα

φυσῶντα καὶ πνέοντα προσκινήσεται,

ἕτεροι δὲ κείσονταί γ' ἀπεψωλημένοι

περὶ ταῖσι καμπαῖς ἡνίοχοι πεπτωκότες.

ἀλλ', ὦ πρυτάνεις, δέχεσθε τὴν θεωρίαν.   905

θέασ' ὡς προθύμως ὁ πρύτανις παρεδέξατο.

ἀλλ' οὐκ ἄν, εἴ τι προῖκα προσαγαγεῖν σ' ἔδει,

ἀλλ' ηὗρον ἄν σ' ὑπέχοντα τὴν ἐκεχειρίαν.

Χο. ἦ χρηστὸς ἀνὴρ πολί-   (ἀντ.

ταις ἐστὶν ἅπασιν ὅσ-   910

τις ἐστὶ τοιοῦτος.

Τρ. ὅταν τρυγᾶτ', εἴσεσθε πολλῷ μᾶλλον οἷός εἰμι.

Χο. καὶ νῦν σύ γε δῆλος εἶ·

σωτὴρ γὰρ ἅπασιν ἀν-

θρώποις γεγένησαι.   915

894 κἄπειτ' van Herwerden: ἔπειτ' codd.

896a Willems proposed to delete this line and retain 896b.

896a ἱστάναι Sommerstein: ἑστάναι codd.

[896b] πλαγίαν καταβάλλειν, ἐς γόνατα κύβδ' ἑστάναι (ἱστάναι conj.
      Meineke) R: om. VΓpt: perhaps an author's variant for 896a.

907 προῖκα pt $^{\lambda}\Sigma^{\Gamma}$: προῖκ' αν RVΓ $^{\lambda}\Sigma^{R}$.

909/910 πολίταις Hermann: πολίτης codd.

88

TRYGAEUS: And *then*, now you've got her, first thing tomorrow you'll   894-5
be able to hold a splendid athletic meeting — to wrestle on the ground,
to stand her on all fours, to anoint yourselves and fight lustily in the
free-style, knocking and gouging with fist and prick at once. After that,
the day after tomorrow, you'll hold the equestrian events, in which jockey   900
will outjockey jockey, while chariots will crash one on top of another and
thrust themselves together puffing and panting, and other charioteers will
be lying with their cocks skinned, having come unstuck in the bends and
twists. Now, Prytaneis, take possession of Showtime! [*He gives Showtime*   905
to the chairman of the Prytaneis.] Look how eagerly the chairman took her
from me! [*To the chairman*] You wouldn't have done that if you'd had to
introduce some business for no reward; no, I'd have found you extending
your . . . armistice.
     CHORUS: Truly any man
                     who is like this one   910-1
                     is good for all citizens.
     TRYGAEUS: When you gather in your vintage, you'll know much better
what a man I am.
     CHORUS: Even now your qualitites are plain:
                     you have become a saviour   914-5
                     to all mankind.

Τρ. φήσεις γ', ἐπειδὰν ἐκπίῃς οἴνου νέου λεπαστήν.

Χο. καὶ πλήν γε τῶν θεῶν ἀεί σ' ἡγησόμεσθα πρῶτον.

Τρ. πολλῶν γὰρ ὑμῖν ἄξιος
    Τρυγαῖος ἀθμονεὺς ἐγώ,
    δεινῶν ἀπαλλάξας πόνων
    τὸν δημότην   920
    καὶ τὸν γεωργικὸν λεών,
    'Υπέρβολόν τε παύσας.

Οι. ἄγε δή, τί νῷν ἐντευθενὶ ποιητέον;

Τρ. τί δ' ἄλλο γ' ἢ ταύτην χύτραις ἱδρυτέον;

Οι. χύτραισιν, ὥσπερ μεμφόμενον 'Ερμήδιον;

Τρ. τῷ δαὶ δοκεῖ; βούλεσθε λαρινῷ βοΐ;   925

Οι. βοΐ; μηδαμῶς, ἵνα μὴ βοηθεῖν ποῖ δέῃ.

Τρ. ἀλλ' ὑῒ παχείᾳ καὶ μεγάλῃ;

Οι.   μὴ μή.

Τρ.   τιή;

Οι. ἵνα μὴ γένηται Θεογένους ὑηνία.

916   φήσεις γ' Dindorf: φήσεις RVΓp̲ Suda: φήσεις τί δῆτ' t̲:
       τί δῆται (sic) Athenaeus: τί δῆτ' Biset.
920   δημότην Dindorf: δημότην ὅμιλον codd.: cf. Zimmermann 183.
924   'Ερμήδιον Schwabe: 'Ερμίδιον codd.: cf. 382.
925   τῷ Blaydes: τί codd.
925   βούλεσθε p̲t̲: βούλεσθαι RVΓ.
926   δέῃ Dindorf: δέοι codd.
928   Θεογένους Dindorf: Θεαγένους codd. Suda.

TRYGAEUS: You'll say that all right when you drink off a goblet of new wine.

CHORUS-LEADER: Yes, and we'll always rank you first of all except the gods.

TRYGAEUS: Yes, for I, Trygaeus of Athmonum,
deserve a rich reward for my services to you,
having freed the common folk   920
and the peasant folk
from terrible hardships,
and having put a stop to Hyperbolus.

SLAVE: Right then, what have we to do next?

TRYGAEUS: What else but to perform the installation of this goddess with an offering of pots?

SLAVE: With *pots*, like a grumbling little Hermes?

TRYGAEUS: Then what do you think it should be with? Do you want it   925
to be with a fatted ox?

SLAVE: An ox? Certainly not; we don't want to have to go on an *oxpedition* anywhere.

TRYGAEUS: Then with a big fat sow?

SLAVE: No, no!

TRYGAEUS: Why not?

SLAVE: For fear we should turn swinish like Theogenes.

Τρ. τῷ δαὶ δοκεῖ σοι δῆτα τῶν λοιπῶν;

Οι.   ὁί.

Τρ. ὁί;

Οι.   ναὶ μὰ Δί'.

Τρ.   ἀλλὰ τοῦτό γ' ἔστ' Ἰωνικὸν   930
τὸ ῥῆμ'.

Οι.   ἐπίτηδές γ', ἵν', <ὅταν> ἐν τἠκκλησίᾳ
ὡς χρὴ πολεμεῖν λέγῃ τις, οἱ καθήμενοι
ὑπὸ τοῦ δέους λέγωσ' Ἰωνικῶς "ὁί"—

Τρ. εὖ τοι λέγεις.

Οι.   —καὶ τἄλλα γ' ὦσιν ἤπιοι·
ὥστ' ἐσόμεθ' ἀλλήλοισιν ἀμνοὶ τοὺς τρόπους   935
καὶ τοῖσι συμμάχοισι πραότεροι πολύ.

Τρ. ἴθι νυν ἄγ' ὡς τάχιστα τὸ πρόβατον λαβών·
ἐγὼ δὲ ποριῶ βωμὸν ἐφ' ὅτου θύσομεν.

Χο. ὡς πάνθ' ὅσ' ἂν θεὸς θέλῃ   (στρ.
χἠ τύχη κατορθοῖ
χωρεῖ κατὰ νοῦν, ἕτερον δ' ἑτέρῳ   940
τούτων κατὰ καιρὸν ἀπαντᾷ.

Τρ. ὡς ταῦτα δῆλά γ' ἔσθ'· ὁ γὰρ βωμὸς θύρασι καὶ δή.

Χο. κατεπείγετέ νυν ἐν ὅσῳ σοβαρὰ
θεόθεν κατέχει πολέμου μετάτροπος

929 δαὶ Meineke: δὴ codd.
931 <ὅταν> Meineke: om. codd.
943 κατεπείγετε Bothe: ἐπείγετε codd.: ἄγ' ἐπείγετε Dindorf.

92

TRYGAEUS: Then other than that, what *do* you think it should be with?
SLAVE: A yow.
TRYGAEUS: A yow?   930
SLAVE: That's right.
TRYGAEUS: But that's a dialect word.
SLAVE: Deliberately so, in order that in the Assembly, whenever someone
says we ought to go to war, his audience should take fright and say in
dialect "yowww!" –
TRYGAEUS: Good idea!
SLAVE: – and be gentle in other ways; so that we shall be like lambs   935
in our behaviour towards each other, and much milder towards our allies.
TRYGAEUS: Go on then, get the sheep and bring it as quickly as you
can; and I'll provide an altar for us to sacrifice on. [*The slave goes inside.*]
CHORUS: See how everthing that God wills
              and that fortune prospers
              goes as one desires, and one such success   940
              leads to another at the right moment!
TRYGAEUS: For sure, that is plainly true. Look, here's the altar outside!
[*He points to the altar on the stage-platform.*]
CHORUS: Hasten now, while the strong winds holds
              which God has caused to veer away   944-5

αὔρα· νῦν γὰρ δαίμων φανερῶς   945
     εἰς ἀγαθὰ μεταβιβάζει.

Τρ. τὸ κανοῦν πάρεστ', ὀλὰς ἔχον καὶ στέμμα καὶ μάχαιραν,
     καὶ πῦρ γε τουτί, κοὐδὲν ἴσχει πλὴν τὸ πρόβατον ἡμᾶς.

Χο. οὔκουν ἀμιλλήσεσθον; ὡς   950
     ἢν Χάρις ὑμᾶς ἴδῃ,
     πρόσεισιν αὐλήσων ἄκλη-
     τος, κᾆτα τοῦτ' εὖ οἶδ' ὅτι
     φυσῶντι καὶ πονουμένῳ
     προσδώσετε δήπου.   955

Τρ. ἄγε δή, τὸ κανοῦν λαβὼν σὺ καὶ τὴν χέρνιβα
     περίιθι τὸν βωμὸν ταχέως ἐπιδέξια.

Οι. ἰδού. λέγοις ἂν ἄλλο· περιελήλυθα.

Τρ. φέρε δὴ τὸ δαλίον τόδ' ἐμβάψω λαβών.
     σείου σὺ ταχέως. σὺ δὲ πρότεινε τῶν ὀλῶν,   960
     καὐτός γε χερνίπτου παραδοὺς ταύτην ἐμοί,
     καὶ τοῖς θεαταῖς ῥῖπτε τῶν κριθῶν.

Οι.   ἰδού.

Τρ. ἔδωκας ἤδη;

Οι.   νὴ τὸν Ἑρμῆν, ὥστε γε
     τούτων ὅσοιπέρ εἰσι τῶν θεωμένων
     οὐκ ἔστιν οὐδεὶς ὅστις οὐ κριθὴν ἔχει.   965

959 δαλίον Σ^V γρ$_Σ$^{R}, Hesychius, Suda: δᾳδίον vel sim. RV Vict.
     γρ$_Σ$^{V} γρ$_{Suda}$.

961 γε Enger: τε RV Vict.

from war; for now it is plain that the deity
is making things change in a better direction.

[*During this the slave has returned with some of the requisites for the
sacrifice, which he gives to Trygaeus.*]

TRYGAEUS: Here's the basket, with barley-grains and ribbons and a knife
— and here's fire too; there's nothing holding us up except the sheep!

[*The slave goes inside again. Trygaeus, after lighting the altar fire,
goes inside also, while the chorus sing.*]

CHORUS: You'd better race for it, then; because   950
            if Chacris sees you,
            he'll come up uninvited
            to play the pipes, and then I know full well
            that he'll puff and labour,
            and of course you'll give him something!   955

[*The slave has now returned leading a sheep, and Trygaeus bringing a basin
of lustral water and two myrtle wreaths which he and the slave place on their
heads. The ribbons from the basket are tied on the animal's horns.*]

TRYGAEUS [*to the slave*]: All right then, you take the basket and the
lustral water, and quickly circle the altar, right-about.

SLAVE [*taking basket and basin*]: Look, I am. [*He carries them round
the altar.*] You can say something else. I've been round.

TRYGAEUS [*taking a brand from the altar fire*]: Now then, let me take
this brand and dip it in. [*He dips the brand in the lustral water and shakes
it over the altar and the sheep. At first the sheep remains motionless.*]
Hurry up, nod your head. [*Eventually the sheep does so. To the slave*] You   960
hand me some of the grains. [*Trygaeus takes some grains from the basket in
the slave's extended hand, and scatters them on the altar and on the sheep's
head. Then he washes his hands.*] Now you hand that to me and wash your
own hands. [*Trygaeus takes the basin, and the slave washes his hands.*] And
throw the spectators some of the barley seeds.

SLAVE [*doing so*]: There you are.

TRYGAEUS: You've given it to them already?

SLAVE: By Hermes, I have, so that of all these spectators there isn't   965
one who hasn't got some seed.

Τρ. οὐχ αἱ γυναῖκές γ' ἔλαβον.

Οι.   ἀλλ' εἰς ἑσπέραν
δώσουσιν αὐταῖς ἄνδρες.

Τρ.   ἀλλ' εὐχώμεθα.
τίς τῇδε; ποῦ ποτ' εἰσὶ πολλοὶ κἀγαθού;

Οι. τοισδὶ φέρε δῶ· πολλοὶ γάρ εἰσι κἀγαθού.

Τρ. τούτους ἀγαθους ἐνόμισας;

Οι.   οὐ γάρ, οὗτινες   970
ἡμῶν καταχεόντων ὕδωρ τοσουτονὶ
εἰς ταὐτὸ τοῦθ' ἑστᾶσ' ἰόντες χωρίον;

Τρ. ἀλλ' ὡς τάχιστ' εὐχώμεθ'.

Οι.   εὐχώμεσθα δή.

Τρ. ὦ σεμνοτάτη βασίλεια θεά,
     πότνι' Εἰρήνη,   975
     δέσποινα χορῶν, δέσποινα γάμων,
     δέξαι θυσίαν τὴν ἡμετέραν.

Οι. δέξαι δῆτ', ὦ πολυτιμήτη,
     νὴ Δία, καὶ μὴ πούει γ' ἅπερ αἱ
     μοιχευόμεναι δρῶσι γυναῖκες.   980
     καὶ γὰρ ἐκεῖναι παρακλίνασαι
     τῆς αὐλείας παρακύπτουσιν,
     κἄν τις προσέχῃ τὸν νοῦν αὐταῖς,
     ἀναχωροῦσιν·
     κᾆτ', ἢν ἀπίῃ, παρακύπτουσ' αὖ.   985

985 παρακύπτουσ' αὖ Hirschig: παρακύπτουσι(ν) RV Suda (Vict.
     omits 983-5).

96

TRYGAEUS: The women haven't had any.

SLAVE: Well, the men will give it to them tonight!

TRYGAEUS [*taking the sacrificial knife from the basket*]: Now let us pray. [*In a loud voice*] Who is here? [*He pauses for a reply, but there is none.*] Where might there be many righteous men?

SLAVE: Here, let me give it to this lot; they're many, and they're sterling fellows. [*He flings the lustral water over the chorus. Some of them break ranks to avoid being showered, but quickly resume their positions when the danger has passed.*]

TRYGAEUS: You reckoned they were sterling fellows, did you?   970

SLAVE: Of course they are. We poured all that water over them, and yet they've come back to stand in exactly the same place!

TRYGAEUS: Well, let us pray straight away.

SLAVE: Yes, let's pray.

[*Trygaeus cuts a few hairs from the forehead of the sheep. He gives some to his slave, and holds the rest himself while he prays.*]

TRYGAEUS:　　O most revered sovereign goddess,

　　　　　　　Lady Peace,   975

　　　　　　　mistress of choral dances, mistress of weddings,

　　　　　　　accept our sacrifice.

SLAVE:　　　Yes, accept it, most highly honoured one,

　　　　　　　yes, by Zeus, and don't do what

　　　　　　　the adulterous wives do.   980

　　　　　　　For they open the front door

　　　　　　　just a little, and peep out,

　　　　　　　and if anyone notices them,

　　　　　　　they withdraw;

　　　　　　　and then if he goes away, they peep out again.   985

τούτων σὺ ποίει μηδὲν ἔθ' ἡμᾶς.

Τρ.   μὰ Δί', ἀλλ' ἀπόφηνον ὅλην σαυτὴν
γενναιοπρεπῶς τοῖσιν ἐρασταῖς
ἡμῖν, οἵ σου τρυχόμεθ' ἤδη
τριακαίδεκ' ἔτη·   990
λῦσον δὲ μάχας καὶ κορκορυγάς,
ἵνα Λυσιμάχην σε καλῶμεν.
παῦσον δ' ἡμῶν τὰς ὑπονοίας
τὰς περικόμψους,
αἷς στωμυλλόμεθ' εἰς ἀλλήλους·   995
μεῖξον δ' ἡμᾶς τοὺς Ἕλληνας
πάλιν ἐξ ἀρχῆς
φιλίας χυλῷ, καὶ συγγνώμῃ
τινὶ πραοτέρᾳ κέρασον τὸν νοῦν.
καὶ τὴν ἀγορὰν ἡμῖν ἀγαθῶν
ἐμπλησθῆναι, 'κ Μεγάρων σκορόδων,   1000
σικύων πρῴων, μήλων, ῥοιῶν,
δούλοισι χλανισκιδίων μικρῶν·
κἀκ Βοιωτῶν γε φέροντας ἰδεῖν
χῆνας, νήττας, φάττας, τροχίλους·
καὶ Κωπᾴδων ἐλθεῖν σπυρίδας,   1005
καὶ περὶ ταύτας ἡμᾶς ἀθρόους
ὀψωνοῦντας τυρβάζεσθαι
Μορύχῳ, Τελέᾳ, Γλαυκέτῃ, ἄλλοις
τένθαις πολλοῖς· κᾆτα Μελάνθιον
ἥκειν ὕστερον εἰς τὴν ἀγοράν,   1010
τὰς δὲ πεπρᾶσθαι, τὸν δ' ὀτοτύζειν,

986 ἡμᾶς R Vict.: ἡμῖν V.
1000 'κ Μεγάρων Hamaker, cf. Σ^V: μεγάλων RV Vict. ^λΣ^V.

Don't do any of that to us any more.

TRYGAEUS: No, indeed; rather reveal thyself fully
and generously to us
thy lovers, who have pined for thee
these thirteen years: 990
and resolve our fights and our broils,
that we may call thee Lysimache.
And put an end to those over-clever
suspicions of ours,
which make us prattle rubbish to one another; 995
blend us Greeks anew,
starting from scratch,
with the juice of friendship, and infuse into our minds
a milder forgivingness.
And may we have our Agora filled
with good things: from Megara, garlic,   1000
early cucumbers, apples, pomegranates,
tiny little woollen cloaks for our slaves;
and from Boeotia may we see men bringing
geese, ducks, pigeons, wrens,
and may there come great baskets of Copaic eels, 1005
and around these may all of us together
be doing our shopping, and jostling
Morychus, Teleas, Glaucetes, and many
another glutton; and then may Melanthius
come late to the Agora,   1010
and may they be sold out, and may he cry out in grief,

εἶτα μονῳδεῖν ἐκ Μηδείας·
"ὀλόμαν, ὀλόμαν ἀποχηρωθεὶς
τᾶς ἐν τεύτλοισι λοχευομένας"·
τοὺς δ' ἀνθρώπους ἐπιχαίρειν.   1015

ταῦτ', ὦ πολυτίμητ', εὐχομένοις ἡμῖν δίδου.
λαβὲ τὴν μάχαιραν· εἶθ' ὅπως μαγειρικῶς
σφάξεις τὸν οἶν.

Οι.   ἀλλ' οὐ θέμις.

Τρ.   τιὴ τί δή;

Οι. οὐχ ἥδεται δήπουθεν Εἰρήνη σφαγαῖς,
οὐδ' αἱματοῦται βωμός.

Τρ.   ἀλλ' εἴσω φέρων   1020
θύσας τὰ μηρί' ἐξελὼν δεῦρ' ἔκφερε,
χοὕτω τὸ πρόβατον τῷ χορηγῷ σῴζεται.

Χο. σέ τοι θύρασι †χρὴ μένοντα τούνυν†   (ἀντ.
σχίζας δευρὶ τιθέναι ταχέως
τά τε πρόσφορα πάντ' ἐπὶ τούτοις.   1025

Τρ. οὔκουν δοκῶ σοι μαντικῶς τὸ φρύγανον τίθεσθαι;

Χο. πῶς δ' οὐχί; τί γάρ σε πέφευγ' ὅσα χρὴ
σοφὸν ἄνδρα; τί δ' οὐ σὺ φρονεῖς ὁπόσα χρε-
ών ἐστιν τόν γε σοφῇ δόκιμον

1023 σέ τοι RV, Heliodorus in Σ^V 939: σὲ δὴ Γ<u>pt</u> ^{γρ}V.
1023 θύρασι Heliodorus: θύραισι codd.
1023 †χρὴ μένοντα τούνυν† codd.: χρή μένειν ὀντ[ ] τινάς Helio-
        dorus: χρη μένοντ' <ἐνθαδὶ μεθ' ἡμῶν> Rogers: perh. e.g.
        χρὴ μένειν κᾆτα νῦν <γε πολλᾶς> or (θυρασιν) <ὦ γέρον>
        (Blaydes) χρὴ μένοντα νυνί.
1029 γε <u>t</u>: om. RVΓ<u>p</u> Suda.

100

and then sing an aria from *Medea*:
"I am undone, I am no more, bereaved
of her who was confined amid the beet!"
And may the people rejoice at his fate.   1015
All this, O most highly honoured one, grant us, we pray thee. [*As he
concludes the prayer, Trygaeus throws the hairs from the sheep's head
on to the altar fire; the slave follows suit. Trygaeus turns to the
slave.*] Take the knife, and then see that you slaughter the sheep in
a professional way.

SLAVE: No, it's not proper.

TRYGAEUS: Oh, why not?

SLAVE: Surely Peace takes no delight in slaughter, "nor is her   1020
altar bloodied".

TRYGAEUS: Very well, take it inside and sacrifice it there, then
cut out the thigh-bones and bring them out here, and that way our sponsor
doesn't lose his sheep! [*The slave, taking the knife from Trygaeus,
leads the sheep back into the house.*]

CHORUS: It is up to you to remain outside
              and quickly put faggots on here
              and everything that is requisite on top of them.   1025

TRYGAEUS [*as he arranges faggots on the altar fire*]: Well, don't you
think I'm arranging the firewood like a real diviner?

CHORUS: To be sure you are! What has escaped you that a wise man
              should know? What are you ignorant of that should
              be known to a man esteemed for his wise

φρενὶ πορίμῳ τε τόλμῃ; 1030

Τρ. ἡ σχίζα γοῦν ἐνημμένη τὸν Στιλβίδην πιέζει.
κοὶ τὴν τράπεζαν οἴσομαι, καὶ παιδὸς οὐ δεήσει.

Χο. τίς οὖν ἂν οὐκ ἐπαινέσει-
εν ἄνδρα τοιοῦτον, ὅσ-
τις πόλλ' ἀνατλὰς ἔσω- 1035
σε τὴν ἱερὰν πόλιν;
ὥστ' οὐχὶ μὴ παύσῃ ποτ' ὢν
ζηλωτὸς ἅπασιν.

Οι. ταυτὶ δέδραται. τίθεσο τὼ μηρὼ λαβών·
ἐγὼ δ' ἐπὶ σπλάγχν' εἶμι καὶ θυλήματα. 1040

Τρ. ἐμοὶ μελήσει ταῦτά γ'· ἀλλ' ἥκειν ἐχρῆν.

Οι. ἰδού, πάρειμι. μῶν ἐπισχεῖν σοι δοκῶ;

Τρ. ὄπτα καλῶς νυν αὐτά· καὶ γὰρ οὑτοσὶ
προσέρχεται δάφνῃ τις ἐστεφανωμένος.

Οι. τίς ἄρα ποτ' ἐστίν; ὡς ἀλαζὼν φαίνεται. 1045
μάντις τίς ἐστιν;

Τρ. οὐ μὰ Δί', ἀλλ' Ἱεροκλέης
οὗτός γέ πού 'σθ', ὁ χρησμολόγος οὑξ Ὠρεοῦ.

Οι. τί ποτ' ἄρα λέξει;

Τρ. δῆλός ἐσθ' οὗτός γ' ὅτι
ἐναντιώσεταί τι ταῖς διαλλαγαῖς.

Οι. οὔκ, ἀλλὰ κατὰ τὴν κνῖσαν εἰσελήλυθεν. 1050

1033 οὖν ἂν οὐκ Dindorf: ἂν οὖν οὐκ RV: ἂν οὐκ Γp: οὐκ ἂν t.
1037 μὴ παύσῃ Elmsley: μὴ παύσει RVΓp: πεπαύσει t.
1043 αὐτά RV: ταῦτα Γpt.

102

mind and resourceful boldness?   1030

TRYGAEUS: Well, anyway, the faggots are alight, and that's crushed
Stillbides. Now I'll bring the table, and I won't need a boy to do it.
[*He goes into the house.*]

CHORUS: Who now would not praise
              a man such as this, who
              has endured many hardships   1035
              and has saved the holy city?
              So you will surely never cease
              to be envied by all.

[*By now Trygaeus has come out again with a table, on which are kitchen
implements, salt, etc. Presently the slave comes out also, bringing the
thigh-bones, rump and tongue of the sheep.*]

SLAVE: That's done. Take the thighs and put them on the fire, and I'll   1040
go for the offals and the meal-offering. [*He puts the things he has brought
into Trygaeus' hands, and turns to go back inside.*]

TRYGAEUS [*calling after him*]: I'll see to this. [*He lays thigh-bones
and rump on the altar, and puts the tongue aside on the table; then calls
again towards the house*] You should have been back by now!

SLAVE [*coming out of the house, carrying in one hand the sheep's offals
on a spit, in the other the meal-offering*]: Look, here I am. You don't
mean to say you think I dawdled?

TRYGAEUS [*taking the meal-offering and sprinkling it over the thigh-bones
and rump*]: Now roast them well, because there's someone here coming this
way crowned with laurel.

SLAVE [*looking towards the side-passage by which Trygaeus has indicated   1045
that the newcomer is approaching*]: Here, who on earth is he? He does look
a quack! Is he a diviner?

TRYGAEUS: No, by Zeus; he's Hierocles, surely, the oracle-monger from
Oreus.

SLAVE: Here, what's he going to say?

TRYGAEUS: Oh, it's plain that he's going to make some objection to the
peace agreement.

SLAVE: No, he's come here drawn by the aroma of sacrifice.   1050

Τρ. μή νυν ὁρᾶν δοκῶμεν αὐτόν.

Οι.   εὖ λέγεις.

ΙΕΡΟΚΛΗΣ
    τίς ἡ θυσία ποθ' αὑτηὶ καὶ τῷ θεῶν;

Τρ. ὄπτα σὺ σιγῇ, κἄπαγ' ἀπὸ τῆς ὀσφύος.

Ιε. ὅτῳ δὲ θύετ' οὐ φράσεθ';

Τρ.   ἡ κέρκος ποιεῖ
καλῶς.

Οι.   καλῶς δῆτ'· ὦ πότνι' Εἰρήνη φίλη.   1055

Ιε. ἄγε νυν ἀπάρχου, κᾆτα δὸς τἀπάργματα.

Τρ. ὀπτᾶν ἄμεινον πρῶτον.

Ιε.   ἀλλὰ ταυταγὶ
ἤδη 'στὶν ὀπτά.

Τρ.   πολλὰ πράττεις, ὅστις εἶ.
κατάτεμνε.

Οι.   ποῦ τράπεζα;

Τρ.   τὴν σπονδὴν φέρε.

Ιε. ἡ γλῶττα χωρὶς τέμνεται.

Τρ.   μεμνήμεθα.   1060
ἀλλ' οἶσθ' ὃ δρᾶσον;

Ιε.   ἢν φράσῃς.

Τρ.   μὴ διαλέγου
νῷν μηδέν· Εἰρήνῃ γὰρ ἱερὰ θύομεν.

Ιε. "ὦ μέλεοι θνητοὶ καὶ νήπιοι—"

Τρ.   εἰς κεφαλὴν σοί.

104

TRYGAEUS: Well, let's pretend not to see him.

SLAVE: Good idea.

[*As the slave busies himself with roasting the offals, and Trygaeus with inspecting the offerings on the altar, Hierocles reaches centre stage. He is warmly dressed in two sheepskins.*]

HIEROCLES: What sacrifice, pray, is this, and to which of the gods?

TRYGAEUS [*to the slave*]: Keep quiet while you roast them, and get away from the rump.

HIEROCLES: But aren't you going to tell me who you're sacrificing to?

TRYGAEUS [*examining the offerings*]: The tail is doing nicely.   1055

SLAVE: Nicely it is indeed! O beloved Lady Peace!

HIEROCLES: Come now, separate the first share and then give it to me.

TRYGAEUS: It's better to do the roasting first.

HIEROCLES [*examining the offals on the spit*]: But *these* are already roasted.

TRYGAEUS: You're being a busybody, whoever you are. [*To the slave*] Cut them up.

SLAVE [*taking the offals away from the fire*]: Where's a table? [*He finds the table, takes the offals off the spit, and begins to cut them up.*]

TRYGAEUS [*calling into the house*]: Bring us the libation.

HIEROCLES: The tongue is cut separately.   1060

TRYGAEUS: We remember that. Do you know what you should do?

HIEROCLES: I will if you tell me.

TRYGAEUS: Don't talk to us at all. We're making a sacrifice consecrated to Peace.

HIEROCLES:

    "O mortals wretched and foolish —"

TRYGAEUS: May those words fall on *your* head!

Ιε. "—οἵτινες ἀφραδίῃσι, θεῶν νόον οὐκ ἀίοντες,
συνθήκας πεποίησθ' ἄνδρες χαροποῖσι πιθήκοις—"   1065

Τρ. αἰβοιβοῖ.

Ιε.   τί γελᾷς;

Τρ.   ἥσθην χαροποῖσι πιθήκοις.

Ιε. "—καὶ κέπφοι τρήρωνες ἀλωπεκιδεῦσι πέπεισθε,
ὧν δόλιαι ψυχαί, δόλιαι φρένες."

Τρ.   εἴθε σου εἶναι
ὤφελεν, ὦλαζών, οὑτωσὶ θερμὸς ὁ πλεύμων.

Ιε. "εἰ γὰρ μὴ Νύμφαι γε θεαὶ Βάκιν ἐξαπάτασκον,   1070
μηδὲ Βάκις θνητούς, μηδ' αὖ Νύμφαι Βάκιν αὐτόν—"

Τρ. ἐξώλης ἀπόλοι', εἰ μὴ παύσαιο βακίζων.

Ιε. "—οὔπω θέσφατον ἦν Εἰρήνης δέσμ' ἀναλῦσαι,
ἀλλὰ τόδε πρότερον—"

Τρ.   τοῖς ἁλσί γε παστέα ταυτί.

Ιε. "οὐ γάρ πω τοῦτ' ἐστὶ φίλον μακάρεσσι θεοῖσιν,   1075
φυλόπιδος λῆξαι, πρίν κεν λύκος οἶν ὑμεναιοῖ."   1076a

Τρ. καὶ πῶς, ὦ κατάρατε, λύκος ποτ' ἂν οἶν ὑμεναιοῖ;   1076b

Ιε. "ἕως ἡ σφονδύλη φεύγουσα πονηρότατον βδεῖ   1077
κώδυνων Ἀκαλανθὶς ἐπειγομένη τυφλὰ τίκτει,

1074 τόδε πρότερον Dindorf, cf. 1107: τότε δὲ πρότερον V: τό γε
       πρότερον R: τότε πρῶτον Γpt.
1074 τοῖς Γpt: τοῖς δ' V: τοῖσδ' R.
1077 ἕως Brunck (as a monosyllable, cf. Iliad 17.727): ὡς codd.
1078 κώδυνων Agar, cf. Σ(i)^VΓ: χἠ κώδων codd. Σ(ii)^VΓ λ_Σ^Γ.

106

HIEROCLES:

    "— men who in your senselessness, not understanding the mind of the gods,
    have made an agreement with fierce-eyed monkeys —"   1065

TRYGAEUS:

    Ha, ha, ha!

HIEROCLES: Why are you laughing?

TRYGAEUS: I liked those "fierce-eyed monkeys".

HIEROCLES:

    "— and like tremulous boobies put your trust in fox-cubs
    who have guileful souls and guileful hearts."

TRYGAEUS [*who has been tasting the roasted offals*] :

                        I only wish,
    you quack, that your lungs were as hot as this is!

HIEROCLES:

    "For if the divine Nymphs deceived not Bacis,   1070
    and Bacis deceived not mortals, and the Nymphs again deceived not
                              Bacis himself —"

TRYGAEUS:

    Blast you to destruction, unless you stop going on about Bacis!

HIEROCLES:

    "— it was not yet ordained that the bonds of Peace should be loosed,
    but this must first happen —"

TRYGAEUS [*to his slave*] :   These have to be sprinkled with salt.

HIEROCLES:

    "For this is not yet pleasing to the blessed gods,   1075
    to cease from warfare, till a wolf shall wed a sheep."

TRYGAEUS:

    And how, curse you, could a wolf ever wed a sheep?

HIEROCLES:

    "So long as the root-beetle in fleeing emits a fart most foul
    and Acalanthis hurries on her birth-pangs and brings forth blind
                              offspring,

τουτάκις οὔπω χρῆν τὴν εἰρήνην πεποιῆσθαι."

Τρ. ἀλλὰ τί χρῆν ἡμᾶς; οὐ παύσασθαι πολεμοῦντας;   1080
ἢ διακαυνιάσαι πότεροι κλαυσούμεθα μεῖζον,
ἐξὸν σπεισαμένους κοινῇ τῆς Ἑλλάδος ἄρχειν;

Ιε. "οὔποτε ποιήσεις τὸν καρκίνον ὀρθὰ βαδίζειν."

Τρ. οὔποτε δειπνήσεις ἔτι τοῦ λοιποῦ 'ν πρυτανείῳ,
οὐδ' ἐπὶ τῷ πραχθέντι ποιήσεις ὕστερον οὐδέν.   1085

Ιε. "οὐδέποτ' ἂν θείης λεῖον τὸν τρηχὺν ἐχῖνον."

Τρ. ἆρα φενακίζων ποτ' Ἀθηναίους ἔτι παύσει;

Ιε. ποῖον γὰρ κατὰ χρησμὸν ἐκαύσατε μῆρα θεοῖσιν;

Τρ. ὅνπερ κάλλιστον δήπου πεποίηκεν Ὅμηρος·
"ὣς οἱ μὲν νέφος ἐχθρὸν ἀπωσάμενοι πολέμοιο   1090
Εἰρήνην εἵλοντο καὶ ἱδρύσανθ' ἱερείῳ.
αὐτὰρ ἐπεὶ κατὰ μῆρ' ἐκάη καὶ σπλάγχν' ἐπάσαντο,
ἔσπενδον δεπάεσσιν, ἐγὼ δ' ὁδὸν ἡγεμόνευον·
χρησμολόγῳ δ' οὐδεὶς ἐδίδου κώθωνα φαεινόν."

Ιε. οὐ μετέχω τούτων· οὐ γὰρ ταῦτ' εἶπε Σίβυλλα.   1095

Τρ. ἀλλ' ὁ σοφός τοι νὴ Δί' Ὅμηρος δεξιὸν εἶπεν·
"ἀφρήτωρ, ἀθέμιστος, ἀνέστιός ἐστιν ἐκεῖνος,
ὃς πολέμου ἔραται ἐπιδημίου ὀκρυόεντος."

Ιε. "φράζεο δή, μή πώς σε δόλῳ φρένας ἐξαπατήσας
ἰκτῖνος μάρψῃ—"

Τρ.   τουτὶ μέντοι σὺ φυλάττου,   1100
ὡς οὗτος φοβερὸς τοῖς σπλάγχνοις ἐστὶν ὁ χρησμός.
ἔγχει δὴ σπονδὴν καὶ τῶν σπλάγχνων φέρε δευρί.

1086 τρηχὺν RV: τραχὺν Γpt ᵡΣ^{ΥΓ}, Macarius 6.78.

108

so long it were not yet right for peace to have been made."
TRYGAEUS:
But what *should* we have done? Never stopped waging war? 1080
Or cast lots for which of us should be made to howl the louder,
when we had the chance to make peace and rule Greece together?
HIEROCLES:
"Never will you make the crab to walk straight."
TRYGAEUS:
Never again will you dine in the Prytaneum in future,
nor compose any of your verses after the event has happened. 1085
HIEROCLES:
"Never can you make the prickly hedgehog smooth."
TRYGAEUS:
Will there yet come a time when you'll stop conning the Athenians?
HIEROCLES:
In accordance with what oracle have you burnt thighs to the gods?
[*By now a libation-bowl and a jug of wine have been brought out of the
house by a servant and placed on the table. As he replies to Hierocles,
Trygaeus takes up the bowl.*]
TRYGAEUS:
The splendid one that is Homer's work, of course:
"So they thrust aside the hateful cloud of war, 1090
chose Peace for themselves, and installed her with a sacrifice.
And when the thighs were burnt up and they had eaten the offals,
they poured libation from cups, and I led the way" —
but nobody gave a gleaming mug to an oracle-monger!
HIEROCLES:
That's got nothing to do with me: it wasn't said by Sibylla. 1095
TRYGAEUS:
But something clever was certainly said, you know, by the wise Homer:
"No clan, no right to justice, no hearth does that man have
who lusts after the horrors of intestine war."
HIEROCLES:
"Lo, beware, lest perchance a kite deceive thine understanding
by guile, and seize —" 1100
TRYGAEUS [*to his slave*]: You be on your guard against that,
because that oracle bodes danger to the offals.
Now pour in a libation, and let me have some of the offals here.

Ιε. ἀλλ' εἰ ταῦτα δοκεῖ, κἀγὼ 'μαυτῷ βαλανεύσω.

Τρ. σπονδὴ σπονδή.

Ιε. ἔγχει δὴ κἀμοὶ καὶ σπλάγχνων μοῖραν ὄρεξον.　　　　1105

Τρ. ἀλλ' οὔπω τοῦτ' ἐστὶ φίλον μακάρεσσι θεοῖσιν,
ἀλλὰ τόδε πρότερον, σπένδειν ἡμᾶς, σὲ δ' ἀπελθεῖν.
ὦ πότνι' Εἰρήνη, παράμεινον τὸν βίον ἡμῖν.

Ιε. πρόσφερε τὴν γλῶτταν.

Τρ. 　　　　　　　σὺ δὲ τὴν σαυτοῦ γ' ἀπένεγκε.

Ιε. σπονδή.

Τρ. 　　　　καὶ ταυτὶ μετὰ τῆς σπονδῆς λαβὲ θᾶττον.　　　　1110

Ιε. οὐδεὶς προσδώσει τῶν σπλάγχνων;

Τρ. 　　　　　　　　οὐ γὰρ οἷόν τε
ἡμῖν προσδιδόναι, πρίν κεν λύκος οἶν ὑμεναιοῖ.

Ιε. ναί, πρὸς τῶν γονάτων.

Τρ. 　　　　　　　ἄλλως, ὦ τᾶν, ἱκετεύεις·
οὐ γὰρ ποιήσεις λεῖον τὸν τρηχὺν ἐχῖνον.
ἄγε δή, θεαταί, δεῦρο συσπλαγχνεύετε　　　　1115
μετὰ νῷν.

Ιε. 　　　τί δαὶ 'γώ;

Τρ. 　　　　　τὴν Σίβυλλαν ἔσθιε.

1111　προσδώσει Bekker: προσδώσει μοι V: προδώσει μοι RΓp: δώσει
　　　μοι t.
1112　προσδιδόναι V^{pc}: προδιδόναι RV^{ac}Γp: πριν διδόναι t.
1114　τρηχὺν Cobet: τραχὺν codd.
1116　δαὶ Blaydes: δὴ RV: δ' Γpt.

110

[*The slave pours wine into Trygaeus' bowl, and hands him a portion of each part of the offals.*]

HIEROCLES:

Well, if it's all right with you, I'll do the job for myself too.

[*He produces a libation-bowl of his own and approaches the table, hoping to have it filled, but Trygaeus and the slave both ignore him.*]

TRYGAEUS: Libation, libation!

HIEROCLES [*holding out his bowl*] :

Pour some in for me too, and hand me a portion of offals.   1105

TRYGAEUS:

No, that is not yet pleasing to the blessed gods,

but this must first happen: we must make libation and you must depart.

[*Praying*]

O Lady Peace, remain with us all our lives long.

HIEROCLES [*as Trygaeus is pouring out the libation on the altar*] :

Please give me the tongue.

TRYGAEUS: You take *your* tongue away from here!

[*At this point Hierocles succeeds in catching the slave off his guard; he seizes the wine-jug and fills his libation-bowl.*]

HIEROCLES: 1110

Libation!

TRYGAEUS: Hurry up and take these with your libation!

[*He flings some of the offals at Hierocles' head.*]

HIEROCLES:

Will no one give me any of the offals?

TRYGAEUS: No, it is not possible

for us to give any, till a wolf shall wed a sheep.

HIEROCLES [*falling at Trygaeus' feet, and trying to touch his knees in
                                                    supplication*] :

Do, I beseech you!

TRYGAEUS: You supplicate in vain, my man;

for never will you make the prickly hedgehog smooth.

[*To the audience*] Come on, spectators, come here and share the offals   1115
with us.

HIEROCLES: And what about me?

TRYGAEUS: You can eat your Sibylla.

111

Ιε. οὗτοι μὰ τὴν Γῆν ταῦτα κατέδεσθον μόνω,
     ἀλλ' ἁρπάσομαι σφῷν αὐτά· κεῖται δ' ἐν μέσῳ.

Τρ. ὦ παῖε παῖε τὸν Βάκιν.

Ιε.   μαρτύρομαι.

Τρ. κἄγωγ', ὅτι τένθης εἶ σὺ κάλαζων ἀνήρ.   1120
     παῖ' αὐτὸν ἐπέχων τῷ ξύλῳ, τὸν ἀλαζόνα.

Οι. σὺ μὲν οὖν· ἐγὼ δὲ τουτονὶ τῶν κῳδίων,
     ἀλάμβαν' αὐτὸς ἐξαπατῶν, ἐκβολβιῶ.
     οὐ καταβαλεῖς τὰ κῴδι', ὦ θυηπόλε;

Τρ. ἤκουσας; ὁ κόραξ, οἷος ἦλθ' ἐξ Ὠρεοῦ.   1125
     οὐκ ἀποπετήσει θᾶττον εἰς Ἐλύμνιον;

Χο. ἥδομαί γ', ἥδομαι   (στρ.
        κράνους ἀπηλλαγμένος
        τυροῦ τε καὶ κρομμύων.
        οὐ γὰρ φιληδῶ μάχαις,   1130
     ἀλλὰ πρὸς πῦρ διέλ-
        κων μετ' ἀνδρῶν ἑταί-
        ρων φίλων, ἐκκέας
        τῶν ξύλων ἄττ' ἂν ᾖ
        δανότατα τοῦ θέρους
        ἐκπεπρεμνισμένα,   1135
     κἀνθρακίζων τοὐρεβίνθου
        τήν τε φηγὸν ἐμπυρεύων,
        χἄμα τὴν θρᾷτταν κυνῶν
        τῆς γυναικος λουμένης.

1135 ἐκπεπρεμνισμένα Bergk: ἐκπεπρισμένα RV: ἐκπεπιεσμένα t:
      om. p.

112

HIEROCLES: By holy Earth, you two aren't going to eat that lot up yourselves. I'll snatch it from you; it's there to be taken. [*He tries to seize the offals from the table, but is intercepted by Trygaeus.*]

TRYGAEUS [*raining blows on Hierocles*]: Hit him, ho! hit Bacis!

HIEROCLES: Witness, everyone!

TRYGAEUS: Witness everyone indeed — that you're a greedy quack of a   1120 man. [*To his slave, who has taken a heavy stick from the pile at the foot of the altar*] Keep on hitting him with the stick, the impostor.

SLAVE [*giving the stick to Trygaeus*]: No, you do that; I'm going to strip him of those sheepskins, which he got dishonestly by cheating. [*To Hierocles*] Drop those sheepskins, soothsayer, will you?

TRYGAEUS [*threateningly*]: Did you hear? [*As Trygaeus is about to strike   1125 him with the stick, Hierocles runs away. Trygaeus turns to the slave.*] What a raven that was that came from Oreus! [*Calling after Hierocles*] Fly off, won't you, to Elymnium, fastish!

[*Trygaeus and the slave go inside.*]

CHORUS: I rejoice, yes I rejoice,
               that I am free from helmets,
               free from cheese and onions.
               For I take no delight in battles,   1130
               but in drinking deep
               by the fire in the company
               of friends, after kindling
               those of the logs
               which have dried best after
               being grubbed up in summer,   1135
               toasting some chickpea
               and roasting acorn,
               and also kissing Thratta
               while the wife is in the bath!

οὐ γάρ ἐσθ' ἥδιον ἢ τυχεῖν μὲν ἤδη 'σπαρμένα,   1140
τὸν θεὸν δ' ἐπιψακάζειν, καί τιν' εἰπεῖν γείτονα·
"εἰπέ μοι, τί τηνικαῦτα δρῶμεν, ὦ Κωμαρχίδη;" —
"ἐμπιεῖν ἔμοιγ' ἀρέσκει, τοῦ θεοῦ δρῶντος καλῶς.
ἀλλ' ἄφαυε τῶν φασήλων, ὦ γύναι, τρεῖς χοίνικας,
τῶν τε πυρῶν μεῖξον αὐτοῖς, τῶν τε σύκων ἔξελε·   1145
τόν τε Μανῆν ἡ Σύρα βωστρησάτω 'κ τοῦ χωρίου.
οὐ γὰρ οἶόν τ' ἐστὶ πάντως οἰναρίζειν τήμερον
οὐδὲ τυντλάζειν, ἐπειδὴ παρδακὸν τὸ χωρίον." —
"κἀξ ἐμοῦ δ' ἐνεγκάτω τις τὴν κίχλην καὶ τὼ σπίνω·
ἦν δὲ καὶ πυός τις ἔνδον καὶ λαγῷα τέτταρα—   1150
εἴ τι μὴ 'ξήνεγκεν αὐτῶν ἡ γαλῆ τῆς ἑσπέρας·
ἐψόφει γοῦν ἔνδον οὐκ οἶδ' ἄττα κἀκυδοιδόπα—
ὧν ἔνεγκ', ὦ παῖ, τρί' ἡμῖν, ἓν δὲ δοῦναι τῷ πατρί·
μυρρίνας τ' αἴτησον ἐξ Αἰσχινάδου τῶν καρπίμων·
χἄμα τῆς αὐτῆς ὁδοῦ Χαρινάδην τις βωσάτω,   1155
ὡς ἂν ἐμπίῃ μεθ' ἡμῶν,
    εὖ ποιοῦντος κὠφελοῦντος
    τοῦ θεοῦ τἀρώματα."

ἡνίκ' ἂν δ' ἀχέτας   (ἀντ.
    ᾄδῃ τὸν ἡδὺν νόμον,   1160
    διασκοπῶν ἥδομαι
    τὰς Λημνίας ἀμπέλους,

1142 τηνικαῦτα Bentley: τηνικάδε codd.
1144 ἄφαυε vel sim. V^{pc}pt: ἄφευε R ^{λ}Σ^{V} Suda: ἄφαυσε ^{γρ}Σ^{V}:
       ἄφαυσον ^{γρ}Σ^{L}: [V^{ac}]: (ἀλλὰ) φαῦζε Paley.
1152 κἀκυδ- L^{2}: καὶ κυδ- RVpt.
1154 ἐξ Αἰσχινάδου codd.: ἐξ παρ' Αἰσχίνου van Leeuwen.
1159 ἡνίκ' ἂν δ' Hermann: ἡνίκ' ἂν t: ἡνίκα δ' ἂν RVp.

114

CHORUS-LEADER: There is nothing more pleasant than for the sowing   1140
to be over and done, and for the god to be sending down gentle rain on the
soil, and for a neighbour to say: "Tell me, Comarchides, since it's like
this, what shall we do?" — "What I'd like to do, since the god is treating
us kindly, is to get drinking! Wife, parch three quarts of the cowpeas,
mix some of the wheat with them, and take out some of the figs; and make   1145
Syra call Manes in from the vineyard. It's quite impossible to work on
the vines or to break up the soil, because the ground's sodden." — " And
from my house will someone fetch the thrush and the two chaffinches? There   1150
was also some beestings in the house, and four helpings of hare — that is
if the ferret didn't take one of them out last evening; it was certainly
making lord knows what kind of a noise and racket in there. Bring us three
of them, boy, and give one to my father. And ask for some myrtle-branches,
the ones with berries on, from Aeschinades' place, and at the same time,   1155
while on that errand, will someone call for Charinades,

                  so that he can join our binge,
                  since the god is doing good
                  and helping the crops."
CHORUS: And at the time when the cicada
                  sounds his sweet tune,   1160
                  it delights me to examine
                  my Lemnian vines

εἰ πεπαίνουσιν ἤ-
  δη—τὸ γὰρ φῖτυ πρῷ-
  ον φύσει—τόν τε φή-   1165
  ληχ' ὁρῶν οἰδάνοντ'·
εἶθ', ὁπόταν ᾖ πέπων,
ἐσθίω κἀπέχω,
χἄμα φήμ' "Ὧραι φίλαι", καὶ
  τοῦ θύμου τρίβων κυκῶμαι·
  κᾆτα γίγνομαι παχὺς   1170
  τηνικαῦτα τοῦ θέρους

μᾶλλον ἢ θεοῖσιν ἐχθρον ταξίαρχον προσβλέπων
τρεῖς λόφους ἔχοντα καὶ φοινικίδ' ὀξεῖαν πάνυ,
ἣν ἐκεῖνός φησιν εἶναι βάμμα Σαρδιανικόν.
ἢν δέ που δέῃ μάχεσθ' ἔχοντα τὴν φοινικίδα,   1175
τηνικαῦτ' αὐτὸς βέβαπται βάμμα Κυζικηνικόν·
κᾆτα φεύγει πρῶτος, ὥσπερ ξουθὸς ἱππαλεκτρυὼν
τοὺς λόφους σείων· ἐγὼ δ' ἕστηκα λινοπτώμενος.
ἡνίκ' ἂν δ' οἴκοι γένωνται, δρῶσιν οὐκ ἀνασχετά,
τοὺς μὲν ἐγγράφοντες ἡμῶν, τοὺς δ' ἄνω τε καὶ κάτω   1180
ἐξαλείφοντες δὶς ἢ τρίς. αὔριον δ' ἔσθ' ἥξοδος,
τῷ δὲ σιτί' οὐκ ἐώνητ', οὐ γὰρ ᾔδειν ἐξιών·
εἶτα προσστὰς πρὸς τὸν ἀνδριάντα τὸν Πανδίονος
εἶδεν αὐτόν, κἀπορῶν θεῖ τῷ κακῷ βλέπων ὁπόν.
ταῦτα δ' ἡμᾶς τοὺς ἀγροίκους δρῶσι, τοὺς δ' ἐξ ἄστεως   1185
ἧττον, οἱ θεοῖσιν οὗτοι κἀνδράσι ῥιψάσπιδες·
ὧν ἔτ' εὐθύνας ἐμοὶ δώσουσιν, ἢν θεος θέλῃ.
πολλὰ γὰρ δή μ' ἠδίκησαν,

1165 οἰδάνοντ' Bentley: οὐδαίνοντ' codd.
1183 προσστὰς Lenting: προστὰς codd.

116

in case they are already
ripening — for nature makes that
an early variety — and to see   1165
the wild fig swelling;
and then, when it's ripe,
I eat and keep on eating
and as I do so, say "Beloved Seasons"
and pound some thyme and mix a drink;
and then I get fat   1170
at that time of the summer —
CHORUS-LEADER: Fatter than if I were staring at some god-detested
taxiarch wearing three crests and a very bright scarlet cloak, which *he*
says is Sardian colour; though if by any chance he has to *fight* wearing   1175
that cloak, then he himself gets dyed Cyzicene colour! And then he's the
first to run away, shaking his crests like a tawny horsecock, while I stand
there like a net-watcher. When they get back home, they do intolerable
things: they enter some of our names on the lists and erase others,   1180
higgledy-piggledy, two or three times. The expedition sets out tomorrow,
and the man's bought no provisions, because he didn't know he was going
on it — and then he stops in front of the statue of Pandion and sees his
name, and rushes off in distress, with a curdling look in his eyes because
of his misfortune. They do all that to us country folk — not so much to   1185
the townspeople — these men whom gods and mortals . . . see throwing their
shields away; and, god willing, they'll yet render account to me for it.
For they have done me many, many injuries,

117

ὄντες οἴκοι μὲν λέοντες,
ἐν μάχῃ δ' ἀλώπεκες.   1190

Τρ. ἰοὺ ἰού·
    ὅσον τὸ χρῆμ' ἐπὶ δεῖπνον ἦλθ' εἰς τοὺς γάμους.
    ἔχ', ἀποκάθαιρε τὰς τραπέζας ταυτηί·
    πάντως γὰρ οὐδὲν ὄφελός ἐστ' αὐτῆς ἔτι.
    ἔπειτ' ἐπιφόρει τοὺς ἀμύλους καὶ τὰς κίχλας   1195
    καὶ τῶν λαγῴων πολλὰ καὶ τοὺς κολλάβους.

ΔΡΕΠΑΝΟΥΡΓΟΣ
    ποῦ ποῦ Τρυγαῖός ἐστιν;

Τρ.   ἀναβράττω κίχλας.

Δρ. ὦ φίλτατ', ὦ Τρυγαῖ', ὅσ' ἡμᾶς τἀγαθὰ
    δέδρακας εἰρήνην ποιήσας· ὡς πρὸ τοῦ
    οὐδεὶς ἐπρίατ' ἂν δρέπανον οὐδὲ κολλύβου·   1200
    νυνὶ δὲ πεντήκοντα δραχμῶν ἐμπολῶ,
    ὁδὶ δὲ τριδράχμους τοὺς κάδους εἰς τοὺς ἀγρούς.
    ἀλλ', ὦ Τρυγαῖε, τῶν δρεπάνων τε λάμβανε
    καὶ τῶνδ' ὅ τι βούλει προῖκα· καὶ ταυτὶ δέχου·
    ἀφ' ὧν γὰρ ἀπεδόμεσθα κἀκερδάναμεν   1205
    τὰ δῶρα ταυτί σοι φέρομεν εἰς τοὺς γάμους.

Τρ. ἴθι νυν, καταθέμενοι παρ' ἐμοὶ ταῦτ' εἴσιτε
    ἐπὶ δεῖπνον ὡς τάχιστα· καὶ γὰρ οὑτοσὶ
    ὅπλων κάπηλος ἀχθόμενος προσέρχεται.

ΚΑΠΗΛΟΣ ΟΠΛΩΝ
    οἴμ', ὡς προθέλυμνόν μ', ὦ Τρυγαῖ', ἀπώλεσας.   1210

Τρ. τί δ' ἐστίν, ὦ κακόδαιμον; οὔ τί που λοφᾷς;

1195 ἐπιφόρει Dobree: ἐπισφόρει R: ἐπεισφόρει VΓp: ἐπείσφερε t:
      ἐπίφερε Blaydes.

118

acting like lions at home
but like foxes in battle! 1190
[*Trygaeus and his slave come out of the house.*]
TRYGAEUS: Whew! What a crowd's come to dinner for the wedding!
Here, wipe the tables clean with this [*handing him a soldier's head-band*]: there's
no use for it any more in any case. Then pile on the sponge-cakes and the 1195
thrushes, and plenty of the hare, and the bread-rolls.
[*The slave goes inside. Trygaeus is going in also, but stops when he
hears his name called. A sickle-maker and a potter have come to see him,
each bringing some of the products of his trade and also a hamper of food.*]
SICKLE-MAKER: Where's Trygaeus, where's Trygaeus?
TRYGAEUS: I'm stewing thrushes.
SICKLE-MAKER: My dear, dear Trygaeus, what great blessings you've
given us by making peace! Until now no one would have paid so much as a mite 1200
for a sickle; but now I sell them for fifty drachmas, and this man sells jars
for the countryside at three drachmas each. So, Trygaeus, please take any
of these sickles and any of these [*indicating the jars brought by his
companion*] that you like, free of charge; and please also accept this
[*the food*]. We bring you these gifts for your wedding out of the sales 1205-6
and profits we have made.
TRYGAEUS: All right then, put these things down next to me, and come
in to dinner as quickly as you can. [*The two visitors lay down their gifts
and go inside.*] Because here comes an arms-dealer, and he's annoyed.
[*Enter an arms-dealer, with his pack of wares, accompanied by a helmet-
maker and a spear-maker, the latter holding several spears.*]
ARMS-DEALER: Damn you, Trygaeus, the way you've completely 1210
ruined me, root and branch!
TRYGAEUS: What's wrong, poor fellow? [*Pointing to two large helmet-
crests protruding from the pack*] You've not by any chance ill with a crest
complaint, are you?

Κα. ἀπώλεσάς μου τὴν τέχνην καὶ τὸν βίον,
καὶ τουτουὶ καὶ τοῦ δορυξοῦ 'κεινουί.

Τρ. τί δῆτα τουτοινὶ καταθῶ σοι τοῖν λόφοιν;

Κα. αὐτὸς σὺ τί δίδως;

Τρ.   ὅ τι δίδωμ'; αἰσχύνομαι.   1215
ὅμως δ', ὅτι τὸ σφήκωμ' ἔχει πόνον πολύν,
δοίην ἂν αὐτοῖν ἰσχάδων τρεῖς χοίνικας.   1217

Κα. ἔνεγκε τοίνυν εἰσιὼν τὰς ἰσχάδας·   1219
κρεῖττον γάρ, ὦ τᾶν, ἐστιν ἢ μηδὲν λαβεῖν.   1220

Τρ. ἀπόφερ' ἀπόφερ' ἐς κόρακας ἀπὸ τῆς οἰκίας.
τριχορρυεῖτον, οὐδέν ἐστον τὼ λόφω.
οὐκ ἂν πριαίμην οὐδ' ἂν ἰσχάδος μιᾶς.

Κα. τί δαὶ δεκάμνῳ τῷδε θώρακος κύτει
ἐνημμένῳ κάλλιστα χρήσομαι τάλας;   1225

Τρ. οὗτος μὲν οὐ μή σοι ποιήσῃ ζημίαν.
ἀλλ' αἶρέ μοι τοῦτόν γε τῆς ἰσωνίας·
ἐναποπατεῖν γὰρ ἔστ' ἐπιτήδειος πάνυ—

Κα. παῦσαι 'νυβρίζων τοῖς ἐμοῖσι χρήμασιν.

Τρ. —ὡδί, παραθέντι τρεῖς λίθους. οὐ δεξιῶς;   1230

Κα. ποίᾳ δ' ἀποψήσει ποτ', ὦμαθέστατε;

Τρ. τηδί, διεὶς τὴν χεῖρα διὰ τῆς θαλαμιᾶς,

1217 αὐτοῖν B: αὐτῶν RV: αὐτὸν Γpt.
[1218] ἵν' ἀποκαθαίρω τὴν τράπεζαν τουτῳί codd. (cf. 1193): del.
    Hamaker.
1229 'νυβρίζων Elmsley: μ' ὑβρίζων codd.

120

ARMS-DEALER: You've ruined my trade and my livelihood, and also this man's and the spear-maker over here.

TRYGAEUS: Well then, what shall I pay you for these two crests?

ARMS-DEALER [*taking out the crests and showing them to him*]: What's   1215
your offer?

TRYGAEUS: What's my offer? I'm ashamed to name it. Still, seeing that a great deal of work went into the collar, I'd give you three quarts of dried   1217
figs for them.

ARMS-DEALER [*handing over the crests*]: Very well, go in and bring the   1219
figs. [*Trygaeus goes inside. The dealer turns to one of his companions*]
It's better than getting nothing, old chap.   1220

TRYGAEUS [*coming out in a rage and flinging the crests back at the dealer*]: Take them away, take the away from my house — to blazes with them!
The crests have their hair falling out — they're rubbish! I wouldn't buy them for so much as one dried fig!

ARMS-DEALER [*displaying a cuirass*]: And what, alack, shall I do with   1224-5
this rounded cuirass, a beautiful fit, worth ten minas?

TRYGAEUS: Well, that one won't make a loss for you, anyway. Give me that at cost price. [*The dealer hands over the cuirass.*] It'll be very convenient to crap in —

ARMS-DEALER: Stop this impudent mockery of my goods!

TRYGAEUS [*who has placed the cuirass on the ground like a chamber-*   1230
pot, and is squatting on it]: — like this, if you put three stones beside it. Isn't that clever?

ARMS-DEALER: But how on earth will you wipe yourself, you stupid fool?

TRYGAEUS [*passing a hand through an armhole of the cuirass from below*]: This way, passing my hand through the oarport — and this way [*same business with the other hand*].

καὶ τῆδ'.

Κα.   ἅμ' ἀμφοῖν δῆτ';

Τρ.   ἔγωγε νὴ Δία,
ἵνα μή γ' ἀλῶ τρύπημα κλέπτων τῆς νεώς.

Κα. ἔπειτ' ἐπὶ δεκάμνῳ χεσεῖ καθήμενος;   1235

Τρ. ἔγωγε νὴ Δί', ὦπίτριπτ'. οἴει γὰρ ἂν
τὸν πρωκτὸν ἀποδόσθαι με χιλιῶν δραχμῶν;

Κα. ἴθι δὴ 'ξένεγκε τἀργύριον.

Τρ.   ἀλλ', ὦγαθέ,
θλίβει τὸν ὄρρον. ἀπόφερ'· οὐκ ὠνήσομαι.

Κα. τί δ' ἄρα τῇ σάλπιγγι τῇδε χρήσομαι,   1240
ἣν ἐπριάμην δραχμῶν ποθ' ἑξήκοντ' ἐγώ;

Τρ. μόλυβδον εἰς τουτὶ τὸ κοῖλον ἐγχέας,
ἔπειτ' ἄνωθεν ῥάβδον ἐνθεὶς ὑπόμακρον,
γενήσεταί σοι τῶν κατακτῶν κοττάβων.

Κα. οἴμοι, καταγελᾷς.

Τρ.   ἀλλ' ἕτερον παραινέσω·   1245
τὸν μὲν μόλυβδον, ὥσπερ εἶπον, ἔγχεον,
ἐντευθενὶ δὲ σπαρτίοις ἠρτημένην
πλάστιγγα πρόσθες, καὐτό σοι γενήσεται
τὰ σῦκ' ἐν ἀγρῷ τοῖς οἰκέταισιν ἱστάναι.

Κα. ὦ δυσκάθαρτε δαῖμον, ὥς μ' ἀπώλεσας,   1250
ὅτ' ἀντέδωκα κἀντὶ τῶνδε μνᾶν ποτε.
καὶ νῦν τί δράσω; τίς γὰρ αὔτ' ὠνήσεται;

1251 κἀντὶ Enger, cf. Σ[VΓ]: ἀντὶ RV: γ' ἀντὶ ΓpL[r]B.

122

ARMS-DEALER: What, with both hands at once?

TRYGAEUS: Certainly; I don't want to be convicted of leaving an oar of my ship unmanned.

ARMS-DEALER: Your're really going to sit on a ten-mina article and shit?   1235

TRYGAEUS: Certainly I am, you damned fool. Do you think I'd sell my arse for a thousand drachmas?

ARMS-DEALER: Go on then, bring out the money.

TRYGAEUS [*standing up; feeling his buttocks as if they were sore*]: No, my good man, it chafes my bottom. [*Giving back the cuirass*] Take it away; I'm not buying it.

ARMS-DEALER [*displaying a trumpet*]: And what, pray, shall I do with   1240
this trumpet, which I bought once for sixty drachmas?

TRYGAEUS [*taking the trumpet and using it to illustrate his suggestions*]: If you pour lead into this hole, then insert a longish rod at the top end, you'll find it becomes one of the knock-off cottabus targets.

ARMS-DEALER: Dammit, you're just laughing at me!   1245

TRYGAEUS: All right, I'll make another suggestion. Pour in the lead, as I said, attach at this end a scale-pan hung on cords, and you'll have the very thing to weigh out figs to your servants, out in the country. [*He returns the trumpet to the dealer.*]

ARMS-DEALER [*displaying a couple of helmets*]: "Inexpiable curse, how   1250
thou didst ruin me" when for these, again, I once paid a mina! And now what shall I do? Who will buy them?

Τρ. πώλει βαδίζων αὐτὰ τοῖς Αἰγυπτίοις·
ἔστιν γὰρ ἐπιτήδεια συρμαίαν μετρεῖν.

Κα. οἴμ', ὦ κρανοποί', ὡς ἀθλίως πεπράγαμεν.   1255

Τρ. οὗτος μὲν οὐ πέπονθεν οὐδέν.

Κα.   ἀλλὰ τί
ἔτ' ἐστὶ τοῖσι κράνεσιν ὅ τι τις χρήσεται;

Τρ. ἐὰν τοιαυτασὶ μάθῃ λαβὰς ποιεῖν,
ἄμεινον ἢ νῦν αὔτ' ἀποδώσεται πολύ.

Κα. ἀπίωμεν, ὦ δορυξέ.

Τρ.   μηδαμῶς γ', ἐπεὶ   1260
τούτῳ γ' ἐγὼ τὰ δόρατα ταῦτ' ὠνήσομαι.

Κα. πόσον δίδως δῆτ';

Τρ.   εἰ διαπρισθεῖεν δίχα,
λάβοιμ' ἂν αὔτ' εἰς χάρακας ἑκατὸν τῆς δραχμῆς.

Κα. ὑβριζόμεθα. χωρῶμεν, ὦ τᾶν, ἐκποδών.

Τρ. νὴ τὸν Δί', ὡς τὰ παιδί' ἤδη 'ξέρχεται   1265
οὐρησόμενα τὰ τῶν ἐπικλήτων δεῦρ', ἵνα
ἅττ' ᾄσεται προαναβάλητ', ἐμοὶ δοκεῖ.
ἀλλ' ὅ τι περ ᾄδειν ἐπινοεῖς, ὦ παιδίον,
αὐτοῦ παρ' ἐμὲ στὰν πρότερον ἀναβαλοῦ 'νθαδί.

ΠΑΙΔΙΟΝ Α
"νῦν αὖθ' ὁπλοτέρων ἀνδρῶν ἀρχώμεθα—"

Τρ.   παῦσαι   1270
ὁπλοτέρους ᾆδον, καὶ ταῦτ', ὦ τρισκακόδαιμον,

1258 μάθῃ ΓpL^rB: μάθῃς vel sim. RV.
1267 -βάλητ', ἐμοὶ Blaydes: -βάληταί μοι codd.

124

TRYGAEUS: Go and sell them to the Egyptians; they're convenient for measuring out laxative.

ARMS-DEALER: My god, helmet-maker, we *have* had wretched fortune!   1255

TRYGAEUS: *This* man hasn't been harmed at all.

ARMS-DEALER: But what way is there for anyone to use helmets any more?

TRYGAEUS: If he learns to make handles like these [*pointing to the helmet-maker's ears*], he'll get a much better price for them than he does now.

ARMS-DEALER: Let's go, spear-maker.   1260

TRYGAEUS: No, don't, because I'll buy those spears off him.

ARMS-DEALER: How much do you offer?

TRYGAEUS: If they could be sawn in half, I'd take them to use as stakes, at a drachma for a hundred.

ARMS-DEALER: We're being insulted. Let's get out of here, old chap. [*He and his companions depart.*]

TRYGAEUS [*as they go*]: Yes, you'd better, because the guests' children   1265
are already coming out here for a piss — if you ask me, it's in order to practice the openings of what they're going to sing. [*While he has been speaking, two boys have come out of the house. Trygaeus beckons to the boy nearer him.*] Stand here beside me, my boy, and right here, before you go in, give us the opening of the song you mean to sing.

FIRST BOY:
    "But now let us begin of younger warriors —"   1270

TRYGAEUS: Stop
    singing of warriors, and that, you utterly wretched creature,

εἰρήνης οὔσης· ἀμαθές γ' εἶ καὶ κατάρατον.

Πα.^α "οἱ δ', ὅτε δὴ σχεδὸν ἦσαν ἐπ' ἀλλήλοισιν ἰόντες,
σύν ῥ' ἔβαλον ῥινούς τε καὶ ἀσπίδας ὀμφαλοέσσας."

Τρ. ἀσπίδας; οὐ παύσει μεμνημένος ἀσπίδος ἡμῖν;   1275

Πα.^α "ἔνθα δ' ἅμ' οἰμωγή τε καὶ εὐχωλὴ πέλεν ἀνδρῶν."

Τρ. ἀνδρῶν οἰμωγή; κλαύσει, νὴ τὸν Διόνυσον,
οἰμώγας ᾄδων, καὶ ταύτας ὀμφαλοέσσας.

Πα.^α ἀλλὰ τί δῆτ' ᾄδω; σὺ γὰρ εἰπέ μοι οἷστισι χαίρεις.

Τρ. "ὣς οἱ μὲν δαίνυντο βοῶν κρέα", καὶ τὰ τοιαυτί·   1280
"ἄριστον προτίθεντο καὶ ἄσσ' ἥδιστα πάσασθαι."

Πα.^α "ὣς οἱ μὲν δαίνυντο βοῶν κρέα, καὐχένας ἵππων
ἔκλυον ἱδρώοντας, ἐπεὶ πολέμου ἐκόρεσθεν."

Τρ. εἶέν· ἐκόρεσθεν τοῦ πολέμου, κᾆτ' ἤσθιον.
ταῦτ' ᾆδε, ταῦθ', ὡς ἤσθιον κεκορημένοι.   1285

Πα.^α "θωρήσσοντ' ἄρ' ἔπειτα πεπαυμένοι—"

Τρ.   ἄσμενοι, οἶμαι.

Πα.^α "—πύργων δ' ἐξεχέοντο, βοὴ δ' ἄσβεστος ὀρώρει."

Τρ. κάκιστ' ἀπόλοιο, παιδάριον, αὐταῖς μάχαις·
οὐδὲν γὰρ ᾄδεις πλὴν πολέμους. τοῦ καί ποτ' εἶ;

Πα.^α ἐγώ;

Τρ.   σὺ μέντοι νὴ Δί'.

Πα.^α   υἱὸς Λαμάχου.   1290

1281 ἄσσ' van Herwerden: ἄττ' RΓp: ἄτθ' V²B (V¹ omits 1280-1).
1281 πάσασθαι RB: μάσασθαι Γp: μασᾶσθαι V².

126

when we're at peace! You *are* a stupid, damnable child!

FIRST BOY:

"And when, advancing against each other, they were at close quarters,
they dashed together their bucklers and their centre-bossed shields."

TRYGAEUS:

Shields? Will you please stop mentioning shields to us?　　　　　　　1275

FIRST BOY:

"And then together rose men's cries of pain and cries of triumph."

TRYGAEUS:

Men's cries of pain? By Dionysus, I'll make you howl
for singing of cries of pain, and centre-bossed ones at that.

FIRST BOY

Well, what *shall* I sing? You tell me what things you enjoy.

TRYGAEUS:

"Thus they feasted on flesh of oxen", and this sort of thing:　　　　1280
"They had breakfast set before them, and whatever is most pleasant
　　　　　　　　　　　　　　　　　　　　　　　　to taste."

FIRST BOY:

"Thus they feasted on flesh of oxen, and loosed from the yoke
their horses' sweating necks, since they were sated with war."

TRYGAEUS: Fine! They were sated with war, and then they began eating.
Sing that, sing that, how they ate after being sated.　　　　　　　1285

FIRST BOY:

"Then when they had finished, they fortified themselves —"

TRYGAEUS:　　　　　　　　　　　　　　And I'm sure they enjoyed it.

FIRST BOY:

"— And poured out from the walls, and clamour unquenchable rose up."

TRYGAEUS: Damn and blast you, little boy, you and your battles! You
sing of nothing but wars. Whose son are you, anyway?

FIRST BOY: Me?　　　　　　　　　　　　　　　　　　　　　　1290

TRYGAEUS: Yes, by Zeus, I mean you.

FIRST BOY: I'm the son of Lamachus.

Τρ. αἰβοῖ·
     ἦ γὰρ ἐγὼ θαύμαζον ἀκούων, εἰ σὺ μὴ εἴης
     ἀνδρὸς βουλομάχου καὶ κλαυσιμάχου τινὸς υἱός.
     ἄπερρε καὶ τοῖς λογχοφόροισιν ᾆδ' ἰών.
     ποῦ μοι τὸ τοῦ Κλεωνύμου 'στὶ παιδίον;   1295
     ᾆσον πρὶν εἰσιέναι τι· σὺ γὰρ εὖ οἶδ' ὅτι
     οὐ πράγματ' ᾄσει· σώφρονος γὰρ εἶ πατρός.

ΠΑΙΔΙΟΝ Β
     "ἀσπίδι μὲν Σαΐων τις ἀγάλλεται, ἣν παρὰ θάμνῳ
      ἔντος ἀμώμητον κάλλιπον οὐκ ἐθέλων—"

Τρ. εἰπέ μοι, ὦ πόσθων, εἰς τὸν σαυτοῦ πατέρ' ᾄδεις;   1300

Πα.ᵝ "—ψυχὴν δ' ἐξεσάωσα—"

Τρ.   κατῄσχυνας δὲ τοκῆας.
     ἀλλ' εἰσίωμεν· εὖ γὰρ οἶδ' ἐγὼ σαφῶς
     ὅτι ταῦθ' ὅσ' ᾖσας ἄρτι περὶ τῆς ἀσπίδος
     οὐ μὴ 'πιλάθῃ ποτ', ὧν ἐκείνου τοῦ πατρός.   1304

     ὑμῶν τὸ λοιπὸν ἔργον ἤδη 'νταῦθα τῶν μενόντων   (στρ.
     φλᾶν ταῦτα πάντα καὶ σποδεῖν, καὶ μὴ κενὰς παρέλκειν.
     ἀλλ' ἀνδρικῶς ἐμβάλλετε
     καὶ σμώχετ' ἀμφοῖν ταῖν γνάθοιν· οὐδὲν γάρ, ὦ πόνηροι,
     λεύκων ὀδόντων ἔργον ἔστ', ἢν μή τι καὶ μασῶνται.   1310

Χο. ἡμῖν μελήσει ταῦτά γ'· εὖ ποιεῖς δὲ καὶ σὺ φράζων.   (ἀντ.
     ἀλλ', ὦ πρὸ τοῦ πεινῶντες, ἐμβάλλεσθε τῶν λαγῴων·
     ὡς οὐχὶ πᾶσαν ἡμέραν

1292 εἴης V²: εις R: ἦς Γ_p̲: ᾖσθα Β: [V¹].
1297 ᾄσει Dawes: ᾄσεις codd. ᵡΣΓ.
1307 ἐμβάλλετε Portus: ἐμβάλλετον (ἐμβάλετον Vᵃᶜ) codd. Suda:
      ἐμβάλλετ' ὦ Bergk.

128

TRYGAEUS: Ugh!
  I was certainly wondering, as I listened, whether you weren't
    the son of some lummock who wants a fight and laments not having one!
Push off and go and sing to the spearsmen. [*The boy goes off by a side
passage.*] Where is Cleonymus' little boy, please? [*The second boy, a fat*   1295
lad, comes up to Trygaeus.] Sing something before you go inside. You, I'm
quite certain, won't sing about trouble and strife; you've got a sensible
father.

SECOND BOY:
  "Some Saian now glories in my shield, the faultless armament
    which I unwillingly abandoned beside a bush —"
TRYGAEUS·
  Tell me, my little cockerel, are you singing about your own father?   1300
SECOND BOY:
  "But I saved my life —"
TRYGAEUS: And put your parents to shame.
Let's go inside. I know very well indeed that you certainly won't ever
forget all that that you've just been singing about the shield — not with
that father you've got. [*They begin to go into the house. Trygaeus turns
to the chorus, directing their attention to the gifts of food left by the
sickle-maker and the potter.*]
      From here on, it's now up to you that are staying out here   1305
        to lay into all this stuff and bang it down, and not let your oars
                                              trail idly.
      So get stuck in like men,
        and chop away with both your jaws; because there's no point, you
                                              silly lot,
      in having white teeth, if they don't actually do some chewing.   1310
CHORUS-LEADER [*as Trygaeus disappears into the house*]:
  We'll make that our business; and thank you too for telling us.
[*To his colleagues*]
      Now, you who have starved till now, get stuck into the hare's meat;
      because it's not every day

129

πλακοῦσίν ἐστιν ἐντυχεῖν πλανωμένοις ἐρήμοις.
πρὸς ταῦτα βρύκετ', ἢ τάχ' ὑμῖν φημι μεταμελήσειν.   1315

Τρ. εὐφημεῖν χρὴ καὶ τὴν νύμφην ἔξω τινὰ δεῦρο κομίζειν,
δᾷδάς τε φέρειν, καὶ πάντα λεὼν συγχαίρειν κἀπικελεύειν·
καὶ τὰ σκεύη πάλιν εἰς τὸν ἀγρὸν νυνὶ χρὴ πάντα κομίζειν
ὀρχησαμένους καὶ σπείσαντας καὶ Ὑπέρβολον ἐξελάσαντας
κἀπευξαμένους τοῖσι θεοῖσιν   1320
 διδόναι πλοῦτον τοῖς Ἕλλησιν,
 κριθάς τε ποιεῖν ἡμᾶς πολλάς
 πάντας ὁμοίως οἶνόν τε πολύν,
 σῦκά τε τρώγειν,
 τάς τε γυναῖκας τίκτειν ἡμῖν,   1325
 καὶ τἀγαθὰ πάνθ' ὅσ' ἀπωλέσαμεν
 συλλέξασθαι πάλιν ἐξ ἀρχῆς,
 λῆξαί τ' αἴθωνα σίδηρον.

δεῦρ', ὦ γύναι, εἰς ἀγρόν,
χὤπως μετ' ἐμοῦ καλὴ   1330
καλῶς κατακείσει.

Χο. Ὑμήν, Ὑμέναι' ὤ.

— Ὑμήν, Ὑμέναι' ὤ.

— ὦ τρίσμακαρ, ὡς δικαί-
ως τἀγαθα νῦν ἔχεις.

— Ὑμήν, Ὑμέναι' ὤ.   1335

— Ὑμήν, Ὑμέναι' ὤ.

1317 κἀπικελεύειν RV[1]p: κἀπιχορεύειν V[2].
1318 νυνὶ Küster: νῦν Rp: om. V.
1332 Ὑμήν, Ὑμέναι' ὤ (twice) p [i]Σ[V] 1329: (once) Π20 RV.

that you can find flat-cakes wandering about unclaimed!
Therefore tuck in, or I say you'll soon regret it! 1315

[*The chorus take portions of food from the pile. Presently Trygaeus
comes out of the house, dressed as a bridegroom.*]

TRYGAEUS:
Let all speak fair, and let the bride be brought out here,
and torches be fetched, and all the folk rejoice with us and cheer us;
and let us now move all our gear back to the country
after dancing, and making libation, and getting rid of Hyperbolus,
and praying to the gods 1320
to give wealth to the Greeks,
and that all of us alike may grow
plenty of barley and plenty of wine,
and figs for dessert,
and that our wives may bear us children, 1325
and that we may gather up once again as of old
all the good things that we have lost,
and that there may be an end of the glittering steel.

[*The sickles and jars brought earlier by well-wishers have by now been
distributed to members of the chorus. Fullfruit now comes out of the house,
escorted, as bride, followed by attendants who distribute lighted torches
to the chorus.*]

TRYGAEUS [*to Fullfruit*]:
This way, wife, to the countryside,
and, pretty one, be sure you lie 1330
prettily at my side.
FIRST SEMICHORUS:
Hymen, Hymenaeus, O!
SECOND SEMICHORUS:
Hymen, Hymenaeus, O!
CHORUS-LEADER [*to Trygaeus*]:
Thrice-happy one, how deservedly
you now enjoy these blessings!
FIRST SEMICHORUS:
Hymen, Hymenaeus, O! 1335
SECOND SEMICHORUS:
Hymen, Hymenaeus, O!

— τί δράσομεν αὐτήν;

— τί δράσομεν αὐτήν;

— τρυγήσομεν αὐτήν.

— τρυγήσομεν αὐτήν.   1340

— ἀλλ' ἀράμενοι φέρω-
   μεν οἱ προτεταγμένοι
   τον νύμφιον, ὦνδρες.

— 'Υμήν, 'Υμέναι' ὤ.

— 'Υμήν, 'Υμέναι' ὤ.   1345

— οἰκήσετε γοῦν καλῶς,
   οὐ πράγματ' ἔχοντες ἀλλὰ συκολογοῦντες.

— 'Υμήν, 'Υμέναι' ὤ.

— 'Υμήν, 'Υμέναι' ὤ.   1350

— τοῦ μὲν μέγα καὶ παχύ,—

—   τῆς δ' ἡδὺ τὸ σῦκον.

Τρ. φήσεις γ', ὅταν ἐσθίῃς
   οἶνόν τε πίῃς πολύν.

Χο. 'Υμήν, 'Υμέναι' ὤ.   1355

— 'Υμήν, 'Υμέναι' ὤ.

Τρ. ὦ χαίρετε χαίρετ', ἄν-
   δρες· κἂν ξυνέπησθέ μοι,
   πλακοῦντας ἔδεσθε.

1337-40 Σ^V reports that some copies omitted these lines.
1342 προτεταγμένοι Bentley: προστεταγμένοι codd.

[*Fullfruit is brought to the chorus, and raised on the shoulders of two of them.*]

CHORUS-LEADER:
  What shall we do with her?
CHORUS:
  What shall we do with her?
CHORUS-LEADER:
  We'll gather her vintage!
CHORUS:
  We'll gather her vintage!   1340
CHORUS-LEADER:
  Now, let's us in the front rank
  lift up the bridegroom
  and carry him, men!
FIRST SEMICHORUS:
  Hymen, Hymenaeus, O!
SECOND SEMICHORUS:
  Hymen, Hymenaeus, O!   1345
[*Trygaeus is likewise raised aloft.*]
CHORUS-LEADER:
  You two *will* live happily,
  having no troubles, just
  cultivating your figs!
FIRST SEMICHORUS:
  Hymen, Hymenaeus, O!
SECOND SEMICHORUS:
  Hymen, Hymenaeus, O!   1350
LEADER OF FIRST SEMICHORUS:
  His is long and thick —
LEADER OF SECOND SEMICHORUS:
  And *her* fig is sweet.
TRYGAEUS:
  You'll say that all right when you're eating
  and drinking plenty of wine.
FIRST SEMICHORUS:
  Hymen, Hymenaeus, O!   1355
SECOND SEMICHORUS:
  Hymen, Hymenaeus, O!
TRYGAEUS [*to the audience*]:
  Good luck, good luck to you, gentlemen!
  And if you follow along with me,
  you'll have flat-cakes to eat!
[*The chorus go off, carrying Trygaeus and Fullfruit aloft.*]

133

NOTES

1.	**for the beetle:** Greek *kantharos* could also be taken as a man's name, and it was in fact the name of a contemporary comic dramatist (*PA* 8247), who probably won first prize at the City Dionysia of 422 twelve months before the production of *Peace* (his name is plausibly restored in *IG* ii²2318.115 and 2325.60). The audience might thus at first be misled into supposing that Ar. was going to satirize this rival of his and portray him as a "shit-eater" (a common term of abuse: cf. *Wealth* 706, Men. *Dysk.* 488); not till line 7 is anything said to indicate positively that the *kantharos* is an actual beetle, and even thereafter it is several times described in quasi-human terms (see on 7).

3.	**may it be the tastiest cake he ever eats:** lit. "may he never eat a cake more pleasant than this"; this is intended as a curse, but it misfires, for the speaker has forgotten that to a dung-beetle dung is not unpleasant at all.

6.	**Eaten it? Why . . . :** lit. "No, by Zeus; rather . . ."; the point is that "eaten" is too weak an expression to describe adequately what the beetle did.

7.	**with his feet:** strictly "with his two feet", since the Greek phrase is in the dual number. The reference to a pair of feet is entomologically accurate, since many dung-beetles do roll balls of dung along with their back legs (see G.Evans, *The Life of Beetles* [London, 1975] 118-120); but in any case Ar. seems intent on investing the unseen creature with a quasi-human personality, endowing it with teeth (34), arms (35), the power of speech (12) and a certain fastidious pride (25-26). In *Clouds* 150 the feet of a flea are likewise spoken of in the dual.

8.	**lots and lots:** or "plenty of them and tightly compressed".

9.	**you dung-collectors:** possibly spoken at the audience, abuse of whom was traditional in comedy (cf. *Clouds* 898, 1096-1100, 1201-3; *Frogs* 274-6). The point of the appeal is that people used to dealing with dung would be better able to endure the smell than the speaker is.

12.	**well pounded:** an allusion to anal intercourse.

14.	**I eat the stuff while kneading it:** naturally a very common misdemeanour among slaves preparing ordinary food; it was sometimes prevented, according to the scholia, by the use of a wide collar which made it impossible for the slave to bring a hand to his mouth.

17-18.	**bilge:** this joke has been explained by C. Carey, *CQ* 32 (1982) 465-6. Greek *antliā*, like English "bilge", can mean either the bottom of a ship (bilge$_1$) or the water that collects there (bilge$_2$). The second slave says "I can't get the better of the bilge$_2$ any longer", using a metaphorical expression that means in effect "I'm abandoning my task as impossible" (like a sailor who finds that water is coming into the ship too fast for him to bail it out). The other slave, however, fails to understand the metaphor, supposes that his colleague is speaking of a bilge$_1$ in the sense of a receptacle containing foul-smelling stuff, and accordingly says "Then I'll take the bilge$_1$ itself in with me" and goes inside with the tub. For such a misunderstanding of a figure of speech Carey compares *Eccl.* 595-6; for misunderstanding of an ambiguous word (on a far larger scale) cf. *Ach.* 770-796 (with my note on 739).

28.	**kneaded into a ball:** this is how many dung-beetles prepare their own food (see Evans [cited on 7]).

28.	**as if to a lady:** implying that women are more particular than men about having their food attractively prepared.

34.	**jaws:** lit. "molars", presumably referring to the insect's mandibles, which are placed laterally and close in from the sides to bite or chew.

35.	**arms:** probably the front legs.
36-37.	**like the men . . . for cargo ships:** the reference is to the "laying" or plaiting of stout ropes by twisting cords tightly together; the worker's arms go round and round the line of the rope as it takes shape. The ropes are said to be for *holkades* (cargo ships propelled only by sails) and are probably tow-ropes by which such ships were brought into and out of harbour; see J.S. Morrison and R.T. Williams, *Greek Oared Ships 900-322 B.C.* (Cambridge, 1968) 244-5.
38-49.	The division of this passage between the speakers is very uncertain; but normal dramatic practice makes it likely (i) that the slave who has been inside the house will come out at a moment clearly determined in the text and speak immediately on his entry, and (ii) that the slave who has been on stage continuously and created a *rapport* between himself and the audience (9-10, 13-14, 20-28) will be the one who eventually explains the situation to them (50-77). It follows that 38ff and 49 must both be spoken by the character whom we are calling the first slave, and that 43ff, which clearly looks forward to the coming exposition of the situation, belongs to the second; and these assignments in turn largely determine the division of the intervening lines.
39.	**this evil visitation:** the slaves suppose that the beetle must have been sent by some god to plague them.
40-41.	**I don't think . . . from the Graces:** so ugly a creature could not have been employed by deities who are patrons of beauty.
42.	**Zeus, the Lord of the Thunder-crap:** in the Greek Zeus is given the invented epithet *Skataibatēs*, a perversion (based on the root *skat-* "dung") of his cult-title *Kataibatēs* "He who descends" (sc. in the thunderbolt). I have been unable to improve on the English rendering of this pun by K. McLeish, *The Theatre of Aristophanes* (London, 1980) 95. On the cult of Zeus Kataibates, which centred mainly on places made holy to him through having been struck by lightning, see A.B. Cook, *Zeus* (Cambridge, 1914-40) ii 13-22.
45-46.	**an Ionian fellow:** a visitor from one of the tributary states in the eastern Aegean, one of many non-Athenians who attended the City Dionysia. He seems to be introduced here mainly so that his alleged words can be quoted in Ionic dialect, whose characteristic features of pronunciation were no doubt heavily exaggerated by the actor.
47.	**he's using it:** "he" is Aristophanes.
47.	**Cleon** (*PA* 8674), son of Cleaenetus of the deme Cydathenaeum, was one of the most influential politicians at Athens from about 427 until his death in battle at Amphipolis in 422, and an inveterate enemy of Ar., whom he tried to prosecute in 426 (*Ach.* 377-382, 502-3) and probably again in 424 (*Wasps* 1284-91), and who caricatured him as Paphlagon in *Knights* and again as the Hound of Cydathenaeum in *Wasps* 894ff. His death has made Ar. no tenderer towards him; indeed more abuse is directed at him in *Peace* than at any living politician (cf. 269-272, 313-320, 647-656, 753-8).
48.	**he's eating muck in Hades:** Cleon was a "shit-eater" in his lifetime (see on 1), and he remains one in the underworld, eating the "ever-flowing dung" (*Frogs* 145) in which the most heinous sinners, according to one belief, were condemned to wallow eternally. The manuscripts have "he/it eats the muck shamelessly"; if this refers to Cleon we are improbably expected to understand, without being told, that the muck-eating is taking place in Hades, while if it refers to the beetle it comes as a weak anticlimax when we would expect a punch-line. It is better therefore to assume what would be a very simple corruption of the text.

49. **give the beetle a drink:** i.e. urinate.

51. **striplings:** lit. "little men".

52. **the men of high position:** possibly referring to magistrates and others who had portions of the theatre reserved for them, such as the *bouleutikon* (*Birds* 794) where the members of the council sat; the words may have been accompanied by a gesture in their direction.

53. **those proud supermen there:** Greek *huperēnoreōn* (which is otherwise found only in Homer) means etymologically "behaving in a superhuman way", but in actual use in epic always bears the derogatory sense "arrogant". Here, coming as the climax of an ascending series, it seems at first to be an extravagant compliment to the men referred to, but those who know their Homer will be aware that it can be taken otherwise. The reference must be to a specific group of men whom the speaker points out in the audience, no doubt the priests, generals and high magistrates who occupied the foremost seats.

55. **the way you are:** this probably does not refer to the Athenians' alleged mania for litigation but is merely generalized abuse of the audience (see on 9).

59. **don't sweep Greece away:** Greek *ekkorein*, like English "sweep away", could be used to mean in effect "utterly destroy", and "may you be swept away" was in Menander's time, and perhaps also earlier, a common malediction (cf. Men. *Georgos* 53).

62. **TRYGAEUS:** the name means "Vintager", appropriate for a man who is a vine-grower (190); it is also appropriate for the hero of a comedy, since one of the Greek words for "comedy" was *trugōidiā*. The name was probably invented for this play, though other names from the same root are occasionally attested, e.g. 'Trygias' at Thespiae (*IG* vii 1888 *i*6) and "Tryges" at Argos (*SEG* xvii 146.5).

63. **uproot:** Greek *ekkokkizein*, properly to squeeze the seeds out of a pomegranate, is used several times by Ar. (*Ach.* 1179; *Lys.* 364, 448) to refer to a variety of violent actions all of which can be seen as involving the forcible removal of something from its resting-place (e.g. the dislocation of an ankle, the tearing out of hair). Here therefore, in relation to the Greek cities, it may mean something like "tear from their foundations". Another possible rendering, however, is "make empty" (of inhabitants). In any case the verb suggests devastation and desolation.

66. **bile-sickness:** one form of insanity was believed by contemporary doctors to be due to overheating of the brain through an excess of bile (Hippocr. *On the Sacred Disease* 18); cf. *Clouds* 833.

73. **an enormous Etna beetle:** Mount Etna was widely believed to be the home of a race of giant beetles (Epicharmus fr. 76 Kaibel; Aesch. fr. 233N = 385M; Soph. fr. 162; Soph. *Ichn.* 300 Pearson = fr. 314.307 Radt; Plato com. fr. 37 who says these beetles are "as big as men"). The city of the same name, founded by Hiero in the 470s, seems to have adopted the beetle as a symbol, for it appears on one of its early coins (see G.K.Jenkins, *Ancient Greek Coins* [London, 1972] 147 and fig. 364). Whether the giant beetles really existed we do not know. See E. Fraenkel, *Beobachtungen zu Aristophanes* (Rome, 1962) 53-57.

74. **to be its groom:** Greek *hippokomein*, the first of several expressions referring to the beetle in terms normally applied to horses.

76. **my little Pegasus, my thoroughbred flier** (lit. "wing"): Pegasus was the winged horse on which the hero Bellerophon attempted to fly to heaven. The line is parodied from one in Euripides' *Bellerophon* (Eur. fr. 306) "Come, my dear winged Pegasus" (lit. "wing of

	Pegasus"); and the whole idea of Trygaeus' flight to heaven is in fact a parody of Belle-rophon's flight in the Euripidean play.
82-101.	Metre: anapaestic. Trygaeus' diction is largely tragic, but there are some obvious and amusing lapses, especially in 87 and 99-101 (see also next note).
82.	**little moke:** Greek *kanthōn*, normally a pet-name for a donkey (cf. *Wasps* 179); there is a pun on *kantharos* "beetle".
83-86.	**do not go . . . your wings:** like a horse, the beetle must not try to go at full speed until he has warmed up.
90.	**O lord and master:** Greek *anax* "lord" is in ordinary fifth-century speech applied only to gods (cf. 180 and *Wasps* 875), and the scholia suggest that the slave addresses Trygaeus in this way "because he has risen into the air and expects to ascend to heaven"; but *anax* is used of men in tragedy, and its use here may be due merely to the mock-tragic context (cf. the mock-lyric *Knights* 1298).
92.	**then:** i.e. if you don't want me to call you crazy.
93.	**on behalf of all the Greeks:** throughout the play it is neither for himself (like Dicaeopolis in *Acharnians*) nor even for Athens that Trygaeus seeks the restoration of peace, but for the Greeks as a whole (105-8, 292-8, 406-413, 435-6, 866, 995-8, 1320-8).
96.	**speak fair:** this injunction to refrain from inauspicious speech (i.e. to refrain from all speech except the responses prescribed by ritual) was regularly uttered at the start of a religious ceremony (cf. 434, *Clouds* 263, *Wasps* 868) or of other actions during which it was especially important that nothing ill-omened should happen (cf. 1316, before a wedding procession).
99-101.	**and shut off . . . their arses:** so that the beetle may not be excited and distracted by the smell of food, and perhaps throw his rider (cf. 157-172).
99.	**alleys:** evidently much used as informal public conveniences.
105.	**to ask him about the Greeks:** it is possible that Bellerophon's ascent to heaven in Euri-pides' play had also been with the intention of questioning Zeus about his seemingly absurd behaviour; in Eur. fr. 286 a character in the play, perhaps Bellerophon himself, argues that the gods do not exist because if they did they would not allow the wicked to flourish and the virtuous to suffer.
107.	**indict:** Greek *grapsomai* implies a literal, not a merely figurative, indictment and an actual prosecution.
107.	**for betraying Greece to the Medes:** because if Greeks continue to fight each other they will soon be in no state to resist a fresh attempt at conquest by the Persians (here called the Medes as was usual in colloquial fifth-century Greek); for the idea cf. 406-413 and *Lys.* 1133.
109.	**never while I live:** the slave is concerned for his master's safety, for it is dangerous to attempt to call the gods to account for their actions: Bellerophon's attempt ended dis-astrously when he was thrown from his horse, and in Euripides' *Andromache* Apollo has Neoptolemus killed because the latter dared to demand satisfaction from him for the death of his father Achilles.
111-149.	The text does not definitely determine the number of children who appear, but since all references to them are in the plural (not dual) number it is likely that there are at least three. It is possible that they sing 114-8 together, but in the ensuing spoken dialogue (124-149) one of them will certainly speak on behalf of all, as chorus-leaders regularly do on behalf of choruses.

139

114-123.	Metre: dactylic, at first in tetrameters but from 118 in hexameters. The passage parodies a lyric exchange between a character and the chorus in Euripides' *Aeolus*; in the original of 114-7 (Eur. fr. 17) the chorus asked whether the rumour was true that Aeolus was marrying his children to one another.
117.	**to the dogs above**: lit. "to the crows", a common expression for "to perdition" (used in 19, 500, 1221): the joke is that Trygaeus is going "to the crows" not only in this meta‑ phorical sense, but also literally by riding through the air among the birds. There is another play on the same phrase in *Birds* 27-29.
119.	**"You may guess, maidens; but the truth"** . . .: a quotation from Euripides' *Aeolus* (Eur. fr. 18), presumably the opening of the reply to the original of 114-7; in Euripides the line ended "but the truth I cannot tell you".
119-121.	**I'm fed up . . . in the house at all**: the girls' importunate wheedling, which has so vexed Trygaeus, is presumably due to their never being adequately fed on account of the poverty and shortages caused by the war; later Trygaeus will pray for the Agora to be full of imported foodstuffs (999-1005), and the chorus, described as "you who have hungered till now" (1312), will be given a magnificent feast, while the very last words of the play are "you'll have flat-cakes to eat".
120.	**calling me daddy**: a child who calls his or her father *pappa, pappiā* or the like is usually trying to wheedle something out of him: cf. *Wasps* 297, 609 and *Odyssey* 6.57.
123.	**a bunch of fives**: Greek *kondulon* "a knuckle, a punch", with a pun on *kandaulos*, a cul- inary delicacy of Lydian origin made of many ingredients (variously listed by Alexis fr. 172; Hegesippus of Tarentum, cited by Athenaeus 12.516d; and Hesychius s.v. *kandūlos*).
124-149.	The diction and metre of this dialogue fluctuates between the high tragic style and the ordinary level of comedy.
124-5.	**And what means . . . on this voyage**: perhaps a reminiscence of *Odyssey* 10.501-2 "Circe, who will guide me on this voyage? No one has yet reached Hades' realm in a black ship."
126.	**A winged colt . . . go by sea**: the line is wholly tragic in style, but is perhaps Euripidean pastiche rather than quotation or parody; for ancient commentators were uncertain whether it derived from Euripides' *Bellerophon* or his *Stheneboea* (in which Bellerophon was also a character).
129.	**Aesop**: the reputed author of numerous animal fables; he was said to have been a slave of Iadmon of Samos in the early sixth century (Hdt. 2.134. 3-4).
130.	**the only winged creature**: perhaps the most extreme example of the Greek tendency to use *monos* "only" loosely and rhetorically (for which cf. 590, Soph. *OT* 299, Eur. *Hipp.* 1282, Isocr. 14.31); for the very same fable which says that the beetle flew to heaven also says that the eagle flew there first (see next note).
133.	**because it was at feud with an eagle**: the story is Aesop *Fab.*3 Perry; the scholia here give a variant version. An eagle once wronged a beetle, either by stealing its young, or by killing a hare which had supplicated the beetle for protection. In revenge the beetle pursued the eagle wherever it nested, rolling its eggs out and breaking them, until the eagle fled for safety to its divine protector Zeus and was allowed to place its eggs in his lap. Thereupon the beetle flew up to Zeus, and either by buzzing round his head or by laying a ball of dung in his lap it made him forget about the eggs and jump up so that they broke. The story is alluded to in *Wasps* 1448 and *Lys.* 695. It is not difficult to

140

see why, on reading or remembering this fable, Trygaeus chose to fly to heaven on a beetle rather than an eagle: in the fable, the beetle's flight to heaven had ended in a success, the eagle's in a failure.

134. **of its nests:** this is not in the Greek but has been added for clarity.

135. **wings:** lit. "wing"; cf. on 76.

136. **like a tragic hero** means "like someone on a serious, not a comic, mission" but also suggests "like Bellerophon in Euripides' play".

139. **I can use again to feed this creature:** lit. "I will feed this (creature) with that very same (food)", i.e. with the excrement into which my body will convert it.

142. **oar:** lit. "steering-paddle"; for phallic (steering-)oars cf. Plato com. fr. 3.4 and probably Theophilus fr. 6.3.

143. **a beetle-boat, made in Naxos:** there are several references to a kind of boat called a *kantharos* "beetle" (Nicostratus com. fr. 10; Sosicrates fr. 2; Men. fr. 286.4-5); our passage is the sole authority for the association between these boats and the island of Naxos.

145. **Beetle Harbour** or "Harbour of Cantharus" (a hero worshipped locally, according to Philochorus *FGrH* 328 F 203) was the official name of the great harbour at Peiraeus (cf. *IG* ii^2 1627.404, 429).

146-8. **that you don't . . . get turned into a tragedy:** Bellerophon's attempt to fly to heaven ended when his winged steed threw him off and he fell to earth; and Euripides' play, which included his flight, also showed him after his fall, lame and in filthy garments (cf. *Ach.* 426-7). On the strength of this and one or two other plays such as *Telephus* and *Philoctetes* it became a standing joke against Euripides that he loved to portray crippled heroes (cf. *Ach.* 411, *Frogs* 846).

151. **for three days:** either this is the expected duration of the flight, or more probably there is an allusion to some three-day period of ritual purification (perhaps involving sexual abstinence, for which abstinence from defaecation is here substituted). A scholium to Lucian's *Dialogues of Courtesans* (p. 276.3-5 Rabe) attests just such a three-day purification period in the case of the *Antletriai*, the women who retrieved certain sacred objects from the "chasms of Demeter and Kore" at the festival of the Thesmophoria.

154-172. Metre: anapaestic. The first few lines parody an anapaestic passage spoken by Bellerophon to Pegasus in Euripides' play (Eur. fr. 307) which began "Go, golden-bitted one, raising your wings".

155-6. **with bright ears pricked:** *phaidros* "bright, glad" is often applied in poetry to faces and eyes, but only a parodist could apply it to ears. Most probably it would be taken to suggest ears pricked up in eagerness and high spirits, but the Greek does not make this explicit. Note that throughout 152-8 the beetle is repeatedly spoken in terms appropriate to a horse ("graze", "ears", "nostrils", etc.).

155-6. **the rattle of cavesson and golden bit:** lit. "the golden-bitted rattle of cavessons". A cavesson is a composite metal nose-band, used for controlling the movement of a horse; J.K. Anderson, *JHS* 80 (1960) 3-6, shows that this is probably what is denoted by Greek *psalion*.

157-8. **Why are you bending your nostrils towards the alleyways?:** or, with another punctuation, "Where are you bending your nostrils? Towards the alleyways?" A dung-beetle could expect to find much food there (cf. 99).

163. **foods:** or, adopting Bentley's emendation, "turds"; this would avoid a slight anticlimax, but the supposed noun *skation* "turd" is not known to have existed.

141

170-2.	the state of Chios will be fined five talents: it is known that if an Athenian citizen met a violent death on the territory of any of the subject states of the Athenian empire, the state in question became liable to a fine of five talents; the same sanction was applied to the killing of certain non-Athenians honoured for their services to Athens (cf. *IG* i³ 19 and 161). There is, however, no apparent reason why under this law Chios should be held liable in the event of Trygaeus' death, and there is probably an allusion to some recent case in which a fine had been imposed on the Chian state by an unduly elastic interpretation of the law; with satirical exaggeration Trygaeus is made to assume that in future, whenever anybody gets killed (no matter how, where or by whom), Chios will be made to pay a fine for it. See R. Meiggs *CR* 63 (1949) 9-12, and D.M.MacDowell, *Athenian Homicide Law in the Age of the Orators* (Manchester, 1963) 127-8.
174.	Mr. Crane Operator: characters in flying scenes speak to the *mēkhanopoios* also in Ar. fr. 160 K-A (from *Gerytades*) and Strattis *CGF* 74. 8-11.
180.	Whence came that mortal voice that — : lit. "Whence struck me a mortal's — "; the scholia are not certain whether the next word would have been "smell" or "voice", but the latter is clearly right: it is true that upon the arrival of Trygaeus and the beetle Hermes might well become aware of a strong smell, but the smell would not be a human one.
181.	hippobeetle: Greek *hippokantharos* "horse-beetle", a comic coinage modelled on *hippokentauros* "centaur", *hippalektruōn* "horse-cock" (see on 1177), and other names of fabulous monsters.
182-3.	You loathsome . . . utter villain: repeated, with a slight change of word-order, in *Frogs* 465-6, again by a divine doorkeeper (at the palace of Pluto) to an unwelcome visitor.
185-7.	What may your name be? . . . Archvillain: Trygaeus is so little impressed by Hermes' bluster that he makes game of him before condescending to answer any questions. Contrast the reaction of Dionysus to similar bluster in *Frogs*: he is so terrified that he faints and soils himself (*Frogs* 479-481).
190.	Athmonum: a deme about six miles north-east of Athens (see Traill 50).
191.	disputes: Greek *prāgmata* "affairs, business", often used with special reference to litigation.
193.	you really came here for that?: the Greek means literally "how [or why] did you come?", but the context suggests that this is not to be taken here as a question expecting an answer but more as an expression of surprise and delight, as it seems to be in Soph. *El.* 1355.
193.	cadger: lit. "clingy one"; the adjective *gliskhros* and its derivatives can be used of importunate beggars, as in *Ach.* 452. Hermes appears as a beggar cadging food in *Wealth* 1134ff, and this role may have been traditional for him in comedy.
199.	cupola: Greek *kuttaros*, a word with several meanings, of which the most apposite here is perhaps "acorn-cup", a comic metaphor for the hemispherical firmament; cf. *Clouds* 95-96, *Birds* 1000-1, where the sky is compared to a dome-shaped cover used in baking.
201.	I'm keeping an eye on the bits of equipment: for Hermes as the divine "servant-boy" cf. *Wealth* 1168-70, [Aesch.] *Prom.* 941-2, Eur. *Ion* 4, and the role of Mercury in Plautus' *Amphitruo*.
202.	odd: lit. "little", the three Greek nouns all being diminutive in form, implying not so much small size as unimportance.
202.	boards: almost anything made of a flat piece or flat pieces of wood can be called a *sanis* (diminutive *sanidion*); here the context suggests that what is meant is a board used as a working surface in the kitchen.

211-2.	**when they repeatedly tried to make peace**: when there arose (as we would say) heaven-sent opportunities for ending the war. The idea that the gods desire peace but are frustrated by human folly appears already in *Ach.* 51ff.
212.	**the Laconians**: a common unofficial term for the Spartan state; Laconia was the south-eastern quarter of the Peloponnese, in which Sparta and her dependent towns were situated.
213.	**gained a small advantage**: as e.g. at the time of the great plague at Athens in 430, when the Athenians sued unsuccessfully for peace (Thuc. 2.59.2).
214.	**by the Twin Gods**: regarded by Athenians as the typical Spartan oath (cf. *Lys*, 81, 86, etc.) The "Twin Gods" are Castor and Pollux, brothers of Helen and patrons of Sparta. Similar oaths are used with reference to different pairs of deities by Thebans (*Ach.* 905) and by Athenian women (e.g. *Wasps* 1396).
214.	**the Attic boys**: Greek (probably) *hāttikiōn* = *ho Attikiōn* "the little Attic (Athenian)", a contemptuous diminutive. Alternatively the transmitted letters might be read as *Attikiōn*, presumably a proper name personifying the Athenian enemy as an individual (compare the use of "Jerry" in the two world wars or of "Charlie Cong" in Vietnam).
214:	**will get what's coming to them**: lit. "will pay a penalty", presumably for the crime of attempting (as Spartan propaganda put it) to enslave Greece (cf. Thuc. 2.8.4, 3.63.3).
215.	**Atticonians**: a comic coinage on the model of "Laconians"; Ar. had already used it in an earlier play, *Merchant Ships* (fr. 437 K-A).
215.	**gained some success**: as at Pylos in 425 (see on 219); the Spartans attempted to make peace while the campaign was in progress (Thus. 4.15-22) and several times after it had ended (665-7; Thuc. 4.41.3-4).
217.	**"We're being tricked"**: when the Spartan embassy of 425 asked to be allowed to negotiate with elected Athenian representatives, rather than having to reply to the Athenian demands in open assembly, Cleon seized on this as proof "that they had no honest intentions" (Thuc. 4.22.2).
219.	**if we hold on to Pylos**: in 425 an Athenian force under Demosthenes had occupied and fortified the promontory of Pylos on the west coast of the Peloponnese, and the Spartan force sent to recapture the place had eventually been compelled to surrender to Demosthenes and Cleon on the neighbouring island of Sphacteria, nearly 300 being taken prisoner. Subsequently the Athenians installed at Pylos a garrison of Messenian exiles, and the fortress became a thorn in the Spartans' flesh as a base for guerrilla raids, as a haven for fugitive helots, and through the fear that the Messenians might be able to foment a general revolt of the helots, most of whom were their compatriots (Thuc. 4.41.2-3; 5.14.2).
222.	**where has she gone?**: with this question, the personification of Peace as a goddess is effected.
223.	**a deep cavern**: on the question how the cavern was represented theatrically, see Introductory Note, p. xvii.
231.	**the Greek states**: lit. "the cities".
235.	**the voice of a martial mortar**: the turn of phrase has a tragic ring (cf. *Ach.* 572), with "mortar" as an incongruous substitute for "trumpet" or the like.
235-6.	Trygaeus' place of concealment may be close to the side wall of the *skēnē*: *Wasps* 138 ("Won't one of you run round here?") shows that there was a passageway down at least one side of the building giving access to the rear.

237.   **how sore you're going to be in the jaws**: i.e. "what a pounding you're going to get", since beating about the jaws was common when a stronger person attacked a weaker (*Clouds* 1324; *Lys.* 360-1; *Frogs* 149-150).

241.   **the fearsome one, the redoubtable one**: the same epithets are applied to Lamachus (see on 304) in *Ach.* 964. The homeric word *talaurīnos*, here translated "redoubtable", seems originally to have meant "bearing a leather shield", but already in Homer it is sometimes little more than a sonorous epithet for a bloodthirsty warrior or a god of war (cf. *Iliad* 5.289).

241.   **the one that gets into your legs**: lit. "the one that is (comes?) down upon the legs", an obsure phrase. Most recent editors follow the scholia in seeing an allusion to involuntary defaecation due to fright (cf. 1176, *Knights* 1057, *Frogs* 479-481), and this may be the meaning of a similar phrase in Men. *Perinthia* 18; but *Lys.* 1258-9 show that in Ar.'s time the expression was at any rate not exclusively scatological. Possibly the reference here is to another effect of terror, namely quaking at the knees: cf. *Lys.* 216 and the Homeric phrase "his knees and inward heart gave way" (e.g. *Iliad* 21.114).

242-252. War intends to pound his ingredients, representing the various Greek peoples, into a savoury mash (*muttōtos*), a popular dish whose components varied somewhat but generally included the four used here as well as eggs, oil and vinegar; the related verb *muttōteuein* (a compound of which is used in 247) is often employed metaphorically in much the same sense as English "make mincemeat of" (cf. *Wasps* 63).

242.   **Prasiae** was a town on the coast of Laconia, sacked by the Athenians in 430 (Thuc. 2.56.6); it had since no doubt been rebuilt, but its position would expose it to further Athenian raids if the war continued, and there was in fact to be such a raid in 414 (Thuc.6.105.2). It is chosen for mention here mainly because its name can be associated with *prason* "leek".

244.   **that doesn't bother us yet**: either Ar. has forgotten, or (more likely) Trygaeus is deliberately closing his eyes to, the fact that there was another Prasiae on the east coast of Attica.

246.   **Megara**, Athens' western neighbour, had suffered twice-yearly Athenian invasions throughout the war (*Ach.* 762; Thuc. 2.31.3, 4.66.1; Plut. *Per.* 30.3), and her south-eastern port of Nisaea and the adjacent island of Minoa were under Athenian occupation (Thuc. 3.51; 4.69). Garlic (cf. 258) was one of Megara's principal export commodities (1000; *Ach.* 521, 761-3, 813).

249.   **wailings**: an unexpected substitute for "heads of garlic".

250.   **Sicily**: the war between Syracuse and Leontini, in which the Athenians had intervened on Leontini's side in 427 but which had been settled in 424, had broken out afresh in 422, and Athens had made diplomatic efforts to enlist other Sicilian states in an anti-Syracusan crusade (Thus. 5.4). She had been unsuccessful, but considerable risk remained of a renewal of general war in Sicily. Sicily was famous for its cheese (cf. *Wasps* 838, 896-7; Hermippus fr. 63.9; Antiphanes fr. 236.4).

251.   **country**: Greek *polis* seems here to mean "territory" regardless of whether that territory is politically unified (Sicily was not); cf. Eur. *Ion* 294, *Bacchae* 58; [*Lys.*] 6.6. The alternative would be to take *polis* as referring to some particular Sicilian state; but how could the audience know which state was meant?

251.   **grated up**: Greek *diaknaiein* means "wear through, destroy", but the cognate verbs *knēn* and *kataknēn* are used of grating cheese.

252.	**let me also pour on this Attic honey:** Ar. avoids making War in so many words condemn Athens to destruction; for similar reticence cf. *Lys.* 33-38. The district of Mount Hymettus, east of the city, was considered to produce the best honey in the world: cf. *Thesm.* 1192, Archestratus fr. 62.17-18 Brandt, Strabo 9.1.23, Plut. *Dion* 58.2.
253.	**Hey, you . . . :** despite this second-person address to War, it seems certain that Trygaeus does not intend to be, and is not in fact, heard by him.
254.	**it costs four obols:** this is probably to be understood as the price of one *kotulē* of honey (about 0.27 litre or just under half a pint). Early in the fourth century (*IG* ii^2 1356) a *kotulē* of honey cost only three obols; in 421, however, after the disruption caused by repeated Spartan invasions, production will probably still have been well below normal.
255.	**Hurlyburly:** Greek *Kudoimos* "tumult, din of battle", personified as a war-demon in *Iliad* 5.593, 18.535.
255.	**really howl:** lit. "howl long". War, it seems, is portrayed as having so savage a temper that he beats his slave for idleness when the latter is merely waiting to receive his orders.
257.	**What a sting!:** R indicates change of speaker after these words, and a number of editors have assigned them to Trygaeus; but this particular comment is more likely to come from the person who is actually smarting from the blow.
258.	**You didn't . . . did you?:** the manuscripts continue these words to the previous speaker (i.e. Hurlyburly), but it is surprising that he should mention "the garlic" when he was not present during 246-9. If Trygaeus is the speaker, his second-person address to War is similar to that in 253-4.
261.	**get one from Athens:** why from Athens, does not become clear until 270. In real life a householder who lacked some utensil might borrow it from a neighbour (cf. *Frogs* 1158-9, Men. *Dysk.* 456-521); hence Hurlyburly's trips to Athens and Sparta occupy no more time than if he had gone round to the two next-door houses.
263.	**poor . . . folk:** Greek *anthrōpia*, a diminutive of *anthrōpoi* "people", here conveying a tone of affection and sympathy.
265-7.	**the boy . . . he . . . he:** referring respectively to Hurlyburly, War and Hurlyburly again. In the Greek the subjects of all the verbs in these lines are left to be understood.
267.	**Dionysus:** possibly Trygaeus chooses to pray to Dionysus because as a vine-grower he regards Dionysus as his special patron: he prays to him again in 442.
270.	**the leather-seller:** this identifies the lost "pestle" as Cleon, whose family's wealth appears to have come from a tanning and shoemaking business, a fact (or allegation) on which Ar. constantly harps (648, 669, 753, *Ach.* 300-2, *Knights* 44, 136, 197, 314-321, 369, 449, etc., *Clouds* 581, *Wasps* 38). Ar. had already called Cleon a pestle (i.e. a creator of chaos and confusion) in *Knights* 984.
270.	**who churned up all Greece:** a similar phrase is applied to Pericles in *Ach.* 531, in connection with the Megarian decree (see on 609). The Greek verb used here, *kukān* "create agitation or confusion", is often applied by Ar. to the activities of Cleon and other "demagogues" (654, *Knights* 692, *Lys.* 491).
[273].	This almost meaningless line ("or before pouring in the savoury mash for us"??) is probably concocted from an explanatory note that was mistaken for part of the text.
274-5.	**get another from Sparta:** most of the audience would probably realize at once that Brasidas was meant (see on 282).
277-8.	**to have been initated at Samothrace:** the island of Samothrace was the home of a celebrated mystery-cult, initiation into which was supposed to be a guarantee that the

initiate's prayers would be answered, especially when he was in danger at sea (cf. Ap. Rh. 1.916-921 with scholia; D.S. 4.43). The gods worshipped in this cult were usually referred to only as "the Samothracian gods"; Herodotus (2.51), who seems to have been an initiate, identified them with the gods called the Cabeiri who were worshipped at Lemnos and elsewhere, but some other ancient authorities disagreed. See W. Burkert, *Griechische Religion der archaischen und klassischen Epoche* (Stuttgart, 1977) 420-6.

279. **that the errand-boy . . . twisted feet**: lit. "that turned away may be the fetcher's two feet", with a pun on the verb *apostrephein* "turn away, avert, twist back". It must have been common to appeal to the Samothracian gods to avert (*apostrephein*) an impending danger; here it is suggested instead that they be asked to twist back (*apostrephein*) the feet of Hurlyburly so that he cannot complete his mission.

282. **their pestle**: the reference is to Brasidas son of Tellis, the outstanding Spartan general of the Peloponnesian War. After saving Megara for the Peloponnesians in 424 (Thuc. 4.70-74) he had conducted operations for two years in the "Thracian Coast area" (283), where he had detached many towns from the Athenian alliance, by persuasion as much as military power. He was fatally wounded in the summer of 422 when leading the successful defence of Amphipolis. Thucydides (5.16.1), like Ar., considers him to have been the main obstacle on the Spartan side to the making of peace, which he opposed "because of the success and honour he was gaining from warfare".

283-4. **some other people**: Brasidas and a small army had gone north at the request of the states in revolt from Athens in the Chalcidic peninsula and of King Perdiccas of Macedon (Thuc. 4.79), who had asked Sparta for an army to help protect them against Athenian attack.

283-4. **the Thracian Coast area**: lit. "the areas in the direction of Thrace", the usual designation for the regions of Greek settlement on the northern shore of the Aegean.

285. **Sons of Zeus** (Greek *Dioskorō*): Castor and Pollux, the special patrons of Sparta (cf. 214): according to the usual story (Pind. *Nem*. 10.49-90) Pollux was son of Zeus, Castor of the mortal Tyndareus, but Pollux gave his half-brother a share of his own immortality and the two were thereafter honoured equally and shared the title "sons of Zeus".

289. **here comes**: i.e. this is an appropriate occasion for.

289. **Datis**: almost certainly the reference is to Datis the Mede, joint commander of the Persian expedition sent against Eretria and Athens in 490 which was defeated at Marathon. In all ages peoples at war have made jokes about the alleged sexual inadequacies of the enemy leaders (as in the once-familiar English song that began "Hitler has only got one ball"); here a joke of this type is combined with one at the expense of Datis' broken Greek, which may have originated in the language of threatening letters sent by him to the Athenians (cf. A.E. Raubitschek in *Charites: Studien zur Altertumswissenschaft E. Langlotz gewidmet* [Bonn, 1957] 236-7). It appears from the scholia here and on *Frogs* 86 that Datis was also the name (or more likely the nickname) of a tragic dramatist, a son of Carcinus (cf. 782-796), most probably Xenocles, the only one of Carcinus' sons known to have been an author; but our Datis here, whose activities are referred to in a past tense, and who makes a typically Asiatic grammatical blunder (see on 291), is hardly to be identified with a native Athenian poet who cannot have been much older than Ar. himself.

290. **of a noonday**: masturbation seems to have been proverbially associated with midday heat and referred to as the behaviour of "a Lydian at noon" or "a goatherd in the heat" (see Suda λ787).

291.	**I'm rejoiced**: Greek *khairomai*, a blunder (middle voice instead of active) for *khairō* "I rejoice". In Timotheus' dithyramb *Persians* (fr. 15.155-6 Page) a Phrygian is made to commit a similar blunder, saying *erkhō* and *kathō* for *erkhomai* "I go" and *kathēmai* "I sit".
293.	**to be rid of broils and battles**: the same phrase appears in *Ach.* 269-270.
296-8:	**you peasants . . . and islanders**: it is well remarked by Dover 138 that we have here "a complete list of the categories of population one would expect to find at Athens"; one may, indeed, be more specific and say that it is a complete list of the categories of adult males that one would expect to find in the theatre at the City Dionysia (except for "privileged" groups such as politicians, priests and generals). We may therefore take it that this summons, like many of Trygaeus' earlier remarks, is spoken straight at the audience. The summons appears to be modelled on a passage in Aeschylus' satyr-play *Netfishers* (*Diktyoulkoi*) (Aesch. fr. 464.18-20M) where "all peasants, vine-diggers . . . and shepherds", and perhaps other groups, are summoned to help in hauling out of the sea a large chest which proves, when opened, to contain Danaë and her infant son Perseus, and/or on similar calls for assistance in other satyr-plays; cf. W. Steffen, *Eos* 55 (1965) 38-43; D.F. Sutton, *Rivista di Studi Classici* 23 (1975) 354; and (on other echoes of satyr-play themes in the ensuing scene) R. Seaford, *Euripides: Cyclops* (Oxford, 1984) 193-4.
297.	**immigrants**: Greek *metoikoi*, free men who, or whose ancestors, had migrated from one state to another and who were consequently not citizens of their state of residence.
297.	**foreigners**: here evidently denoting foreign *visitors* who did not reside permanently in Attica.
298.	**islanders**: inhabitants of the many Aegean islands that belonged to the Athenian empire. Since these islands were one of the most important components of the empire, and the nearest to Athens, Ar. several times (760; *Knights* 170, 1034, 1319) uses "the islands" to refer to the empire as a whole, and it may be that here "islanders" is used in the same loose fashion to mean "citizens of the subject states".
298.	**ye people**: Greek *leōi*, a form of address normally used only by heralds making proclamations (551; *Ach.* 1000; *Birds* 448).
299-345.	Metre: trochaic tetrameters, ending (from 339) in a long continuous trochaic run or *pnīgos*. The shift of metre in mid-speech and mid-sentence at 299 is exactly paralleled at 553 in another "proclamation", with the same phrase (*hōs takhista* "as quickly as you can") at the point of transition.
300.	**to have a pull at**: the manuscripts' reading *harpasai* means "to seize, to grab", which is not very appropriate either to the hauling-out of Peace from her cave or to the drinking of wine (see next note). It is likely that the text originally contained the verb *spasai* "to pull; to suck, to drink" or some compound of it, and that Ar. intended to pun on the two meanings of the verb; but no emendation has been proposed that is convincing in detail (van Herwerden's *au spasai* introduces an adverb to which it is hard to assign an appropriate meaning).
300.	**the Good Spirit's cup**: after a meal the first libation was poured to the Good Spirit (*Agathos Daimōn*) from a cup of neat wine; since this marked the transition from the meal to the drinking and entertainments that followed, "now we can drink from the Good Spirit's cup" means in effect "now we can start enjoying ourselves". The pun mentioned in the previous note may be continued in this phrase, since "good spirit" could

147

301. (with a change of gender) be taken to refer to the goddess of Peace.
For the question of the dramatic identity (or identities) of the chorus, see Introductory Note, p. . For the time being they represent the whole Greek people (302); but the reference to Lamachus (304) and the epithet "most vine-loving" applied to Peace (308) already foreshadow their later and more specific identity as Athenian peasants.

302. **liberation:** Greek *sōtēriā* "salvation, escape from danger".

303. **smart scarlet cloaks:** these cloaks (called *phoinīkides*) were worn by officers in the Athenian army (1173-6); a similar garment was part of the standard uniform of the Spartan soldier (*Lys.* 1140; Xen. *Lac.* 11.3; Arist. fr. 542). The adjective *kakōn* "bad, wretched", offered by the manuscripts, is rightly said by Platnauer to be weak; I suggest Ar. wrote *kalōn* "smart, attractive", conveying (as in 395 and 1172-90) the common soldier's resentment of his brightly-clad, crest-bedecked, strutting (and often cowardly) superiors.

304. **Lamachus,** son of Xenophanes, probably of the deme Oë (*PA* 8981), was a distinguished officer more noted, however, for personal courage than for intellectual power (Pl. *La.* 197c); he had been a general at least twice (Plut. *Per.* 20; Thuc. 4.75) and probably on several other occasions. Both in this play (473-4, 1290-4) and earlier in *Acharnians* (270, 566-625, 959-968, 1071-1149, 1174-1226) Ar. represents him as eager for the continuation of war, not so much for the sake of glory as of financial gain (*Ach.* 597-617); against this it should be noted that Lamachus was one of those who took the oath and made the peace with Sparta in 421 (Thuc. 5.19.2) and that some years later he was still a poor man (Plut. *Nic.* 15.1, *Alc.* 21.9). In 415, though getting on in years (Plut. *Alc.* 18.2), Lamachus was made one of the three commanders of the Sicilian expedition; the following year he characteristically over-exposed himself in battle and was killed (Thuc. 6.101.6). After Lamachus' death he is twice referred to by Ar. with admiration as a model of the soldierly virtues (*Thesm.* 841, *Frogs* 1039).

308. **vine-loving:** in peacetime vines are tended and grow; in war they are destroyed by the invading enemy (612-3; *Ach.* 231-3, 512, 979-987).

310. **rekindle War in there:** there is a slight clash between the natural metaphor of war as a destructive fire (cf. 610-1) and the personification of war as a demon (implied by "in there").

312. **"come with three days' rations":** the usual mustering order for a military expedition (cf. *Ach.* 197, *Wasps* 243).

313. **that Cerberus in the underworld:** Cleon, who seems to have spoken of himself as the people's "watchdog" or protector (cf. *Knights* 1017-24), in mockery of which Ar. brings him on stage in *Wasps* (894-994) as "the Hound of Cydathenaeum" and several times refers to him as "the jag-toothed one" (754 = *Wasps* 1031; *Knights* 1017) or as "Cerberus" the watchdog of Hades (*Knights* 1030); the latter designation is even more appropriate now that Cleon has actually gone to Hades.

314. **spluttering:** or "bubbling" (Greek *paphlazōn*), alluding to Cleon's style of oratory. In *Knights* Cleon is portrayed as a slave named *Paphlagōn*.

314. **screaming:** Ar. constantly refers to Cleon's loud, raucous voice (757; *Knights* 137, 256, 274-6, 286, etc.; *Wasps* 36, 1228).

314. **up here:** on earth; it is forgotten that the action is supposed to be taking place in heaven. Similarly in *Frogs* 783, where the scene is in Hades, a character says "There aren't many good folk ⟨in Hades⟩, no more than there are here", where "here" means "in Athens".

316-7. **There is no one . . . into our possession:** adapted from Euripides' *Heracleidae* (976-7) "Now that this man has come into my hands, there is no mortal who will snatch him

148

away". In the Greek the opening words of the couplet give no satisfactory sense ("now too"?) and are almost certainly corrupt; Meineke's conjecture (see critical note) gives the meaning "(There is no one who will take her away . . .) with impunity", Richter's "(There is no one) even from there [i.e. the underworld] (who will take her away)".

319. **he:** War (not Cleon), as "rush out" (sc. of the stage-house) shows.

320. **let him make chaos, let him make confusion:** possibly a reminiscence of [Aesch.] *Prom.* 994 where this is said of Zeus.

323. **dances:** strictly "dance-figures".

335. **I fart:** for breaking wind as a sign of contentment and satisfaction cf. *Knights* 115 (with 103-4), *Clouds* 9, *Wasps* 1305, *Eccl.* 464, *Wealth* 176.

336. **escaped from my shield:** cf. *Ach.* 58, 279, where those who have finished with soldiering are said to "hang up their shields".

336. **cast off my old age:** the Greek phrase is the same as that used of a snake that sheds its old skin.

338. **her:** Peace.

341. **to travel or stay at home:** i.e. to have a choice between the two. Greek *plein* means strictly "travel *by sea*": in wartime one might be forced to sail out on campaign when one would rather have stayed at home, or (on the Peloponnesian side) be forced to stay at home because the enemy dominated the seas.

342. **international festivals:** Greek *panēgureis* "general assemblies", often used in reference to the Olympic games (Plato, *Hipp.Mi.* 363c) and other panhellenic religious and athletic gatherings. The first clause of the Peace of Nicias provided that at these gatherings "whoever so wishes may sacrifice and visit and consult oracles and be a spectator, going by land or by sea, without fear" (Thuc. 5.18.2), implying that during the war Athenians had not always been allowed to do so (despite the tradition of the "sacred truce").

343. **cottabus:** a game played at symposia, which "consisted of throwing wine-lees at·a target set in the midst of the diners' couches" (B.A. Sparkes, *Archaeology* 13 [1960] 203).

344. **be a regular Sybarite:** i.e. live a life of ease and pleasure; the south Italian city of Sybaris, destroyed by its neighbour Croton about 510, was a byword for the luxurious effeteness of its inhabitants (Ar. fr. 216 Kock = 225 K-A; Hdt. 6.127.1).

346-360 ≏ 385-399 Metre: a mixture of trochaic (based on the unit - υ -x) and cretic-paeonic (based on -υ- or -υυυ).

348. **palliasses:** straw mattresses, such as soldiers or sailors might use when on active service.

348. **of which Phormio is patron saint:** lit. "which Phormio has had alloted to him": Phormio is humorously spoken of as if he were a god who had palliasses (i.e. campaigning and its discomforts) under his special protection (cf. Pind. *Nem.* 11.1 "Child of Rhea, Hestia, to whom *prytaneia* [civic hearths] are allotted"; Pl. *Tim.* 23d "the goddess [Athena] to whom have been allotted both your city and this one"). Phormio, son of Asopius (*PA* 14958), was an outstandingly successful Athenian admiral in the early years of the Peloponnesian War, winning more than one victory against heavy odds (Thuc. 2.83-92); he probably died in the winter of 429/8 (cf. Thuc. 3.7.1). He was remembered as a tough and hardy fighter (cf. *Lys.* 804); in Eupolis' comedy *Taxiarchs* he was shown trying to teach the unwarlike and effeminate god Dionysus to endure the hardships of a soldier's or sailor's life (see A.M. Wilson, *CQ* 24 [1974] 250-2), and it is natural to suppose that he was particularly notable for being ready to share these hardships with the men under his command, unlike some other officers (cf. 1172-90 and see on 303).

349.	**a fierce or ill-tempered juryman**: Ar. regularly presents the typical Athenian juror as an irascible old man ever ready to condemn and reluctant to acquit: cf. *Wasps* passim, *Ach.* 375-6, *Knights* 808.
355.	**killing ourselves**: the context suggests that this is merely an exaggerated complaint of the rigours and annoyances of hoplite training.
356.	**the Lyceum**: a gymnasium and exercise-ground just to the east of the city walls at Athens, used for cavalry displays (Xen. *Hipparch.* 3.1, 3.6-8) and as a mustering and training ground for the army (cf. Xen. *Hell.* 1.1.33).
357.	**"with spear, with shield"**: a quotation from Achaeus' tragedy *Momus* (fr. 29), which Ar. had previously used in *Wasps* 1081.
363.	**the same as Cillicon**: Cillicon (or Callicoön as he seems to have been called by Hellenistic poets: Callimachus fr. 607, Euphorion fr. 82 Powell) was a semi-legendary traitor, a byword for wickedness. When he came under suspicion of planning to betray his city (variously identified as Samos, Miletus and Syros) to its enemies, and was questioned as to what he was doing or intending to do, he gave the evasive reply *panta agatha* "nothing but good"; and that in effect is the reply Trygaeus gives to Hermes here.
364.	**if the lot falls on me**: "when the Athenians condemned several men to death, they did not execute them all in one day, but lots were cast for each of them day by day, and the one on whom the lot fell was put to death, so that only one died each day" (scholia). This custom is not directly attested elsewhere, but no better explanation of our passage has been offered; and there is some evidence (Ant. 5.69-70) that men who had been condemned at the same time might be executed at different times.
[365]	Here the manuscripts have the line "For, being Hermes, you will do it by lot, I know" (Hermes being the patron god of lotteries). The phrase translated "do it by lot" is dubious Greek, and the line is quite unnecessary: if the scholia's interpretation of 364 (see previous note) is correct, it would be worse than pointless to add another and conflicting explanation; if, on the other hand, no custom existed such as the scholia allege, it is hard to see what sense an audience could make of the vague expression "do it (i.e. make me perish) by lot". The line, like [273], was probably made up from an explanatory note.
367-8.	**I haven't yet bought any groats or cheese**: Trygaeus pretends to understand "you are doomed to perish" as meaning "you have been ordered to go on campaign" (as if being ordered to join an expeditionary force were the equivalent of a death sentence) and protests that he has not had time to buy his "three days' rations" (see on 312).
369.	**you are utterly ruined and crushed**: the Greek perfect tense is here anticipatory, meaning "you are certain to be . . . ", "you are doomed to be . . . ", like the perfect tenses used by Hermes in 364 and 366; Trygaeus however pretends to understand it as a true perfect ("you have already been . . .") and moreover affects to regard being "ruined and crushed" as a great blessing. He is determined to give no sign of taking Hermes' menaces seriously; he changes his tone only when Hermes seems about to call down on him the thunderbolt of Zeus (376)
374-5.	**Then please lend me . . . before I die**: initiates of the Eleusinian Mysteries were promised happiness in the afterlife, provided they observed a simple moral code (cf. *Frogs* 449-459); and one of the preliminary rites that a candidate for initiation had to perform was the sacrifice of a sucking-pig (cf. *Ach.* 747, 764, *Frogs* 338, Pl. *Rep.* 2.378a).
376.	**O Zeus, lord of thunder . . .** : Hermes is about to denounce Trygaeus and the chorus to

	Zeus as violators of his edict against the rescue of Peace, and to ask him to strike them with his thunderbolt.
376-8.	**in the name of the gods . . . in the name of the meat:** Greek *pros tōn theōn . . . pros tōn kreōn.*
380-1.	**be annihilated . . . shrill this out . . . cry it aloud:** the Greek verbs are all strongly poetic in flavour: none of them is found in vernacular Attic, and two of the three are too elevated even for tragedy.
383-4.	Metre: trochaic tetrameters.
387.	**given by me:** as a sacrifice.
395.	**Peisander**, son of Glaucetes, of the deme Acharnae (*PA* 11770), was a significant figure in Athenian politics for at least fifteen years; as early as 426 Ar. was accusing him of favouring war from corrupt motives (Ar. fr. 81 Kock = 84 K-A), a charge which is also implicit in our passage and which reappears in *Lys.* 490-1. Elsewhere he is satirized as a big, clumsy man (Hermippus fr. 9; Eupolis fr. 182; Phrynichus fr. 20), a glutton (*com. adesp.* 64; Aelian *VH* 1.27) and above all as a coward (*Birds* 1556-64; Eupolis fr. 31; Xen. *Symp.* 2.14) — an allegation which as in the case of Cleonymus (see on 446) may well derive from a single incident. The reference here to "crests" shows that there is no foundation for the gibe in Xenophon (loc.cit.) that Peisander avoided military service; indeed he may well have been a taxiarch in 422/1 (cf. 1173). In the following year he was elected to a three-man board supervising the making of two statues for the temple of Hephaestus (*IG* i^3 472.1-3). Being considered "very loyal to the people", he was chosen in 415 as one of the commission of inquiry to investigate the mutilation of the Hermae and other acts of sacrilege; he showed great determination to seek out the truth by all means, and was one of the strongest propagators of the belief that the mutilation was the work of anti-democratic conspirators (Andoc. 1.27, 36, 43). By 412/1, however, he had himself become a supporter of oligarchy, and he did more than anyone to pave the way for, and then to carry out, the *coup d'état* by which the Four Hundred took power in the summer of 411 (Thuc. 8.49-56, 63-68). On the fall of their regime he escaped, with others, to the Spartan camp at Deceleia (Thuc. 8.98.1) and was condemned to death in his absence and his property confiscated (Lys. 7.4; Lycurgus, *Against Leocrates* 120-1). For a favourable view of his career, see A.G. Woodhead, *AJPh* 75 (1954) 131-146.
395.	**brows:** either Peisander, like Cleon (Cratinus fr. 228 K-A), had frighteningly bushy eyebrows, or else he was thought haughty or arrogant (the gesture of raising the eyebrows was considered a mark of haughtiness: cf. Cratinus fr. 355 Kock = 348 K-A; Alexis fr. 16, 116; Men *Sik.* 160).
402.	**because they're bigger thieves:** Hermes was the patron god of thievery (*Wealth* 1139-45; *Iliad* 24.24; *Odyssey* 19.395-7; *h.Hom.Herm.* 175, 292; Hipponax fr. 3a West = 2 Degani).
408.	**trying to betray Greece to the barbarians:** cf. 107-8.
410.	**you:** the Olympian gods.
411.	**the barbarians:** the reference is specifically to the Persians, who according to Herodotus (1.131.) did not believe in anthropomorphic gods and sacrificed to the sky, to the sun and moon, and to earth, fire, water and winds. In point of fact the sun and moon had a comparatively minor place in contemporary Persian religion, whose chief god was the Zoroastrian deity Ahuramazda; see J.M.Cook, *The Persian Empire* (London, 1983) 147-157.

411-3.	it's natural . . . for themselves: the alleged scheme of the Sun and the Moon is to have the Greeks weaken themselves so much by fighting each other that it will be easy for the Persians to conquer and destroy them, whereupon Persian cults of the Sun and Moon will presumably be instituted in place of the Greek cults of the Olympians.
414.	Ah, that's why . . . : the "stealing of days" by the Sun and Moon (see next note) is now perceived by Hermes as being the first stage of a much larger plan to deprive the other gods of the honours to which they are entitled.
414.	stealing some of the days: the reference is to irregularities in the Athenian calendar. Such irregularities probably arose most often when the archon ordered the calendar to be "stopped" at a particular date so that a festival could be postponed and yet still be held on its proper calendar date: *SEG* xiv 65.3-4 (third century) is a decree passed at a time when the calendar had been stopped at 9 Elaphebolion for five days, presumably in order to complete preparations for the City Dionysia. After such a retardation of the calendar it would be necessary to compensate by suppressing calendar days later in the year, possibly making the final month or months noticeably shorter than normal. The calendar might also be tampered with for other reasons: in 419 the Argives stopped their calendar so that the sacred month of Karneios would not begin until they had completed their invasion of Epidaurus (Thuc. 5.54.3-4). In our passage, as in *Clouds* 615-626, the irregularities are regarded as offensive by the gods, who apparently do not realize that it is the Athenians who are responsible for them and instead blame them on the heavenly bodies. For fuller discussion of the intercalation and suppression of calendar days, see W.K. Pritchett, *BCH* 81 (1957) 269-301; W.K. Pritchett and B.L. van der Waerden, *BCH* 85 (1961) 19-23.
416-7.	help us . . . in hauling up Peace: the text here is uncertain in detail, but the general sense must be as given.
418.	the Great Panathenaea: the Panathenaea was one of the most important Athenian festivals, held in honour of Athena towards the end of the month Hecatombaeon (roughly July); every fourth year it was designated the Great Panathenaea and celebrated with special splendour, with many athletic, artistic and other competitions. See Parke 33-50. Trygaeus rightly assumes that Hermes will have no compunction about betraying his fellow-gods for gain: cf. *Wealth* 1147-51.
420.	the Mysteries: the Eleusinian Mysteries in honour of Demeter and Persephone, held from the 15th to the 21st of Boedromion (roughly September); see Parke 55-72.
420.	the Dipolieia: a festival of Zeus, held on the 14th of Scirophorion (roughly June), and noted for its archaic and bizarre rituals; see Parke 162-7.
420.	the Adonia: the festival commemorating the death of Adonis, the mortal youth who was loved by Aphrodite. In the fifth century this festival may not yet have been officially recognized by the Athenian state, since a meeting of the Assembly could be held to the inauspicious accompaniment of the Adonis-dirges (*Lys*. 389-397); but it was already very popular especially with women, who sowed seeds of quickly-growing, quickly-withering plants in trays called "gardens of Adonis" which they carried up to the house-roofs. The date of the festival is not clear: Pl. *Phdr*. 276b seems to imply that in Greece, as in the Orient, it fell in high summer, but this is hard to reconcile with the evidence of *Lys*. 389-397 that in 415 the Adonia fell at a time when the Sicilian expedition had not yet sailed (see Dover *HCT* iv 271). See generally N. Weill, *BCH* 90 (1966) 677-698; M. Detienne, *Les jardins d'Adonis* (Paris, 1972).

422.	the Averter of Evil: Greek *Alexikakos*, properly a title of Heracles (cf. *Wasps* 1043, Hellanicus *FGrH* 4 F 109, Luc. *Alex.* 4) and Apollo (Paus. 1.3.4): again Hermes is being promised honours that have hitherto belonged to other gods.
426-430.	Metre: trochaic tetrameters.
429.	you be in charge . . . what we need to do: cf. 305; the superintendence of the work rescuing Peace, there entrusted to Trygaeus, is now transferred to Hermes.
432.	boldly is not in the Greek, but has been added to help reproduce the pun on *phialē* "bowl" and *(e)phialoumen* "we can get on with".
433-457.	The assignment of lines in this passage has been much disputed, but the crucial fact is that Hermes is holding the libation-bowl; hence it is he who must call for silence, lead the prayers and pour the libations. Thus at 456 Hermes pours a libation to himself; cf. *Birds* 1614 where Poseidon swears by Poseidon. (For another view see B. Marzullo, *Museum Criticum* 18 [1983] 98-108.)
433-4.	These ritual calls are not metrical.
434.	Speak fair!: i.e. refrain from inauspicious speech, so that the ritual can be properly performed: see on 96.
435-6.	that this day . . . for all the Greeks: alluding no doubt to the words of the Spartan Melesippus, who was sent to Athens in 431 in a last-minute attempt at negotiation when the Peloponnesians were ready to invade Attica; he was refused a hearing and ordered to leave Attica at once, and at the border he took leave of his escort with the words "This day will be the beginning of great evils for the Greeks" (Thuc. 2.12.1-3).
440.	poking the coals: the surface meaning of this is "sitting by the fire" (cf. 1131-7), but the phrase can also easily be understood in a sexual sense: the female genitals are called a hearth or fireplace in *Knights* 1286 and *Thesm.* 912, an oven in *Peace* 891.
443.	extracting arrowheads: always a difficult and painful procedure, because arrowheads had backward-pointing barbs (cf. *Iliad* 4.214).
444.	a taxiarch: the commander of one of the ten tribal divisions of the Athenian infantry. The *number* of taxiarchs (and of generals [450]) was the same in war as in peace; but in war, owing to casualties, the *turnover* of high officers would be much greater, and an ambitious man would thus have better prospects of obtaining a taxiarch's or general's position.
445.	thee, O Lady: Peace.
446.	suffer the same fate as Cleonymus: put himself to public shame by fleeing from the battle and throwing away his shield. Cleonymus (*PA* 8680) seems to have done this some time in 424, probably at the battle of Delium when the Athenian army was routed, and Ar. harps on the incident for ten years afterwards (*Clouds* 353-4; *Wasps* 15-27, 592, 822-3; *Peace* 673-8, 1295-1304; *Birds* 290, 1473-81). He was a minor politician, active from 426 to 415 (*IG* i³ 61.34; 68.5; 69. 3-4; Andoc. 1.27); he is elsewhere satirized as an obese glutton (*Ach.* 88; *Knights* 958, 1290-9; *Wasps* 16, 592; *Birds* 1477) who had once been very poor (*Clouds* 675) but had enriched himself by perjury (*Clouds* 400) and other criminal methods.
447.	any maker of spears or seller of shields: cf. 545-9, 1208-64.
451.	a slave ready to run away: in wartime a runaway slave would be safe if he reached enemy territory; so in *Clouds* 6-7 Strepsiades damns the war because he cannot punish his slaves properly for fear they will abscond.
452.	stretched out on the wheel: a severe form of torture (cf. *Lys.* 846, *Wealth* 875, Ant. 5.40,

Andoc. 1.43); the references, though laconic, suggest that the victim was bound, face upwards, to the broad rim of a fixed wheel, and his extended limbs pulled downwards with cords — a variant on the principle of the rack. Antiphon *loc. cit.* describes this kind of torture as "the ultimate compulsion", but Trygaeus wants to make it even worse by having the victim simultaneously flogged. He is presumably thinking more of the would-be runaway slave than of the would-be general, since the torture of Athenian citizens was forbidden by law.

453. **strike up the paean**: the Greek has simply "hail Paean", a ritual cry to Apollo (cf. *Wasps* 874, Soph. *OT* 154); I have altered this in the translation so as to reproduce the pun on the name *Paiōn* and the verb *paiein* "strike" (cf. next note).

454. **leave out the striking**: Trygaeus objects to the use of the name *Paiōn* because it reminds him of the verb *paiein* "strike, smite, wound" and therefore warfare and its sufferings.

456. **the Graces**: Greek *Kharites*, goddesses of beauty and delight.

456. **Desire**: Greek *Pothos*, a deity elsewhere named in association with the Graces (*Birds* 1320, Eur. *Ba.* 415) and with Aphrodite (Aesch. *Supp.* 1039).

457. **Enyalius**: a war-god, sometimes identified with Ares (e.g. *Iliad* 13.519-522) but regarded by the Athenians as distinct from him. In the list of gods by whom young Athenians, on attaining their majority, swore to defend their country and its institutions, Enyalius appears directly preceding Ares (Tod *GHI* 204.17-18; see P. Siewert, *JHS* 97 [1977] 102-111).

458. **put your backs into it**: lit. "strain ⟨your backs⟩ underneath ⟨the ropes⟩".

458. **bring her in**: Hermes speaks as if he were giving orders for hauling in a ship to be beached.

459-472 = 486-499. Metre: **the short** exclamations are metrically irregular, but strophic responsion is maintained; the comments by Trygaeus and the chorus-leader are in anapaestic metre, with a heavy preponderance of spondees giving the impression of toilsome effort. The speaker-assignments here adopted are based on the assumption that in 459-463 and 467-8 (and the corresponding lines in the antistrophe) it is regularly the "foreman" who speaks first, in effect giving an order to haul, and the "workers" who respond, confirming that they are obeying the order; this assumption is supported by the oath *nē Dia* "by Zeus" in 489, which normally accompanies statements, not commands, and the scholia show that the ancient commentators interpreted the passage in this way. They identified the "foreman" as Hermes; but 484-5 suggests that although Hermes is in general charge of the work, it is the chorus-leader who gives the specific orders to the men, standing in much the same relation to Hermes as the boatswain (*keleustēs* or "order-giver") stood to the captain of a warship. (For another view see Marzullo [cited on 433-457] 109-113, 117-9.)

466. **you'll howl**: a threat of a beating.

466. **you Boeotians**: the Boeotians disapproved of the Peace of Nicias (Thuc. 5.17.2), largely because it required them to return to Athens the border fort of Panactum (Thuc. 5.18. 7) which they had captured some months before. The result was that they refused to subscribe to the Athenian-Spartan peace treaty and instead made a separate truce with Athens which could be denounced at any time on ten days' notice (Thuc. 5.26.3, 5.32.4); they also refused for over a year to repatriate their Athenian prisoners of war, and although under Spartan pressure they did in the end evacuate Panactum, they first demolished the fortifications (Thuc. 5.35.5, 5.39.2-3, 5.42).

154

470. **I'm pulling:** Trygaeus can hardly in fact be hauling very assiduously, since he seems to spend most of his time supervising and criticizing the efforts of others; if at this point he takes part in the actual work himself, his contribution is probably of short duration and small value.

473-483. In this passage it is hardly possible to tell which speaker is Hermes and which is Trygaeus; it may also be that there are fewer changes of speaker than have here been assumed.

473. **obstruct the work:** lit. "sit in the way", an idiomatic expression (cf. Pherecrates fr. 19) meaning "be a hindrance".

474. **that bogy of yours:** the hideous Gorgon which Lamachus bore as a device on his shield (cf. *Ach.* 574, 964, etc.), and which Ar. uses as a symbol of his fierce martial nature, is here (as in *Ach.* 582) called not *Gorgō* but *Mormō*, after a monster whom mothers and nurses invoked to frighten children (*Knights* 693, Theocr. 15.40). Whereas in *Ach.*582 the speaker is pretending to be terrified, here the tone is derisive.

475. **these Argives:** Argos had been neutral in the war, and had reaped considerable benefits by her neutrality (Thuc. 5.28.3), so that she had no strong incentive to help bring the war to an end; moreover, since her own thirty-year peace treaty with Sparta was about to expire, it was not in her interest that Sparta and Athens should be on friendly terms.

477. **their daily groats:** from barley groats was made the kneaded, uncooked cake called *māza* which was the staple food of the poorer Greek; hence *alphita* "groats" is often used in the sense of a person's "daily bread".

477. **drawing pay from both sides:** the mention of pay (*misthos*) suggests that the reference is to Argives serving as hired rowers in the Athenian and Peloponnesian fleets, both of which made considerable use of foreign manpower (cf. Thuc. 1.31.1, 1.35.3, 1.121.3).

478. **the Laconians:** on the strong Spartan desire for peace at this time, see Thuc. 5.13-15.

479. **those of them who are gripped tight by stocks and gyves:** the text here is corrupt and the restoration I have adopted is by no means certain, but the reference is in any case to the Spartans who had been captured on Sphacteria in 425 (see on 219) and who had been imprisoned at Athens ever since: for them peace would bring freedom. The words translated "by stocks and gyves" mean literally "in the wood"; a similar phrase is used, in reference to the same prisoners, in *Knights* 394; the meaning may be that they had their ankles locked in a board.

480. **the smith won't let them:** i.e. they are unable to help because of their iron shackles.

481. **the Megarians:** the Megarians, like the Boeotians, rejected the peace treaty (Thuc. 5.17.2), in their case because it did not require the Athenians to give up the Megarian port of Nisaea which they had captured in 424. Ar. however seems to be saying here that the Megarians were eager for peace but too weak to strive hard for it; and their weakness at this time is certainly shown by the fact that the Spartans felt able to concede Nisaea to the Athenians over the Megarians' heads, this being the only one of their conquests that the Athenians were allowed by the treaty to retain.

483. **they're perishing with hunger:** this is meant to explain the Megarians' inability to help effectively in the rescue of Peace, as well as their facial expression described in the preceding line. The Megarid had been repeatedly devastated by Athenian invasions during the war (Thuc. 2.31.3; 4.66.1; Plut. *Per.* 30.3), and in 425 Ar. had made a starving Megarian and his children characters in *Acharnians* (729-835).

491. There is an irregularity of strophic responsion here, the antistrophe being one anapaestic *metron* shorter than the strophe; but the sense requires no supplement, and in Ar. "such

instances of omission, always in neat segments . . . , are far too numerous to admit of wholesale emendation" (Dale 207, who gives a list of examples).

500-2.   **you Megarians . . . with your garlic:** it is surprising that the Megarians are here charged with being responsible for the war, when in 605-611 responsibility is pinned on Pericles and the war's origins traced to an attempt by him to avoid prosecution; but "panhellenic affection for Megarians is too much to ask of Attic comedy" (Dover 137).

502.   **to smear her with your garlic:** i.e. to anger her: fighting-cocks were fed with garlic to make them more aggressive (cf. *Ach.* 166; *Knights* 494, 946). There is also a suggestion that the Megarians transformed the sweet fragrance of Peace (cf. 525-538) into the pungent and unpleasant odour of war. For the connection between Megara and garlic see on 246.

505.   **judge in the courts:** we expect "hinder the work" or the like, but the complaint suddenly changes into an irrelevant gibe at the Athenian love of judging, which Ar. had satirized the previous year in *Wasps*.

507.   **withdraw a little towards the sea:** during the war, especially from 425 onwards, Athens had to some extent repeated the attempt she made in the "first Peloponnesian war" of 459-446 to acquire a land-empire in Greece in addition to her maritime empire, as witness the ambitious scheme of 424 to gain control of Boeotia, which came to grief at Delium (Thuc. 4.76-77, 89-101); Ar. had represented Cleon as holding out the prospect that Athenians would one day "judge cases in Arcadia" (*Knights* 798). Now, if Peace is to be established, Athens must give up all such ambitions, and be content to be supreme at sea while Sparta is supreme on land; then the two great powers will be able to "rule Greece together" (1082).

508-511.   Metre: iambic tetrameters. The assignment of lines to speakers is uncertain: it is possible (see M. Landfester, *Handlungsverlauf und Komik in den frühen Komödien des Aristophanes* [Berlin, 1977] 296-7) that 508 should be given to Trygaeus and 511 (as well as 509) to Hermes. This would imply that Trygaeus took a full and active part in the final stage of the hauling work (in contrast to earlier stages: see on 470, and note his use of "you" in 497). Against this, note that (i) the chorus do not hereabouts ask for Trygaeus' help, as they did at 469, and (ii) whereas the chorus, seemingly exhausted by their efforts, fall silent as soon as Peace appears, not speaking until 556 and not greeting Peace until 582, Trygaeus is ready at 520 to address the goddess immediately. I prefer therefore to retain the traditional assignments.

508.   **us peasants . . . all by ourselves:** we are thus to suppose that the Megarians, Argives and others who have been impeding the work have now been dismissed. If we reject (as we probably should: see Introductory Note p. xviii) the assumption that these were represented by supernumerary performers, then Ar. and his *chorodidaskalos* must have arranged the movements and grouping of the chorus in this passage in such a way as to give the *impression* that the number working on the ropes had been reduced even though in fact it had not. Possibly this might have been contrived (as my tentative stage direction suggests) by concentrating the same number of choreutae in a smaller space.

512-9.   Metre: iambic, except for the first line which is anapaestic. In 518-9 the text is very uncertain: with most recent editors I have adopted Richter's emendations, but the ancient metrical analysis on which they are based has survived only in an incomplete and ambiguous form.

156

520. **Grape-giver:** Peace is given this title because her restoration will enable the country people to plant, tend and harvest their vines in security. The theme of return to the country-side and its fruits and flowers is prominent throughout the ensuing scene (to 600), and recurs in the second parabasis (1127-71) and at the end of the play (1316-56).

521. **million-gallon:** lit. "ten-thousand-amphora", an amount equivalent to about 400,000 litres or over 85,000 gallons. Trygaeus would have liked to be able to address Peace in terms of an amplitude and joyfulness comparable to that quantity of wine.

523. **Fullfruit:** Greek *Opōrā* "(season of) fruit harvest".

523. **Showtime:** Greek *Theōriā*, which can be taken to mean either (i) a public spectator-event of any kind (e.g. a theatrical performance, a religious procession, an athletic contest) or (ii) a delegation sent to represent a state at one of the panhellenic festivals such as the Olympic games.

524. **What a face you've got, Showtime:** according to the transmitted text, Trygaeus from here to 538 praises the charms of Showtime while not mentioning those of Peace herself; and it is certainly tempting to suppose that Showtime's name has found its way by acci-dent into this line from the preceding one, displacing e.g. "dear Peace" (Meineke). Rogers however points out that "it is difficult to believe that Trygaeus addressed the words ['And what a fragrance'], &c. to an artificial statue", and it would be quite like him to pay more attention to a flesh-and-blood female (cf. 706-728, 856-908). I there-fore on balance retain the traditional text.

526. **perfume and demobilization:** the Greek has the two nouns in the reverse order (for their combination cf. *Clouds* 1007 "fragrant with green-brier and freedom from cares and catkin-shedding poplar"). The word translated "demobilization" is *astrateiā* "exemp-tion from (or avoidance of) military service".

528. **"I spurn that odious man's most odious pouch":** a quotation from Euripides' *Telephus* (fr. 727) with *plekos* "pouch, wickerwork bag" substituted for *tekos* "child". In their new context the words "that odious man's" have lost all meaning, though they still contribute emphasis to the expression. The word translated "I spurn" is *apeptusa* "I spit out, I abominate".

529. **onions and indigestion:** one word in the Greek, an *ad hoc* compound meaning something like "acid belching caused by eating onions". For onions as part of a soldier's or sailor's regular diet cf. 1129; *Ach.* 550, 1099; *Knights* 600.

530-8 **She smells . . . many other good things:** there is a similar recital of the blessings of peace, mentioning some of the same items (sheepflocks, new wine, thrushes), in Ar. fr. 387 Kock = 402 K-A (from the possibly spurious *Islands*).

530. **fruit-harvest:** the Greek word is *opōra*, identical with the name of one of Peace's atten-dants, and corruption has therefore been suspected; but the sense is unobectionable.

530. **the Dionysia:** this could well refer *both* to the City Dionysia, the major dramatic festival at which *Peace* itself was produced, *and* to the Country Dionysia which was celebrated some three months earlier in and by the individual demes of Attica, and which in at least some of them was likewise an occasion for dramatic competitions (see Pickard-Cambridge[2] 42-56).

531. **the pipes:** a piper regularly provided an accompaniment to the sung and chanted portions of dramatic performances.

531. **thrush** either stewed (1197) or roasted (*Ach.* 1011-2) was a popular culinary delicacy; men-tioned here, in a context concerned with dramatic performacnes, it may evoke the idea

of the banquet traditionally given by a *choregos* for those involved in the production he had sponsored.

532. **you'll be for it**: lit. "you'll howl", i.e. "you'll be severely punished".

534. **a composer of little phrases from the lawcourts**: alluding to the strong rhetorical elements in Euripides' style, and his fondness for set debates in which his characters employ the methods, and some of the language, of contemporary forensic oratory.

536. **the bosoms of women running errands to the fields**: this phrase seems to have been found hard to understand by some ancient scholars, and there was a variant reading "to the kitchen" or "to the oven", favoured apparently by scholars who thought that the line referred to women carrying dough for baking in the folds of their garments. The interpretation here adopted is based on two passages of Menander (*Dysk.* 557, *Epitr.* 462) where the verb *diatrekhein* used here seems clearly to mean "run an errand" (see Gomme-Sandbach on these passages). For the sort of errand of which Trygaeus may be thinking cf. 1146 where a female slave (Syra) is sent to call a male slave (Manes) home from the vineyard. Trygaeus seems to be picturing to himself the bouncing breasts of a woman hurrying on such an errand.

537. **an overturned jug**: the kind of accident that is likely to occur during a lively drinking party.

542. **cupping-vessels**: bronze vessels (cf. Arist. *Probl.* 890b7-26) applied to the skin for the relief of bruises and swellings.

543. **here**: in the theatre.

544. **Good grief, what an idea!**: the exclamation *aiboi talās* seems to combine amazement (at the idea that anyone should imagine it possible to deduce a man's occupation from his face) with self-pity (at the prospect of having to perform this task).

545-9. The contrast here drawn between the rejoicing of makers of agricultural tools and the grief of makers of military equipment reads like a preliminary sketch for the more elaborate treatment of the same theme in 1197-1264.

549. **and how he gave the spear-maker the long finger**: this may alternatively be an interjection by Trygaeus, continuing and enlarging upon what Hermes has said, as he does in 541-2. The gesture referred to is the extending of the middle finger in token of contempt (cf. *Ach.* 444, *Clouds* 651-4).

551. **Hear ye, O people!**: the conventional opening for a proclamation by a herald (cf. *Ach.* 1000, *Birds* 448).

553-581. Metre: trochaic tetrameters, ending (from 571) in a trochaic *pnīgos*. As at 299 (see note there) the change from iambic to trochaic metre occurs in mid-sentence.

554. **mellowed old peace**: by this phrase (*eirēnē saprā*) the delights of peace are compared to those of the particularly choice wine, called *sapros* or *sapriās*, that was made from overripe grapes; the taste and bouquet of this wine are lavishly praised in Hermippus fr. 82. 6-12.

555. **the paean**: either the ritual cry "hail Paean" (cf. 453) or a hymn, usually but not always to Apollo, which was often sung in thanksgiving for victory, success, or deliverance (cf. *Knights* 1318, *Iliad* 22.391, Thuc. 2.91.2).

561. **of crests and Gorgons**: i.e. of arrogant, bellicose officers who wear elaborate crests on their helmets (cf. 395, 1173; *Ach.* 575, 965, 1109) and bear a Gorgon's head on their shields (see on 474).

563. **buying some good salt-fish**: the countryman can provide most kinds of food from local

	resources, but if he wants fish he must buy it in the town market before going home.

564-7.   The parade of the chorus with their agricultural "weapons" is described in notably military language (*stĭphos... puknon* "serried ranks .. compact", *gorgon* here perhaps "spirited" but often "fierce" in relation to warriors, *exŏplismenē* here "ready for action" but literally "fully armed"); it is as if the Greeks who have so long been waging war *destructively* upon each other are now turning to wage war *constructively* upon the devastation their countryside has suffered. Cf. F. Heberlein, *Pluthygieia: Zur Gegenwelt bei Aristophanes* (Frankfurt, 1980) 89.

565.   **like barley cake or a feast of plenty**: the sight of the ranks of peasants, ready to work the land again, is as pleasing as the sight of a square meal of the uncooked barley cake (*māza*) that was the ordinary Greek's staple food, or of a table spread with dishes of every kind (*pandaisiā*, literally "feast of everything").

566.   **beetle-maul**: Greek *sphūra*, a heavy mallet used for breaking clods.

568.   **the lanes of a vineyard**: Greek *metorkhion* "space between two rows of vines", which needs to be kept clear of weeds, dead wood, etc., and have its soil well cultivated.

574.   **pressed figs**: Greek *palasia*, brick-shaped cakes made from pressed dried fruit.

582-600.   Metre: similar to, but not an exact repetition of, 346-360 and 385-399.

594.   **without cost**: cf. *Ach.* 33-36 "my village, which never cried 'buy charcoal' or 'buy vinegar' or 'buy oil'; it knew not 'buy', it produced everything itself". The town-dweller, on the other hand, has to pay for everything he consumes.

595.   **boiled grits**: Greek *khīdra*, unripe whole grains of wheat or barley, eaten boiled or in the form of gruel. Since unripe corn would not be available in the city, *khīdra* were thought of as a typically rural item of diet, and they are mentioned in *Knights* 806 as something the Athenian people will rejoice to eat again when peace is made and they can return to the countryside.

598.   **young fig-trees**: or "young fig-slips" (cf. *Ach.* 996); Greek *sūkidion* could be the diminutive either of *sūkē* "fig-tree" or of *sūkis* "fig-slip" (a third possible derivation, from *sūkon* "fig", is ruled out by 599 which shows that a plant, not a fruit, is mentioned here).

601-656.   Metre: trochaic tetrameters, ending (from 651) in a trochaic *pnīgos*.

603-4.   **"O indigent peasants, mark well my words"**: quoted from a poem by Archilochus (fr. 109) with "peasants" substituted for the original "citizens"; the same passage was quoted by Cratinus fr. 198 Kock = 211K-A (from *The Wine-flask*, produced in 423) and imitated by Eupolis fr. 357. The rare word *lipernētes*, which Archilochus and Cratinus had used, was believed in Hellenistic times to have meant "indigent, poor" (cf. Callimachus fr. 254 and *ep. adesp.* 4.17 Powell); this may have been based on information not available to us, or it may have been a guess (in which case we are in no position to improve on it). The manuscripts of Ar. here have not *lipernētes* but *sophōtatoi* "most wise"; this however is far less appropriate (there is no reason why Hermes should wish to flatter the chorus), and *lipernētes* is found in both the quotations of this passage by ancient historians and may well therefore have been the reading known to their probable source, Ephorus (cf. *FGrH* 70 F 196), who was writing no more than half a century after Ar.'s death.

605-624.   With this account of the origins of the war compare the quite different version of *Ach.* 509-539; the two accounts agree only in asserting that the war was caused by the "Megarian decree" and that this decree was proposed by Pericles from personal motives which had nothing to do with the public interest.

605.   **started it all:** this is approximately the meaning required by the context; the manuscripts
        and the quoting historians offer various phrases meaning "began her", which can only
        be understood on the improbable supposition that it stands for "began her disappearance".

605.   **Pheidias:** the famous sculptor, son of Charmides (*PA* 14149). His "trouble" was an accu-
        sation that he had embezzled some of the materials intended for the great chryselephan-
        tine statue of Athena in the Parthenon. The evidence of the ancient sources (Philochorus
        FGrH 328 D 121; D.S. 12.39, derived from Ephorus; Plut. *Per.* 31) as to the outcome of
        this accusation has been re-examined by J. Mansfeld, *Mnemosyne* 33 (1980) 22 -76, who
        reconstructs the sequence of events thus: the charge was first considered by the Assem-
        bly, who remitted it to a court for trial and meanwhile ordered Pheidias to be held in
        prison; either before or after the trial, he escaped and fled to Elis (where he later had
        charge of the making of the statue of Zeus at Olympia); his flight was taken as an admis-
        sion of guilt, and a decree of immunity was passed in favour of the man who had informed
        against him. Pericles was potentially implicated because he was not only a personal
        friend of Pheidias but also a member of the board of magistrates (*epistatai*) responsible
        for ensuring that the work on the statue of Athena was properly and honestly carried
        out. The idea, however, that this scandal had anything to do with the Megarian decree
        or the origin of the war is an invention of Aristophanes, as is virtually admitted in 615-
        8, when both Trygaeus and the chorus-leader say they had never heard anything of the
        sort before; and indeed the accusations against Pheidias and his flight are almost certainly
        to be dated, with Philochorus, to 438/7, fully six years before the outbreak of war
        (though for another view see C. Triebel-Schubert, *MDAI(A)* 98 [1983] 101-112).

607.   **your hard-biting temper:** angry jurymen (cf. 349) are often said to "bite" the defendants
        who appear before them (*Ach.* 376; *Wasps* 778, 943).

609.   **a Megarian decree:** the reference is to the decree passed by the Athenian Assembly, pro-
        bably in 433/2, whereby citizens of Megara were forbidden to enter "the harbours in
        the Athenian empire and the Attic market" (Thuc. 1.67.4). In the diplomatic exchanges
        of 432/1 the Spartans repeatedly demanded the repeal of the decree, saying that if this
        demand were acceded to there would be no war (Thuc. 1.139.1), but Pericles strongly
        opposed any such concession (cf. Thuc. 1.140-144). As a result the Megarian decree and
        the refusal to repeal it became established in the popular mind as the main cause of the
        great war (cf. 500-2, *Ach.* 515-556, Andoc. 3.8), though Thucydides disagreed. The
        motives, purpose, scope and effects of the decree remain matters of controversy: see
        G.E.M. de Ste Croix, *The Origins of the Peloponnesian War* (London, 1972) 225-289;
        R.P. Legon, *Megara: The Political History of a City-State to 336 B.C.* (Ithaca, 1981)
        210-227; B.R. MacDonald, *Historia* 32 (1983) 385-410.

610.   **fanned up so great a war:** into an otherwise metaphorical sentence is inserted the one word
        "war" to remind us of the reality that lies behind the metaphor.

611.   **those over there and those over here:** the Peloponnesians and the Athenians. Hermes
        speaks throughout as if addressing a purely Athenian audience (619, 621, 641) in Athens
        (626, 638).

612-3. **and as soon as . . . at another jar:** i.e. as soon as the Peloponnesians had begun to ravage
        Attica and the Athenians to make retaliatory raids on the Peloponnese; the reluctance
        of the peasants to go to war, and their determination to take revenge once their lands
        had been devastated (cf. *Ach.*223-233), are here by a "pathetic fallacy" ascribed also
        to their vines and wine-jars. At first sight these lines may seem chronologically out of

160

place, since what follows in 619-624 is an account of events allegedly leading up to the Spartan decision to make war, while in 610-4 the war is already raging; but 610-4 is not so much a part of the narrative as a graphic reminder of the terrible consequences of a decision taken by Pericles from petty personal motives. The "and then" of 619 resumes the narrative not from 614 but from 609. Cf. A.C. Cassio, *RFIC* 110 (1982) 29.

616-8. **connected with Pheidias ... a relation of his:** Greek *prosēkein* has among its meanings "be concerned with" and "be related to": Trygaeus uses the verb in the former sense, the chorus apparently understand it in the latter, since the adjective *sungēnes* which they use means only "related, kindred".

619-620. **you were enraged ... at one another:** this has often been taken to refer to the mutual hostility of Athenians and Spartans, but Cassio *loc. cit.* rightly insists that "you" here, as in the preceding and following clauses, can only mean "you Athenians", and that the reference is therefore to internal political dissensions at Athens, dissensions which according to 606-8 looked as though they might well lead to the fall of Pericles.

621. **they were afraid of the tribute:** in the context (cf. preceding note) this must mean that the allies were afraid that the party strife at Athens would eventually result in an increase in their tribute assessments. Such an increase would of course be likely in the event of war, but it cannot have been war that the allies feared, otherwise they would hardly have reacted by taking steps intended to bring a war on. We are to understand, rather, that they feared lest rivals of Pericles might outbid him for popular support by promising lavish new building programmes, increased payments to jurymen and others, etc., to be financed by exacting increased tribute from the allies.

622. **sought to win over ... among the Laconians:** the implication is that the allied states intended to revolt from Athens, and wished to induce the Spartans to declare war and invade Attica in order to make it as difficult as possible for the Athenians to suppress such a revolt. Such approaches to Sparta had often been made by Athenian allies contemplating rebellion (cf. Thuc. 1.40.5; 1.101. 1-2; 1.114; 3.2.1); but in the period 433-431 we hear only of one such request, from Poteidaea (Thuc. 1.58.1), and Sparta's favourable response to this request may well have had less to do with bribery than with the fact that Poteidaea was a colony of Corinth, one of Sparta's most important allies.

623. **being avaricious:** the same reproach against the Spartans is found in Eur. *Andr.* 451; and an alleged oracle quoted in the Aristotelian *Constitution of the Lacedaemonians* (Arist. fr. 544) predicted that "love of money and nothing else will destroy Sparta". Spartans had little opportunity to be avaricious in dealings with their fellow-citizens; but ever since the Persian wars it had been remarked that "any Spartan who goes abroad conforms neither to the Spartans' own standards of conduct nor to those of the rest of Greece" (Thuc. 1.77.6; cf. Thuc. 1.95, 1.139, Xen. *Lac.* 14).

633. **treacherous towards outsiders:** an accusation even more constantly levelled at the Spartans: cf. 1064-8, 1083, 1086; *Ach.* 308 "men with whom no covenant, no handclasp, no oath stands firm"; *Lys.* 628-9, Eur. *Andr.* 445-453 "lords of the lie ... always found to be saying one thing with your tongue and thinking another", *Supp.* 187; Hdt. 9.54.1. In Thuc. 5.105.4 the Athenians are made to say that while the Spartans behave virtuously towards one another, in their dealings with outsiders "they make it more obvious than any other men we know of that they equate pleasure with honour and self-interest with justice". In the present passage the reference is explicitly restricted to "the greatest men" among the Spartans, exonerating the majority of the population; in other Aristo-

phanic passages where the Spartans are condemned indiscriminately on this score, the speaker is an opponent of the hero or heroine and evidently meant to be regarded as prejudiced.

624. **threw this goddess out**: Peace is thought of as a foreigner resident in Sparta, whom the Spartan leaders "being . . . treacherous towards outsiders" unceremoniously expelled. It was a regular practice at Sparta from time to time to expel aliens from the country in what were called *xenēlasiai* (cf. *Birds* 1012-3; Thuc. 1.144.2; Xen. *Lac.* 14.4; Pl. *Prot.* 342c).

625. **the peasants**: the agricultural population of Laconia is here, most misleadingly, represented as a united social group which can be regarded as parallel with the Attic peasantry who are the subject of 632ff. In reality it consisted of two wholly distinct classes: the Helots, who were serfs of the Spartiate ruling class, and the Perioikoi, inhabitants of the non-Spartiate portions of Laconia, who were free but had no voice in political decisions (hence they are said in 627 to be "totally innocent" of responsibility for the war). Most of the Athenain naval raids on Laconia during the war will have been on Perioikic territory (cf. Thuc. 3.16.2), and Cythera, captured by the Athenians in 424, was inhabited by Perioikoi (Thuc. 4.53.2). On Ar.'s fiction of a unified Laconian peasantry see A.C. Cassio, *RFIC* 110 (1982) 38.

627. **the warships kept coming from here to retaliate**: from 431 to 424 Athenian naval expeditions repeatedly raided and ravaged the coastal regions of Laconia.

627. **devouring the fig-sprays**: the ravages wrought by the Athenian expeditions are described "as if locusts or other winged predators were being spoken of" (van Leeuwen): in reality, of course, rather than being stripped bare the fig-trees will have been cut down.

628. **raven-fig tree**: a variety evidently named from the colour of its fruit.

630. **bushel**: Greek *medimnos*, equivalent to about 52 litres or nearly one and a half English bushels.

632. **and back here**: the manuscripts have "and then", but this would not make it clear that Hermes has passed from describing the misfortunes of the Peloponnesian peasants (625-7) to those of the Attic peasants.

633. **they were being sold out in just the same way**: i.e. the interests of the Attic peasants, like those of the Peloponnesian peasants, were being callously disregarded by corrupt politicians bent on personal gain, in a manner described in detail in 635-647.

634-5. **because they were . . . to the orators**: the country people, cut off as they were from their land, their fruit trees and their accustomed way of life, had no alternative but to rely on the promises of politicians to maintain them and promote their interests.

634. **raisins**: strictly "grape-husks", what remains of a grape when the juice has been completely pressed out.

636. **groats**: see on 477.

637. **bawlings**: a surprise for "pitchforks" or the like; for "expel with a pitchfork" = "expel brutally and ignominiously" cf. Lucian, *Timon* 12; Catullus 105.2; Cicero *Ad Att.* 16.2. 4; Horace *Ep.* 1.10.24. The word "bawlings" hints at the loud-voiced oratory of Cleon (see on 314), whose opposition to peace is described and analysed in *Knights* 792-809 in terms rather similar to those of the present passage.

638. **she repeatedly appeared of her own accord**: the reference is to the three Spartan attempts to make peace after the Pylos-Sphacteria campaign (cf. 665-7): the story has therefore now moved forward to the period 425-424.

638. **because she pined for this land**: cf. Aesch. *Eum.* 851-2 (Athena to the Furies) "if you go to a foreign country, you will long for this land like lovers". Even a goddess could find no lovelier place to dwell than Attica.

639. **took to shaking up . . . among the allies**: the allegation is that Cleon and his associates prosecuted rich citizens of the allied states on false charges of treason (cf. *Knights* 326, 1408; *Wasps* 281-9), partly in order to fill the state treasury with the victims' confiscated property so that the money would be available for distribution to their own supporters in the form of jury-pay (cf. *Knights* 1359-60), but mainly in order to frighten others, who might be in danger of similar prosecutions, into purchasing immunity by substantial bribes (644-6; cf. *Knights* 66-68, 775, 802, *Wasps* 669-671, 971-2).

640. **"he's a supporter of Brasidas"**: an accusation that was often on the lips of Cleon and his followers in 423/2 (cf. *Wasps* 288 "one of those who betrayed the Thracian Coast", 473-5 "you enemy of the people . . . who consorts with Brasidas").

642. **the city was all pale, it sat in fear**: the meaning seems to be that the politicians had terrified the people with tales of a vast conspiracy against them among the allied states, directed by Brasidas, and aimed at the destruction of the Athenian empire and Athenian democracy; in *Wasps* any opponent of Cleon is seen by the chorus as an anti-democrat and would-be tyrant (*Wasps* 342-5, 408-419, 463-507). For pallor as an outward sign of terror cf. *Lys.* 1140, *Frogs* 307.

643. **any scraps of slander that were thrown to it**: the Greek has a pun on *diaballein* "slander" and *paraballein* or *proballein* "throw food to an animal", the Athenian people being depicted as a pack of hungry dogs (cf. 641).

644. **the foreigners**: the rich citizens of the allied states.

645. **to stuff shut . . . who were doing it**: the metaphor whereby buying a man's silence is called "stuffing his mouth with money" appears again in *Wealth* 379; it gains added point in Greek from the fact that it was common to carry money in one's mouth (cf. *Wasps* 791-6, *Birds* 502-3, *Eccl.* 818).

646. **them**: the Athenian politicians.

648. **a leather-seller**: Cleon (see on 270).

650. **he's yours**: Hermes was often spoken of as an underworld deity (e.g. Aesch. *Pers.* 629, *Cho.* 1, 124, 727; Soph. *El.* 111), especially with reference to his function of conducting departed souls to Hades (*Odyssey* 24.1-10; Soph. *Aj.* 832).

651-6. **so whatever you say . . . one of your own**: "Trygaeus, under pretence of forbidding Hermes to revile the dead, takes the opportunity of doing it himself to his heart's content" (Rogers).

654. **an agitator and a trouble-maker**: the two Greek nouns used here are derived from the verb *kukān* (see on 270) and its synonym *tarattein*, which Ar. had likewise often used to describe Cleon's activities (*Knights* 66, 247, 309, 431, 692, 867; *Wasps* 1285).

662. **shield-band-hating**: the armband (*porpāx*) of a shield was a detachable bronze strip, usually running from edge to edge of the shield's inner face, through which the bearer passed his left arm: see A.M. Snodgrass, *Arms and Armour of the Greeks* (London, 1967) 53 and plate 18. A shield without its band could not be used (cf. Critias fr. 37 D-K) and hence a hater of war may be comically described as a hater of shield-bands.

665. **the events at Pylos**: see on 219.

665. **she came here of her own accord**: after their defeat on Sphacteria the Spartans repeatedly sent embassies to Athens in the hope of making peace, regaining Pylos, and securing the

release of the Spartans held prisoner (Thuc. 4.41.3-4).

666.   **a hamper full of treaties**: "of treaties" (*spondōn*) is a surprise for "of treats, of good things" (*agathōn*) or the like.

667.   **three times**: Thucydides says more vaguely "several times". On one of these occasions the Milesian-born Athenian politician Archeptolemus spoke in support of the Spartan proposals but was routed by Cleon (*Knights* 794-6).

669.   **our brains were in our shoe-leather**: the phrase "to have your brains in your heels instead of your head" (cf. [Dem.] 7.45) meant "to be extremely stupid"; here it is adapted to incorporate an allusion to Cleon's connection with the leather trade, so that the meaning becomes in effect "we stupidly followed the advice of Cleon".

671.   **was**: the past tense probably implies "while the war was on"; it is dropped in favour of the present once the joke about Cleonymus is finished.

673.   **Cleonymus**: see on 446.

678.   **deposititious**: Greek *apobolimaios* "inclined to throw away", a word coined by Ar. for the sake of a pun on *hupobolimaios* "supposititious child, changeling" and of referring yet again, but in an original manner, to the occasion when Cleonymus threw away his shield.

680.   **the rock on the Pnyx**: the hill of the Pnyx, in the west of the city close to the walls, was the meeting place of the Athenian Assembly; the "rock" (so called also in *Knights* 956 and *Eccl.* 87) is the speaker's platform (*bēma*). See Travlos 466-476 and H.A. Thompson, *Hesperia* Suppl. 19 (1982) 133-147.

681.   **Hyperbolus** (*PA* 13910), son of Antiphanes, of the deme Perithoidae, entered politics at an early age (Cratinus fr. 262K = 283K-A; Eupolis fr. 238) in the middle 420s, at first as a prosecutor in the courts (*Ach.* 846-7, *Wasps* 1007) but before long also as a speaker in the Assembly (*Knights* 1303-15). After Cleon's death he became not only the leading radical politican but also the favourite victim of comic satire (cf. *Clouds* 551-8, written for the revised version of the play some time after 420); to say, however, that he dominated the Assembly in early 421 is unlikely to be an objective assessment (Thuc. 5.16.1 indicates rather that Nicias was the most influential politician at this time – but Ar. did not want to satirize Nicias). Probably in spring 416 (cf. Andrews on Thuc. 8.73.3) Hyperbolus was banished by ostracism, as the result of a temporary coalition between Nicias and Alcibiades (Plut. *Nic.* 11; *Alc.* 13); in 411 he was murdered by an oligarchic group at Samos.

682.   **Where are you turning your head?** it is not clear how it was contrived that the statue of Peace should seem to turn away of its own accord as if alive; possibly, as is suggested by S. Halliwell, *Personal Jokes in Aristophanes* (Diss. Oxford 1980) 266-7, the actor playing Hermes, being close to the statue, was in a position to move its head (by pulling a concealed string? his action must not be detectable by the audience).

684.   **chosen**: lit. "inscribed for themselves, registered". At Athens every resident alien had to register the name of an Athenian citizen as his *prostatēs* (patron, sponsor), and he would wish if possible to choose a man of good standing and reputation; but *prostatēs* also meant "political leader" (especially in the phrase *prostatēs tou dēmou* "champion of the people, leading radical politician": cf. *Knights* 1128, Thuc. 4.66.2, Arist. *Ath.Pol.* 28.1-3) and here Ar. plays on the two senses of the word. On resident aliens and their *prostatai* see D. Whitehead, *The Ideology of the Athenian Metic* (Cambridge, 1977) 89-92.

685.   **we're not going to have any more to do with him**: yet in 688-692 the likely effects on the city of Hyperbolus' leadership are discussed in the future tense. Trygaeus must there-

164

fore mean here that the Athenians will look to Hyperbolus as their leader only "for the time being" (687) and will discard him as soon as the temporary need for his services has passed.

687. **have wrapped themselves in this man:** as if Hyperbolus were a piece of cloth, which a man robbed of his clothes might use as an emergency garment; just so that the Athenian people, feeling "naked" and vulnerable after losing their "guardian" Cleon, have turned to Hyperbolus as a temporary substitute.

690. **he happens to be a lamp-maker:** cf. *Knights* 739, 1315; *Clouds* 1065. As in the case of Cleon the "tanner" or "leather-seller", it is impossible to determine the real nature of Hyperbolus' connection, if any, with this banausic occupation.

694. **then:** at the oubreak of war, when Peace left Athens.

697. **Simonides** of Ceos (c.556-468) was one of the greatest of Greek lyric and epigrammatic poets. Already in his lifetime he had a reputation for avarice (cf. Xenophanes fr. 21 D-K); on the subsequent development of this tradition, and the many anecdotes it spawned, see J. Bell, *QUCC* 28 (1978) 29-86 and M.R. Lefkowitz, *The Lives of the Greek Poets*(London, 1981) 50-53.

698. **he's old and decayed:** in 421 Sophocles was about seventy-five.

699. **"for profit's sake he'd go to sea upon a mat":** seemingly a blend of two lines from different plays by Euripides (fr. 397, from *Thyestes*; fr. 566.2, from *Oeneus*). The suggestion here that Sophocles would do anything for money is out of keeping with all our other information about him, and has never been satisfactorily explained. S. Halliwell, *LCM* 7 (1982) 153, has suggested a connection with the story told in the ancient *Life of Sophocles* 12 of how Sophocles claimed the reward of a talent which had been offered for information leading to the recovery of a gold crown stolen from the Acropolis, after its whereabouts had been revealed to him in a dream; but since he is said to have used the money to build a shrine of Heracles, the affair would hardly justify Trygaeus' statement. Moreover the phrase "go to sea upon a mat" carries a strong suggestion of *taking risks* to make money. Had Sophocles perhaps been involved in a hazardous and unsuccessful business venture?

700. **Cratinus** (*PA* 8755), son of Callimedes, was the leading comic dramatist of the generation before Ar., winning nine victories between 453 and 423. In Ar.'s early plays (*Ach.* 848-853, 1173; *Knights* 400, 531-4) he is contemptuously portrayed as a played-out, drunken, incontinent, dirty old man, though it is admitted (*Knights* 526-530, 535-6) that he had *formerly* gained and deserved great success. In *Frogs* 357, however, long after his death, he is referred to as almost a tutelary god of comedy.

700-1. **he died when the Laconians invaded:** this cannot be literally true, since Cratinus was alive in 423 (when he was victorious at the City Dionysia, defeating Ar.'s *Clouds*) and there had been no Spartan invasion of Attica since 425. Hence it has been widely supposed that Cratinus had not died at all, and that Ar. intended these words to be taken as implying that he had been "dead" *as an artist* ever since 431. Against this it should be noted (i) that Cratinus' fragments give no indication that he remained active after 423, (ii) that the tone of the present passage is far friendlier than those in *Acharnians* and *Knights* cited in the previous note, and the statement that Cratinus is "a fine artist" is allowed to remain uncontradicted — altogether not the way one would expect Ar. to speak of a living rival (contrast *Clouds* 551-560, *Frogs* 1-18). Probably Cratinus died in 423/2, and Ar. is here antedating his death in order to make the manner and cause of it

165

appropriate both to Cratinus' own character and to themes of the present play (wine and war).

704. **a jar full of wine being smashed**: cf. 613, *Ach*. 979-987. Cratinus' love of wine was notorious; in 423 he made it the subject of, and himself a character in, his successful comedy *The Wine-flask*.

705. **after that experience**: lit. "with the result that".

706. **on that understanding**: that you will never again let Peace depart.

708. **grapes**: a surprise for "children".

711. **to indulge in**: sexually, he means; but in the Greek the verb (whose literal meaning is "thrust up") comes last in the sentence and is a surprise substitute for "eat freely of, stuff myself with" or the like, and Hermes accordingly answers as if he had been asked about the possible effects of heavy fruit-eating on the digestion!

712. **an infusion of pennyroyal**: pennyroyal (*Mentha pulegium*) was much used as a herbal remedy for digestive and other disorders; see Pliny *NH* 20.152-5.

714. **the Council, whom she used to belong to**: Showtime (Theoria) is to be given back to the Council "because the Council used to send out the state delegations (*theōriai*)": so the scholia, probably rightly (cf. Dem. 19.128). On the two senses of *theōriā* see on 523.

716-7. **how much soup . . . you'll be eating**: the surface meaning is that in honour of the good news that peace has been restored, a three-day celebration will be held, with sacrifices and feasting on a large scale (cf. *Knights* 652-663) in which the councillors will take a prominent and privileged part; but *zōmos* "soup" can also mean "vaginal secretion" (cf. 885), and *kreas* "meat, flesh" can denote the genitals of either sex (cf. *Ach*. 795), so that Trygaeus is also promising the councillors the opportunity to practise unlimited cunnilingus upon Showtime (see Henderson 144, 145, 186).

720. **O beetle, homeward, homeward let us fly**: the repetition of *oikade* "homeward" suggests that this line is modelled on (probably a parody of) some poetic original, but this original cannot be identified.

722. **"Yoked to the car of Zeus, it bears the lightning"**: a quotation from Euripides' *Bellerophon* (fr. 312), where it presumably referred to Pegasus.

723. **where's the poor creature going to get food from?**: it is assumed that gods do not defaecate.

724. **Ganymede**, a Trojan prince, son of Tros (*Iliad* 20.231-2) or Laomedon (*Little Iliad* fr. 6 Allen) and "the most beautiful of mortal men", was taken up into heaven to be Zeus' cupbearer and catamite (Latin *catamitus* is derived, via Etruscan, from Ganymede's name).

724. **ambrosia**: the food of the gods, which they apprently could digest without residue but Ganymede could not.

726. **right past the goddess**: since, on the stage-arrangements here assumed, Peace is standing on the *ekkyklēma* just outside the central portal, Hermes must be directing the travellers through that portal (cf. Dover 135).

729-818. Parabasis, consisting of: prelude, 729-733; leader's speech, 734-774 (765-774 forming a *pnīgos*); strophe, 775-795; antistrophe, 796-818. The usual epirrhema and antepirrhema are omitted.

729-733. Metre: four anapaestic tetrameters and a trochaic tetrameter (for the change of rhythm cf. *Wasps* 1009-14).

729. **Go, and good luck to you**: formulaic at the start of a parabasis (*Knights* 498; *Clouds* 510, 1113; cf. *Ach*. 1143).

730. **the attendants:** presumably the same stage-hands who gave them the implements between 552 and 563.

733. **"the path of words that is ours, and all that is in our minds":** Ar. elsewhere uses phrases like "path of words" only in lyrics and oracles (*Knights* 1015, *Birds* 1374, *Frogs* 897), and it may well be that this line is a quotation or parody of an unknown poetic source.

734-774. Metre: anapaestic tetrameters, ending (from 765) with a *pnīgos*.

734-5. **Really the stewards . . . before the audience:** cf. *Ach.* 628-9 "Ever since our producer has had charge of comic choruses, he has never come forward to the audience to say that he is clever." In fact Ar. praises himself in the parabasis of each of his five earliest surviving plays.

734. **the stewards:** Greek *tous rhabdoukhous* "the rod-bearers", evidently officials whose function was to keep order in the theatre and who carried rods for this purpose.

735. **the anapaests:** Ar.'s usual term for the first long speech by the chorus-leader to the audience in a parabasis, which was normally, as here, in anapaestic metre (cf. *Ach.* 627, *Knights* 504, *Birds* 684).

736. **if it is proper . . . and is the best:** adapted, according to the scholia, from an elegiac poem by Simonides (fr. eleg. 9 West) written in honour of an Athenian or of the Athenian people.

736. **daughter of Zeus:** i.e. "Muse" as in *Odyssey* 1.10.

737. **comic producer:** as in *Ach.* 628ff the words *didaskalos* "producer" and *poiētēs* "poet" are used interchangeably to denote the same person.

740. **making fun of rags and waging war on lice:** i.e. making fun of poor people for being squalid and verminous; Ar. in contrast (he says) satirizes not "the little man or woman" but "the greatest monsters" (751-2). As often, Ar.'s criticism of his rivals is disingenuous; he himself quite frequently invites his audience to laugh at someone's poverty (e.g. *Ach.* 857-9, *Knights* 1268-73, *Wasps* 1267-74, *Thesm.* 948-952).

741. **those Heracleses who kneaded dough or went hungry:** "Heracles being cheated of his dinner" (*Wasps* 60) was a stock figure of the comic stage, criticized also by Cratinus (fr. 308 Kock = 346 K-A). Ar. however was to create just such a Heracles himself in *Birds* 1574-1692. We do not know of a comedy in which Heracles "kneaded dough", but a dramatist might well have shown him engaged in this servile activity (cf. 1-18) during one of his periods of enslavement: Euripides in his satyr-play *Syleus* depicted Heracles as a slave working in a vineyard (cf. *Prolegomena* XI.a.ii.62-70 Koster).

743-742. **the slaves who were always running away from someone:** the reference is to the stock figure of comedy whom later Roman commentators called the *servus currens*, of whom our best Greek example is Pyrrhias fleeing from Cnemon in Men. *Dysk.* 81-87. Ar. has a similar scene in *Ach.* 175-203, though the fleeing character there is not a slave; cf. also *Wasps* 1292ff where Xanthias is evidently fleeing from his drunken old master.

742. **deceiving someone:** the *servus callidus* of the Romans; in Greek comedy compare e.g. Daos' deception of Smicrines in Menander's *Aspis* and the two deceptions, seemingly by a slave Syrus, which gave his *Dis Exapaton* its name. Our passage shows that the *servus callidus* as a type goes back to Old Comedy, but he does not appear in the surviving plays of Ar.

742/745. **getting beaten . . . make fun of his bruises:** cf. in general terms *Knights* 1-10, where however *both* slaves have just had a beating.

[744]. This line ("whom they always brought out howling, and that for this purpose") is a doublet

167

of 742 ("who were always . . . just in order"); either by itself would make good sense, but not both together. Evidently the two lines were originally alternatives to one another, both of which were mistakenly retained in the text. Though similar in content, the two lines differ so greatly in expression that it is hard to suppose the doublet originated in the process of transmission; it is perhaps preferable to assume that Ar. originally wrote 744 and later (in revising his script either before or after production) inserted 742 in its place, without however obliterating the original line, which was therefore retained by the copyists. Such a history might also account for the misplacement of 742 in the manuscrips (including Π11 of the third century A.D.), if in the author's autograph it was written out of place (e.g. at the top or bottom of a column) with a mark (which might be misinterpreted) to show where it belonged in the text. I assume that 744 was the first draft and 742 the improved version, because 744 is much the weaker and flabbier: *kai toutous* "and that" is mere padding, while the subject of *exēgon* "they brought out" has to be understood from 739, four or five lines back. On author's variants in Ar. see K.J. Dover *ICS* 2 (1977) 150-6.

745.   **his bruises:** the change from the plural "slaves" (743) to the singular "his" is made because the speaker, having previously spoken in a general way about stock characters and scenes, is now imagining one specific scene with two slaves on stage, one of whom has been beaten. For the change of number within a sentence cf. *Wasps* 564-5.

746.   **bristle-whip:** Greek *hustrikhis* (lit. "porcupine"), according to the scholia a whip whose lash was made of pig-bristles. In *Frogs* 619 flogging with a *hustrikhis* is mentioned as a form of torture.

747.   **in great strength:** lit. "with a large army", continuing the military metaphor begun by "invaded".

747.   **laid waste:** lit. "tree-felled" like the Peloponnesian invaders of Attica (cf. previous note).

749.   **for us:** i.e. for the performers of comedy (cf. *Birds* 789); but Blaydes' conjecture "for you" is tempting, since in parabases it is regular to praise the poet for the benefits he has conferred *on the audience* (cf. 759-761, *Ach.* 633-658, *Wasps* 1017, 1037-43).

749.   **built it up to towering dimensions:** in *Frogs* 1004 similar language is used of Aeschylus' contribution to the art of tragedy.

752-760.   is repeated, with a few changes, from *Wasps* 1030-7.

752.   **with a spirit like that of Heracles:** Heracles was the greatest legendary destroyer of monsters. In its new context the phrase may imply a contrast with the paltry, unworthy Heracles-figures created by other dramatists (741): Ar. represents far better the true spirit of the great hero.

753.   **striding through:** one does not stride through "smells" or "menaces", but the image is of a hero traversing marsh and mire, streams and snows, to fulfil his mission of cleansing Greece of evil monsters.

753.   **leather:** this word identifies the principal "monster" as Cleon (cf. 270).

753.   **the menaces of a muckraker's rage:** lit. "muddy-angered menaces": Cleon is elsewhere called a "mud-churner" (*Knights* 308, 864-7) and the torrents of his abusive oratory are likened to a filthy stream (*Ach.* 380-2). It is easy to see how this rather difficult metaphor, presupposing acquaintance with earlier comic characterizations of Cleon, might have been corrupted into the ancient variant known to us from the scholia, in which "muddy-" is replaced by "barbarian-" with reference to the presentation of Cleon in *Knights* as a barbarian slave; the reverse corruption would be much harder to

account for. The reading of the mss. should therefore be retained.

754. **I fought**: the sudden change from third to first person has been thought surprising, but there is a similar shift in *Ach.* 660. In the parallel passage in *Wasps* Ar. is spoken of in the third person throughout, with the result that an important change of subject between 1034-5 (which are about the Cleon-monster) and 1036-7 (which are about Ar.) is not marked by any clear grammatical signal. Thus Ar. may have shifted to the first person in *Peace* for the sake of greater clarity.

754. **the Jag-toothed One**: Cleon is made to use this canine epithet of himself in *Knights* 1017. There may well be an allusion to Cerberus (see on 313) whom Heracles carried off from the underworld.

755-8. The description here of the Cleon-monster is based partly on Cerberus, who in Hesiod (*Thg.* 311-2) had fifty heads and a voice like brass, in Pindar (fr. 249b) a hundred heads, and whom Horace (*Carm.* 3. 11.17-18) describes as having a hundred snakes around his head, but mainly on another mythological monster, Typhoeus, son of Earth and Tartarus, who is thus described by Hes. *Thg.* 824-830: "From his shoulders rose a hundred snake-heads . . . licking with their dark tongues; from his eyes . . . flashed fire, and fire blazed from all his heads as he glanced; and in all his terrible heads there were voices that sent forth monstrous sounds of every kind." According to Hesiod (ib. 837) he was laid low by Zeus with a thunderbolt, but in another account (cf. Eur. *HF* 1271-2) his defeat was ascribed to Heracles. Cleon is compared to Typhoeus (or Typhos) in *Knights* 511.

755. **like those of the Bitch-star**: the Dog-star (Sirius) began to rise before the sun in late July, and its rays were believed to cause the fevers that attacked men in the hottest part of summer: cf. *Iliad* 22.31; Hes. *Works* 586-8; Archilochus fr. 107. Hence "rays like those of the Dog-star" would mean "deadly rays"; but for *Kunos* "of the Dog-star" Ar. substitutes *Kunnēs* "of Cynna", a well-known courtesan (cf. *Knights* 765), thus suggesting that Cleon deserved to be no better esteemed than a prostitute (for this estimate of Cleon's worth cf. *Knights* 1400-3).

756. **accursed flatterers**: in Ar. the most notable of these alleged lickspittles of Cleon is Theorus (*Wasps* 42-46, 419, 1236-42); Cleonymus too (for whom see on 446) is called *Kolakōn-umos* "Flatter-onymus" in *Wasps* 592.

757. **the voice of a torrent**: cf. on 314; a similar comparison is made in *Ach.* 381 and *Knights* 137.

757. **in destructive spate**: lit. "which had given birth to destruction".

758. **the smell of a seal**: regarded as nauseating (cf. *Odyssey* 4.435-443).

758. **a Lamia**: Lamia was an ogress or bogy who ate children (cf. Duris, *FGrH* 76 F 17; D.S. 20.41; and the scholia here). Since Lamia is elsewhere always female, "the balls of a Lamia" may mean "no balls at all", in which case this short phrase would be making three separate insinuations about Cleon — that he was bloodthirsty, that he was sexless, and that his nether regions were dirty.

760. **the islands**: cf. on 298. In the corresponding passage in *Wasps* there is no mention of the subject states, and Ar. seems to have added a reference to them because many of their citizens would be present at the City Dionysia to see *Peace* (whereas at the Lenaea, at which *Wasps* was produced, the audience contained few or no visitors from outside Attica). For Cleon's alleged harassment of subject states and their citizens, see the passages cited on 639.

169

761. **pay your debt of gratitude**: by audibly demonstrating your appreciation of the present play, thereby putting pressure on the judges to award it first prize.

762-4. **after all . . . the way it should be**: the point seems to be "you need not be deterred from supporting me by any fear that if I win the competition I may then make a nuisance of myself".

762-3. **I didn't tour . . . making passes at boys**: a near-repetition of *Wasps* 1025. The wrestling-school appears to have been a common place for making homosexual pick-ups; see K.J. Dover, *Greek Homosexuality* (London, 1978) 54-55.

763. **packed up my gear and went on my way**: if this is to be taken literally, it implies that Ar.'s home was outside Attica, and confirms the interprestation of *Ach.* 652-4 according to which he lived on Aegina; but the expression may be metaphorical, Ar. likening himself to an itinerant entertainer who must not overstay his welcome in any one place if he wants to make a good living.

766. **both the men and the boys**: i.e. the whole audience (cf. 50-53).

767. **all bald men**: for Ar.'s baldness cf. *Knights* 550, *Clouds* 545, and Eupolis fr. 78.

772. **dessert**: beans, chickpeas, figs, etc., eaten as an accompaniment to the wine at a symposium: cf. 1136-7, *Eccl.* 44-45, *Wealth* 798, Pl. *Rep.* 2.372c.

775-796 = 797-818 Metre: at first essentially dactylo-epitrite, based on the units $-\cup\cup-\cup\cup-$ and $-\cup-$; then by the lengthening of one syllable the first of these units becomes the aristophanean $-\cup\cup-\cup--$ (785-7 = 807-9), after which abuse is heaped on the families of Carcinus and Morsimus in dactylic metre (788-794 = 810-6) until finally the dactylo-epitrite rhythm is briefly revived and the song ends with an ithyphallic ($-\cup-\cup--$) as does another Aristophanic dactylo-epitrite composition, *Knights* 1264-73 = 1290-9. See Dale [2] 182-3.

775-780. **O Muse . . . the festivities of the blest**: quoted or adapted, according to the scholia (on 775 and 797), from the *Oresteia* of Stesichorus (fr. 33 Page).

782. **Carcinus** (*PA* 8254; *TrGF* 21), son of Xenotimus of the deme Thoricus, was a tragic dramatist, active since at least 446 when he won first prize at the City Dionysia (*IG* ii^2 2318.81); he had also held public office as one of the generals in 432/1 (Thuc. 2.23.2; *IG* i^{3}365. 30-40).

784. **his children**: Carcinus apparently had four sons (Pherecrates fr. 14), at least three of whom were well known to the public in 422/1: these three were all of small stature (790, *Wasps* 1513, Pherecrates fr. 14) and were talented dancers. Two of them also achieved some distinction in other ways. Xenotimus (*PA* 11269), probably the eldest, appears in the 390s as a shipowner trading to the Crimea and a friend of the local king (Isocr. 17.52). Xenocles (*PA* 11222; *TrGF* 33) was the youngest of the three (*Wasps* 1510-1) and was a tragic dramatist: he is condemned by Ar. as a bad poet (*Thesm.* 169, *Frogs* 86), but he defeated Euripides' *Trojan Women* and its companion plays in 415 (Aelian *VH* 2.8). He and his brothers seem also to have taken some part in public life, as their father did (cf. *Thesm.* 440-2, Pherecrates fr. 14). In *Wasps* 1500-37 they are brought on stage as dancing crabs (a play on the name Carcinus which means "Crab"). On the family see Davies 283-5.

788. **home-bred quails**: quails were commonly domesticated and kept as pets (cf. *Birds* 707; Pl. *Lys.* 211e) and for the gambling sports of quail-fighting and quail-tapping (cf. *Birds* 1297-9; Eupolis fr. 250; Plut. *Ant.* 33.4; J. Pollard, *Birds in Greek Life and Myth* [London, 1977] 108). The sons of Carcinus are compared to quails because of their diminutive size (similarly in *Wasps* 1513 they are compared to wrens), and to *home-bred* quails

perhaps, as Rogers suggests, because of a belief that quails reared in captivity were less spirited and pugnacious, and therefore less valuable, than those captured in the wild.

789. **with hedgehogs' necks:** i.e. with little or no distinguishable neck separating head from shoulders; for this interpretation of the unique word *guliaukhenas* see E.K. Borthwick, *CQ* 18 (1968) 50.

790-1. **snippets of dung-balls:** i.e. tiny, offensive, and worthless.

791. **hunters after gimmicks:** Greek *mēkhanodīphās.* The scholia take the reference to be to the use of theatrical machinery for spectacular effects in Xenocles' plays, but this would not be relevant to the other two brothers, and the meaning may rather be that the three were constantly seeking to contrive strikingly novel dance-figures.

792-6. **for their father . . . by a ferret:** this difficult passage, alluding presumably to an event well-known to the audience but not to us, has been well elucidated by S. Halliwell, *Personal Jokes in Aristophanes* (Diss. Oxford 1980) 164. Carcinus had unexpectedly been awarded a chorus for one of the dramatic festivals (perhaps at rather short notice) and had failed to complete all his plays in the time available; he is maliciously supposed to have offered (to the magistrate in charge of the festival?) the explanation regularly given when meat disappeared from the household stores (but in this case absurd) that "it must be the ferret's fault". Perhaps, too, there is an insinuation that a play that could be killed by a ferret must in any case have been something of a *ridiculus mus.* The scholia offer several unsatisfactory interpretations, one of which is that there is an allusion to a play by Carcinus called *Mice*; but such a title would be plausible only for a comedy, not a tragedy or a satyr-play, and Carcinus was not a comic dramatist.

795. **he'd . . . got a booking for:** lit. "he . . . had". A dramatist who was given the right to produce plays at a forthcoming dramatic festival was said to "have a chorus" for that festival (cf. 808); here apparently the phrase "have a play" is used with the same meaning.

796. **a ferret:** Greeks often kept polecats in their homes to catch mice (cf. *Wasps* 1182), but they were notoriously thievish animals, much given to stealing meat (1151; *Wasps* 363; *Thesm.* 558-9).

797-802. **Such songs as these . . . her songs of spring:** again adapted from Stesichorus' *Oresteia* (fr. 34 and 35 Page).

800-2. **the perching swallow . . . with her voice:** or, with Bergk, "the swallow . . . with joyful voice"; but the transmitted text is supported by the parallel of *Frogs* 682, in a song that both verbally and metrically contains other echoes of this one.

803. **Morsimus** (*PA* 10416; *TrGF* 29) was son of Philocles the tragic poet and great-nephew of Aeschylus; he himself was not only a tragic poet but also an eye-doctor (Ar. fr. 704 Kock = 723 K-A; schol. *Frogs* 151). Ar. regards him as a very bad poet. to be a member of his chorus is a ghastly fate (*Knights* 401) and to copy out a speech from one of his plays is a sin deserving eternal damnation (*Frogs* 151).

803. **does not get a chorus:** see on 795. The joy of the City Dionysia is all the greater if Morsimus and Melanthius are not producing plays at it.

804. **Melanthius** (*PA* 9767; *TrGF* 23) was another tragic dramatist, who is mentioned several times in comedy between about 430 and 400, often with reference to his love of expensive fish and other culinary delicacies (cf. 1009-15; Pherecrates fr. 139; Eupolis fr. 41; Archippus fr. 28); he was also satirized as a passive homosexual (Eupolis fr. 164), as a sufferer from a skin disease (*Birds* 150-1), and as a "babbler", i.e. probably a writer of drivel (Plato com. fr. 132). He may well have competed at the City Dionysia of 422,

since he was mentioned in at least three comedies produced in 421 (cf. Eupolis fr. 164; Leucon fr. 2). The present passage makes it probable, but not certain, that he was a brother of Morsimus (see on 807-9). The Melanthius who wrote elegiac poetry in honour of Cimon (Plut. *Cim.* 4.1, 4.7, 4.9) is likely in any case to be a different person, since he will certainly have been writing before 449 and probably before 462: see A. Dihle, *RhM* 119 (1976) 144-6.

804-6.   **he whose . . . shrilling out:** Melanthius was either acting in one of his own or his brother's plays, or else demonstrating to the performers at a reherarsal how he wished a particular speech or song to be delivered.

807-9.   **his brother:** the scholia seem to take it for granted that this brother of Melanthius is *not* to be identified with Morsimus. If they are right, however, Morsimus surprisingly disappears from the song after a single mention and escapes the colourful insults of 810-4, while the brother of Melanthius becomes completely unidentifiable. It is preferable to assume that Melanthius and Morsimus were indeed brothers; this results in a close balance between strophe and antistrophe, each being directed against the members of one particular theatrical family.

810.   **Gorgons:** i.e. ugly and fearsome fiends.

811.   **skate-eyeing Harpies:** the Harpies were the hideous winged beings (represented in art as birds with women's faces) who persecuted the Thracian king Phineus by snatching food from his table or even from his mouth (Aesch. fr. 258N = 432M); in Aesch. *Eum.* 48-51, as here, they are mentioned alongside the Gorgons. Melanthius and his brother too are hideous food-snatchers, looking out for and seizing the best skate in the fish-market; for skate as a favoured delicacy cf. *Wasps* 510, Ar. fr. 318 Kock = 333 K-A.

812.   **scarecrones:** Greek *grāosobai* "scarers away of old women"; the idea may be that Melanthius and his brother are so horrifically ugly that even the tough old women who keep stalls in the market (cf. *Wasps* 1388-1414, *Lys.* 456-460, *Wealth* 426-8) are terrified at the sight of them; cf. *Lys.* 563-4 where a woman selling figs is frightened at the sight of an armed Thracian soldier who thereby gets an opportunity to steal and eat some of her stock.

813.   **with goat-scented armpits:** cf. *Ach.* 852-3 "his armpits smelling vilely of his Goatlandish father".

820.   **I'm thoroughly sore in the legs:** Trygaeus flew up to heaven, but he has had to walk all the way back!

824.   **SLAVE:** in the remainder of the play only one slave has a speaking part, and for convenience he will be designated simply as "Slave", though he may very well be the same person (i.e. have the same mask and costume) as the Second Slave of 1-149.

824.   **well, so someone's told me:** a silly answer to a silly question.

829.   **dithyrambic composers:** lit. "dithyrambic producers" (see on 737). The dithyramb was a choral performance of song and dance, originally in honour of Dionysus; at the City Dionysia there were competitions in dithyramb for choruses of boys and men. Dithyrambic poets had a reputation for nebulous grandiloquence, and Ar. often mocks them as vaporous creatures whose natural home is up among the clouds: cf. *Clouds* 333-9, *Birds* 1372-1409.

830.   **flitting about collecting ideas:** we seem to have here a blend of the notion of the poet as a bird, a singer of winged songs (e.g. Pind. *Nem.* 3.80-83; Bacchyl. 3.96-98; Pratinas fr. 1.5 Page) with that of the poet as a bee flitting from flower to flower collecting the honey

of the Muses (e.g. *Birds* 748-752; Pind. *Pyth.* 10.53-54; Pl. *Ion* 534a-b). See Taillardat 430-3.

831. **air-haunting-swiftly-soaring:** Greek *endiāeriaurinēkhetous*, a vast compound adjective of a kind allegedly typical of dithyramb. Its components seem to be *endiān* "haunt (a place)" (cf. *Endiagros* "she who haunts the wild", an epithet of Artemis), *āerios* "of the air", *auri-* "swiftly" (cf. *auribatās* "swiftly striding", Aesch. fr. 280N = 207M), and *nēkhes-thai* "swim, float, glide" (cf. *āeronēkheis* "floating in the air" in an alleged quotation of dithyramb at *Clouds* 337). The adjective might be suitably applied e.g. to high-flying birds.

832-3. **we die:** lit. "one dies".

832 -3. **we become stars in the sky:** this popular belief (not otherwise attested at so early a date) seems to combine two ideas well known in other literature. (1) That certain star-groups and constellations were originally men, women or animals to whom the gods had granted immortality is a belief that can be traced back to the very beginning of Greek literature; it is implicit in the very name of the constellation Orion (*Odyssey* 5,274; Hes. *Works* 598) and is attested in the fifth century for at least the Pleiades and Hyades (Pherecydes *FGrH* 3 F 90; Hellanicus *FGrH* 4 F 19) and probably also for Virgo (Hellanicus, cited by schol. Aratus 97; see D. Ambaglio, *Athenaeum* 62 [1984] 657). (2) In Euripides (e.g. *Suppl.* 532-6, *Helen* 1013-6) and also in some fifth-century epitaphs (e.g. *IG* i² 945 945) there appears the notion that at death the soul escapes to rejoin the aether whence it originally came: see Kannicht on *Helen* 1013-6.

835. **Ion of Chios:** an extremely versatile writer, who composed poetry and prose in a dozen different genres; he was born about 480, visited Athens many times from the 460s to the 420s, and presumably died not long before *Peace* was produced. He was probably also a man of considerable political influence in his own island, where his son Tydeus later became leader of the pro-Athenian party and was put to death on that account by the Spartans in 412 (Thuc. 8.38.3). See F. Jacoby, *CQ* 41 (1947) 1-17, and H.B. Mattingly in K.H. Kinzl (ed.) *Greece and the Eastern Mediterranean in Ancient History and Prehistory: Studies presented to Fritz Schachermeyr* . . . (Berlin, 1977) 236-9.

836. **The Star of Dawning:** the reference is to a dithyramb by Ion that began "We have awaited the star of dawning that ranges through the air on brilliant wing, forerunner of the sun" (Ion fr. 6 Page).

841. **lanterns:** Greek *hipnoi*, described by Aelian *NA* 2.8 as "small hollow braziers containing a lively fire, and transparent, so as to protect the fire without concealing the light". These would be more convenient for carrying out of doors (especially perhaps in the upper air!) than ordinary lamps, which could be hard to keep alight in a strong wind (cf. *Lys.* 1003).

843. **rinse the bathtub and heat water:** an important preliminary to a wedding was the ritual bathing of bride and groom: cf. *Lys.* 378, Eur. *Phoen.* 347-8, Thuc. 2.15.5.

844. **nuptial couch:** Greek *kouridion lekhos*, a highly poetic phrase (cf. *Iliad* 15.39-40) neither word of which is used in Attic prose or in normal comic style.

846. **give . . . back:** cf. 713-4.

848. **I wouldn't give three obols for the gods:** i.e. "I think the gods are worth very little".

849. **if they go in for pimping:** the implication is that Fullfruit and Showtime are prostitutes; and Showtime is certainly spoken of and treated like one in 871-908. Yet Fullfruit is to be *married* to Trygaeus with full ritual and feasting, which a prostitute could never

173

be. Trygaeus is doing what no one could do in real life: he is taking a *wife* who also has (and being immortal, will always retain) all the qualities one could wish for in a *mistress*. On the ambivalent nature of Fullfruit see M.M. Henry, *Menander's Courtesans and the Greek Comic Tradition* (Diss. Minnesota 1983) 21-22.

850.   **it's not like that:** i.e. "the gods" as a group are not pimps — only some individuals among them.

855.   **something for her to lick:** he may well have *fellatio* in mind, and the audience will certainly think of it.

856-867. = 909-921 **Metre:** each of the sections sung by the chorus consists of two telesilleans (x–uu–u–) and a reizianum (x–uu––), metrical forms that seem to have had a traditional association with weddings (cf. 1329ff; *Birds* 1731ff; Sappho fr. 141.1). Trygaeus' interjections and the replies by the chorus-leader are in recitative iambic tetrameters, after which Trygaeus sings in lyric iambics.

864.   **Carcinus' young spinning-tops:** we expected "all other men" or the like, and what we have instead is distinctly anticlimactic, since after 782-796 we are clearly meant to think of the sons of Carcinus as a pretty miserable crew. They are called "spinning-tops" because of the pirouettes that were a feature of their dances (cf. *Wasps* 1517, 1523, 1528-31).

865.   **all alone:** the reinterpretation of the transmitted letters (*heis* "one, all alone" instead of *eis* "to, into") by G. Nenci, *QUCC* 3 (1979) 81-84, removes an unwanted and inappropriate preposition and introduces a contrast between "the one" (here the lone hero) and "the many" (here the Greek people) beloved of fifth-century poets (cf. *Ach.* 493, *Knights* 861-2, Aesch. *Ag.* 1456-67, Eur. *IA* 1387-90)

867.   **screw and sleep:** cf. 341.

869.   **sesame-balls:** "spherical cakes made of honey, roasted sesame seeds, and oil" (Athenaeus 14.646f), which it was the custom to eat at weddings (cf. *Birds* 159-161).

870.   **only the prick's missing:** i.e. everything needed for the wedding is ready in the house, except the bridegroom.

873-4.   **the Showtime . . . to Brauron:** lit. "the *theōriā* which (whom) we at one time used to knock to Brauron"; the expression is hard to analyse grammatically, but *epaiomen* "used to knock, used to screw" seems to be a surprise substitute for e.g. *epoioumetha* "used to make". The meaning is apparently that in pre-war days Trygaeus and his slave had been in the habit of visiting Brauron to watch (*theōrein*) the celebration of the four-yearly festival there (see next note), and that on these expeditions drink had flowed freely and casual sex had been readily available.

874.   **Brauron:** a sanctuary in eastern Attica, where every four years (Arist. *Ath.Pol.* 54.7) the festival of the Brauronia was celebrated in honour of Artemis. On this festival see Parke 139-140; H. Lloyd-Jones, *JHS* 103 (1983) 91-95; S.G. Cole, *ZPE* 55 (1984) 238-244.

876.   **quadrennial:** lit. "quinquennial", since the Greeks usually reckoned intervals of time "inclusively" and spoke of the Olympic games, the Brauronia, etc., as taking place every *fifth* year, when modern usage would say they were held every fourth year. The compound *prōktopenteteris* "quadrennial bum" may be merely a "million-gallon word" (521) coined to provide a magnificent description of a magnificent object without much concern for semantic precision, or it may also carry the suggestion that Showtime's bottom is the sort of delight that is worth waiting four years to enjoy.

879-880. **staking a claim . . . for the Isthmian games:** visitors coming from far and wide to attend the great athletic festivals, one of which was held every alternate year at the Isthmus of

174

Corinth, usually stayed in tents (referred to as *skēnai theōrikai* in Heniochus fr. 5.8), and would try to arrive early in order to claim a space for their tent not too far away from where the events were held. The speaker here of course has "games" of a rather different sort in mind; the "isthmus" *he* is thinking of is the narrow strip of territory between the two broad expanses of Showtime's thighs. This sense of "isthmus" was probably well established in popular speech, for it seems to be alluded to in Aesch. fr. 17.29-31M (from the satyr-play *Theoroi* or *Isthmiastai*).

882.   **them:** as 887 shows, this refers not to the audience as a whole but to the councillors, who sat in a special section of the theatre called the *bouleutikon* (*Birds* 794).

883.   **nodding:** in belated response to Trygaeus' request for some member of the audience to take charge of Showtime.

883.   **Ariphrades** (*PA* 2201), son of Automenes, is several times attacked by Ar. for his addiction to cunnilingus (*Knights* 1274-89; *Wasps* 1280-3; Ar. fr. 63 Kock = fr. dub. 926 K-A). Since the same practice is not condemned when indulged in by other people (cf. 716-7, *Eccl.* 846-7), it is likely that Ar. had some other and more personal reason for animosity towards Ariphrades; the explanation may be that Ariphrades was a comic poet (cf. Arist. *Poet.* 1458b31) and therefore a rival of Ar. See further *CQ* 27 (1977) 276.

885.   **lap up her broth:** cf. on 716-7.

886.   **your things:** on the text here see R. Seager, *CQ* 31 (1981) 244-5, who shows that if we retain the manuscripts' reading *ta skeuē* "your equipment" (which cannot refer to clothing) it is hard to envisage plausibly what things Showtime could have been carrying or why she should now be asked to discard them. It is more satisfactory to adopt Meineke's emendation *tēn skeuēn* "your things, your attire"; this gives full value to the following line — the councillors are being invited to gaze on Showtime's full beauty, now for the first time revealed. (In point of fact, as in other scenes where nude women appear as mutes, the performer was probably "a man padded with false breasts and wearing a leotard painted with nipples, a navel and pubic hair" [Stone 150].)

887.   **Prytaneis:** the members of the business committe of the Council, which held office for one-tenth of the year and was composed of all the fifty councillors from one of the ten tribes.

890.   **have a feast of a time:** lit. "celebrate an *anarrhusis*". *Anarrhusis* "sacrificing" (from *anarrhuein* "draw back the head of a sacrificial victim") was the name given to the second day of the festival of the Apaturia (on which see Parke 88-92); here, however, the word is evidently intended to be taken as meaning "sexual intercourse", as if derived from *anarrhein* "well up, flow forth" with reference to ejaculation (cf. *IG* xii [7] 115.11 where this verb is used of blood flowing from a wound).

891.   **this oven of hers:** for "oven" = "female genitals" cf. Hdt. 5.92η.2-3 where "to put one's loaves on a cold oven" is interpreted as meaning "to have intercourse with a corpse".

892-3.   **Ah, that's why . . . before the war:** as if the "oven" were a real oven, blackened by repeated exposure to fire. Showtime's "oven" is black with pubic hair.

893.   **used to keep their trivet here:** Greek *lasana*, here translated "trivet", meant a stand on which pots were placed for cooking. The meaning is thus that before the war the Council did a great deal of "cooking" in Showtime's "oven"; for the use of verbs of burning and cooking in relation to sexual activity, see Henderson 177-8.

896-904.   The description of the "athletic meeting" is one long series of double-entendres and word-plays on sporting and sexual activities.

896a-b.   After 896a ("to wrestle on the ground, to stand her on all fours") R alone has an additional line "to throw her down sideways, to stand (her) on her knees bending over". The omission of this line in the other mss. is probably accidental, due to the fact that it ends with the same word as 896a; nevertheless it is surprising to find so repetitious a couplet in this varied, imaginative and lively passage, and it is likely that one line or the other should be deleted. Willems' deletion of 896a has been supported with strong arguments by B. Marzullo, *Museum Criticum* 5-7 (1970-2) 93-97; but 896a is essential **to** the passage, because it alone clearly identifies the first event of the "games" as wrestling, just as subsequent events are identified as *pankration* (897), horse-racing (*kelēs* 900), and chariot-racing (901). It is preferable therefore, with Rogers, to delete 896b as a rejected author's variant mistakenly retained in the text (cf. on 744). Whichever of the lines we retain, its last word must be *histanai* "to stand her", not *hestanai* "to stand": all the other infinitives in the context describe the actions of the men, not of the woman.

896a.   **to stand her on all fours:** an allusion to the coital position called "lioness" (*Lys.* 231, in which the woman stood bending forward and was penetrated from behind (cf. Henderson 179-180; add *Wealth* 152).

897.   **to anoint yourselves:** as one would do before wrestling (*com. adesp.* 401, Thuc. 1.6.5) and also before making love (*Lys.* 938-947).

897.   **free-style:** Greek *pankration*, a form of wrestling in which punching, striking, kicking, jumping and throttling were all permitted, "unarmed combat converted into a scientific sport" (H.A. Harris, *Greek Athletes and Athletics* [Lond, 1964] 106).

898.   **with fist and prick at once:** according to the scholia, "with fist and *leg* at once" was a phrase in common use, no doubt referring to a tactic in the *pankration*.

899.   **after that, the day after tomorrow:** or possibly "on the next day but one after that"; but 716 suggests that a continuous three days' sexual feast (today, tomorrow, the day after) is envisaged.

900.   **jockey will outjockey jockey:** Greek *kelēs* actually means "horse ridden by a jockey"; it was also the name given to the coital position in which the woman is above the man, straddling him (cf. *Wasps* 501-2; *Lys.* 60, 676-8).

901.   **chariots will crash . . . :** the sentence continues as if the word used had been not *harmata* "chariots" but *sōmata* "bodies".

903.   **skinned:** i.e. erect, with the foreskin retracted; cf. *Lys.* 953, 1136, *Wealth* 295.

904.   **having come unstuck in the bends and twists:** lit. "having fallen in (at, around) the *kampai*", which can mean either 'bends, turning-points" of a race-track or "bendings, twistings" of violent love-making (cf. Pherecrates fr. 145.9, 14, 26).

906.   **the chairman:** lit. "the Prytanis", which could refer to an ordinary member of the business committee (as probably at *Thesm.* 923) but which here may well denote (as in Thuc. 6.14.1 and probably also Pl. *Gorg.* 516d-e) the member who was chosen by lot to be chairman (*epistatēs*) of the Prytaneis for the day. It is true that in Aristotle's time the *epistatēs* was forbidden to leave the building called the Tholos during his day of office (Arist. *Ath.Pol.* 44.1), but this cannot have been true in the fifth century when he presided over meetings of Council and Assembly (cf. Xen. *Mem.* 1.1.18); what was essential if he was to perform his duties properly was not that he should always be in a particular place, but that it should always be known where he was to be found. On the *epistatēs* see P.J. Rhodes, *The Athenian Boule* (Oxford, 1972) 23-24.

907.   **if you'd had to introduce some business:** i.e. if I had asked you to bring before the Council some matter of concern to me.

907. **for no reward**: in the present case his "reward" will be to participate in the "games" described in 896-904 — in addition to which we may safely assume that Showtime is even now sitting on his knee.

908. **extending your . . . armistice**: a surprise for "extending your hand" (to receive a bribe, cf. *Thesm.* 936-7, [Lys.] 6.29), *kheira* "hand" being replaced by *ekekheiriā* "truce, armistice", whose point resides solely in its being a surprise and in its similarity to *kheira* in sound, for it makes no sense in the context (attempts to extract the sense "raising the pretext of a legal holiday" fail because *hupekhein* does not mean "raise the pretext of" and *ekekheiriā* does not in classical Greek mean "legal holiday").

916. **You'll say that all right when . . .** : Athenaeus 11.485a seems to have read "what about when . . .?" (cf. 859, 863); but the chorus-leader's reply, beginning *kai . . . ge* "yes, and . . .", cannot be a response to a "what" question, only to a "yes/no" question or to a statement.

916. **a goblet**: Greek *lepastē*, a broad, deep drinking vessel (see the quotations collected by Athenaeus 11.484f-486a).

921. **Hyperbolus**: see on 681. He has been "put a stop to" in the sense that now peace has been made "his crimes will be more easily detected and his slanders less readily believed" (Thuc. 5.16.1, speaking of Cleon). Ar. likes to mention the removal of Hyperbolus as the last of a series of blessings: cf. 1319, *Knights* 1363, *Wasps* 1007.

923. **perform the installation of this goddess**: the goddess is Peace, and her statue is to be "installed" as a cult-image in the place it has occupied since 520, in front of the centre of the *skēnē*.

923. **with an offering of pots**: at the installation of a cult-image in a temple or shrine, or at the dedication of an altar, it was customary (at least if there was no animal sacrifice) to offer pots of boiled vegetables to the god: cf. *Wealth* 1197-8, Ar. fr. 245 Kock = 256 K-A.

924. **a grumbling little Hermes**: the slave is thinking of the images of Hermes that sood in front of many Athenian houses (cf. *Clouds* 1478, Thuc. 6.27.1): the unique and treasured goddess Peace deserves a grander kind of installation ceremony than was given to these commonplace images of a rather roguish god. The word *memphomenon* "grumbling, criticizing, complaining" may possibly refer to the propensity of Hermes, when he appears on the comic stage, to rail in condemnation of mortals (182-191, 362-381, *Wealth* 1099-1116) and to complain of his own ill-fortune (*Wealth* 1118-32); alternatively *memphomenon* might be passive and mean "contemptible", though a passive use of *memphesthai* is otherwise unknown in classical Greek.

925. **do you want**: the Greek verb is plural, indicating that at this moment Trygaeus is speaking to the chorus as well as to his slave; in 929, however, "you" is singular.

926. **to go on an oxpedition**: Greek *boēthein* "to go to someone's help" (often used of military expeditions sent to assist allies), with a pun on *boï* "with an ox".

928. **Theogenes** (*PA* 6703) of the deme Acharnae (cf. *CQ* 27 [1977] 273-4) was a merchant and shipowner (Eupolis *CGF* 92.5-7; schol. *Birds* 822) who had the reputation of a vain boaster pretending to be much richer than he was (*Birds* 822, 1127) and was accordingly nicknamed "Smoke" (schol. *Birds* 822). He was also satirized as a dirty boor, and his name linked with faeces and flatus (*Wasps* 1183-4; Ar. fr. 571 Kock = 582 K-A; Eupolis *CGF* 92.9). In politics, Theogenes was prominent enough by 425 to be chosen with Cleon to investigate the situation at Pylos (Thuc. 4.27.3); in 421 he was among those who swore

177

to the peace and alliance with Sparta (Thuc. 5.19.2; 5.24), and he remained prominent at least until 412 when he was mentioned in Eupolis' *Demes*. We last hear of him (if it is the same Theogenes) in 409 when he was a member of an abortive embassy to Persia (Xen. *Hell*. 1.3.13).

929.   **yow** (the Scottish and northern English dialect equivalent of standard English *ewe*) is meant to correspond to Greek *oῖ*, the Ionic dialect form of the dative case of *ois* "sheep".

930.   **dialect:** lit. "Ionic"; so also in 933.

932.   **his audience:** lit. "those seated".

933.   **"yowww!":** the Greek is again *oῖ*, this time as a typically Ionic exclamation of distress; the exclamation is not otherwise attested, but presumably corresponds to the Attic *oi* found in Aesch. *Ag*. 1257, Soph. *El*. 674, etc., and in the common *oimoi*.

935.   **we:** probably the Athenians and the Spartans (cf. 996, 1080-2); possibly the Athenians alone, with reference to their internal politics; not the Greeks generally, since the mention of allies in 936 shows that the reference must be to a hegemonial state or states.

939-955 ≏1023-38 Metre: the chorus begin in iambic rhythm but soon move to lyric anapaests, returning to iambics at the end of their second section (947 = 1030) and remaining mainly in that rhythm thereafter, to conclude with a reizianum (see on 856-867). In the antistrophe two of their iambic dimeters are replaced by telesilleans (1035-6), possibly for the sake of a musical reminiscence of 909-915, another passage praising Trygaeus as a public benefactor (cf. Zimmermann 185). The interjections by Trygaeus in strophe and antistrophe are in recitative iambic tetrameters.

942.   **here's the altar outside:** Trygaeus pretends to be surprised to find an altar already in position in front of the house, regarding it as evidence of divine favour that he does not have to go and fetch one. In fact the altar was probably a permanent stage-property; see P.D. Arnott, *Greek Scenic Conventions in the Fifth Century B.C.* (Oxford, 1962) 43-53, and Dearden 46-48.

948-1018. The sacrificial ritual is only partly and sketchily indicated by the spoken words, but it can be reconstructed (as I have attempted to do in the interpolated stage-directions) with the help of various passages of epic and tragedy, especially *Odyssey* 3.430-463, Eur. *El*. 798-839, *HF* 926-9, *IA* 1563-9. The evidence is conveniently summarized by Denniston on Eur. *El*. 791ff.; see also W. Burkert, *Homo Necans* (Berlin, 1972) 10-12.

948-9.   **Here's the basket . . . except the sheep:** M.G. Bonanno, *Museum Criticum* 4 (1969) 48-49, gives these two lines to the slave; this entails the assumption that the slave has brought not only fire for the altar and the ritual basket (*kanoun*) but also the sacrificial animal (as indeed he was ordered to do), and that his statement that the sheep is "holding us up" refers to its resistance to being led to the altar (a theme more fully developed in Men. *Dysk*. 393-9). If however the sheep is already on stage at this point, why is it necessary for *both* Trygaeus and the slave to go inside for the two or three items still needed, as the dual verb *hamillēsesthon* "you (two) had better race" (950) implies that they do? I prefer therefore to give 948-9 to Trygaeus, who reminds the slave (not too sternly) that the most important requisite for the sacrifice is still missing.

948.   **ribbons:** for adorning the victim: cf. P. Stengel, *Die griechischen Kultusaltertümer* (Munich, 1920), Tafel III fig. 11.

951.   **Chaeris:** a musician who (according to the comic dramatists) played as atrociously on the pipes as he did on the lyre: cf. *Ach*. 15-16, 866, *Birds* 857, Cratinus fr. 118 Kock = 126 K-A, Pherecrates fr. 6. The statement of schol. *Ach*. 866 that he was a Theban is

| 952. | **to play the pipes:** the pipes were as regular a feature of Greek sacrifices as ribbons or barley-grains (cf. Hdt. 1.132.1). Music for the present sacrifice would most naturally be provided by the piper who had been playing accompaniments to song and recitative throughout the performance (cf. *Thesm.* 1175, *Eccl.* 890-2, Men. *Dysk.* 880), and the chorus fear that any delay in the proceedings may give Chaeris the opportunity to come up and demand that *he* should have the job. In *Birds* 858, on the other hand, at another sacrifice, the chorus actually invite Chaeris to play for them. |

no more than a bad guess based on the text of that passage: a Theban could hardly have performed at Athens in 426/5 (*Ach.* 15 "this year").

952.   **to play the pipes:** the pipes were as regular a feature of Greek sacrifices as ribbons or barley-grains (cf. Hdt. 1.132.1). Music for the present sacrifice would most naturally be provided by the piper who had been playing accompaniments to song and recitative throughout the performance (cf. *Thesm.* 1175, *Eccl.* 890-2, Men. *Dysk.* 880), and the chorus fear that any delay in the proceedings may give Chaeris the opportunity to come up and demand that *he* should have the job. In *Birds* 858, on the other hand, at another sacrifice, the chorus actually invite Chaeris to play for them.

955.   **you'll give him something:** probably a portion of the sacrificial meat (cf. 1102ff). The Greek verb used, *prosdidonai*, carries the suggestion that anything given to Chaeris will not be a payment for services rendered, but rather the sort of gift one makes to a persistent beggar.

957.   **right-about** probably means "anticlockwise", the direction one will take if one first faces the altar and then turns right to circle it: see A.F. Braunlich, *AJPh* (1936) 245-260.

960.   **hurry up, nod your head:** it was essential that the animal should do this, thus in appearance consenting to be sacrificed: cf. Plut. *Mor.* 729f and the oracle cited by Porphyry, *On Abstinence* 2.9.3.

962.   **throw the spectators some of the barley seeds:** I can find no evidence that it was ever the practice at sacrifices to scatter barley-grains over the worshippers, and we should rather suppose with Platnauer that Ar. is parodying the practice of some other comic dramatists who made their characters throw nuts, figs, etc., into the audience (*Wasps* 58-59, *Wealth* 794-801).

964-7.   **of all these spectators . . . will give it to them tonight:** the joke has had to be slightly altered in translation; in the Greek it is a play on the word *krīthē* which means both "barley-grain" and "penis" (see Henderson 119-120).

966.   **the women haven't had any:** this remark does not help to establish whether or not women were present at the dramatic performances, for it might imply "because there are no women present" or might equally well imply "because the women are sitting too far to the rear for the grains to reach them". However, *Lys.* 1049 and several passages of Plato (*Gorg.* 502b-d; *Laws* 658a-d, 817b-c) show that some women (not necessarily or even probably the wives and daughters of citizens) did attend the theatre.

968.   **Who is here?:** at a public sacrifice the officiant, or a herald, would ask this question, and the public would respond "Many righteous men", thus assuring him that no one was present who was polluted by homicide or otherwise and whose participation in the sacrifice might make it unacceptable to the gods (cf. *Wasps* 654, Ant. 5.82-84).

968.   **where might there be many righteous men?:** evidently he can see none in the audience; for similar denigration of the spectators' moral character cf. 822-3, *Clouds* 1096-1100, *Thesm.* 810-829, *Frogs* 274-6, 783, *Eccl.* 436-440.

969.   **sterling fellows:** the Greek adjective (*agathos*) is the same as that translated "righteous" in 968; there is a play on the ambiguity of the word – in the ritual formula of 968 it means "virtuous", but in 970-2 the slave is taking it to mean "courageous".

969.   For the sprinkling of lustral water over the worshippers at a sacrifice, cf. Athenaeus 9.409b; a polluted person was said to be "excluded from lustral water", i.e. forbidden to attend sacrifices (Dem. 20.158; cf. Aesch. *Eum.* 656, Soph. *OT* 240). Here, instead of the customary sprinkling, the chorus are unexpectedly and comically given a drenching.

973.   The cutting of hairs from the victim's head, which were then thrown on the altar fire, was the last ritual act before the actual slaughter (cf. *Odyssey* 3.446, 14.422-3; Eur. *El.* 811-2). It cannot be determined with certainty from the text at what moment this act is performed in our scene; but noting that in both the *Odyssey* passages prayers are said to be uttered while the hairs are being thrown on the fire, and that in *Iliad*. 3.273-4 hairs from several sacrificial lambs are distributed to the Greek and Trojan leaders to hold while they take an oath, I tentatively assume that the regular practice was for the officiant to hold the hairs in his upraised right hand while making his prayer, and to cast them on the fire at the prayer's conclusion.

974-1015.   Metre: anapaestic.

978.   **Yes, accept it, most highly honoured one:** It is possible that this line should be given to the chorus (or their leader on their behalf), the slave then chipping in with 979-986.

990.   **these thirteen years:** Trygaeus is evidently dating the disappearance of Peace not from the actual outbreak of war with Sparta, but from the beginning of Athenian military involvement in the disputes that led up to this, i.e. the Athenian decision to send ships to defend Corcyra against Corinth in 433. (Thuc. 1.44-45). The first squadron sailed very early in the Athenian year 433/2 (*IG* i³ 364.1-2), and it is therefore likely that the decision to send it was taken before the end of 434/3; from 434/3 to 422/1 by inclusive reckoning is thirteen years. Cf. H.R. Rawlings III in G.W. Bowersock et al. (ed.), *Arktouros : Hellenic Studies Presented to Bernard M. W. Knox*... (Berlin, 1979) 276 n.8. It may, however be preferable not to press Trygaeus' phrase as a chronological datum, in view of the evidence that the number thirteen could be used as a round figure, "an indefinite number with a sinister tinge" (J.P. Postgate, *CR* 19 [1905] 438; cf. J. Elmore, *ib.* 437), as in *Wealth* 846, 1083, *Iliad* 5.387, Pind. fr. 135.

992.   **Lysimache:** the name means "resolver of fights". There is probably an allusion to the incumbent priestess of Athena Polias, Lysimache daughter of Dracontides of Bate (*PA* 9470; cf. Davies 170), who according to much recent opinion was also in some sense the original of Lysistrata in the play of that name. On this Lysimache see D.M. Lewis, *ABSA* 50 (1955) 1-12, and N.V. Dunbar, *CR* 20 (1970) 270-2.

993-4.   **put an end to those over-clever suspicions:** this wish was not fulfilled: Thuc. 5.26.3 calls the years after 421 a period of "suspicious truce", and in 411 (*Lys.* 1231-5) Ar. is again complaining about Athenians' suspicions of Spartan intentions which lead them to hunt misguidedly for hidden meanings between the lines of Spartan diplomatic statements.

996-8.   **blend us Greeks anew . . . a milder forgivingness:** the metaphor seems to be from the blending and flavouring of wine (so Taillardat 325): cf. *Wasps* 878. An infusion of the sweet juices of friendship and kindness will put an end to the bitterness and harshness the Greeks have shown towards one another.

966.   **starting from scratch:** or "all over again".

999.   **we** now denotes the Athenians, as is shown by the mention of the Agora, the market-place and main public square of Athens.

1000.   **from Megara:** cucumber and woollen cloaks are mentioned as typical Megarian products in *Ach.* 519-521; for garlic, see on 246. In *Ach.* 729-835 Dicaeopolis reaps the first benefits from his private peace-treaty when a Megarian comes to trade in the private Agora he has set up, to be followed (*Ach.* 860-958) by a Boeotian.

1002.   **tiny little woollen cloaks:** the Greek word for "cloaks" used here, *khlaniskidia*, is a diminutive of *khlanides*, and since the *khlanis* was a luxury garment (cf. *Wasps* 677, *Birds* 1693,

Eccl. 848) it has occasioned surprise that slaves should be envisaged as wearing them; but the point is that peace will bring such prosperity that even slaves will wear rich men's clothes (cf. *Wealth* 816-8, and see Stone 164).

1004. **geese, ducks, pigeons, wrens**: all these are among the animals and birds bought by Dicaeopolis in *Ach.* from the Boeotian trader (*Ach.* 875-8, 1104).

1005. **Copaic eels**: from Lake Copais in north-west Boeotia. They were a much prized delicacy at Athens (*Ach.* 880-894; *Lys.* 36, 702; Ar. fr. 364 Kock = 380 K-A).

1008. **Morychus** (*PA* 10421) is mentioned again as a lover of good food and luxury in *Ach.* 887; *Wasps* 506, 1142; Plato com. fr. 106. There is also a reference to him as active in politics (Telecleides fr. 11) and to his having served on an embassy to Persia (schol. *Ach.*61).

1008. **Teleas** (*PA* 13500), son of Telenicus, of the deme Pergase, was a minor politician, who held the office of secretary to the Treasurers of Athena in 415/4 (*IG* i³ 308.65, 331.32-33, etc.) It was in this capacity, no doubt, that he drafted the "rotten bit of paper" that sent an Athenian imperial inspector grumbling to Cloudcuckooville (*Birds* 1024-5). Comedy regards him as deceitful and unreliable (*Birds* 168, Plato com. fr. 161); in Phryn. com. fr. 20 he is one of the four men dubbed "great apes". The present passage is probably the earliest reference to him, and the only one that calls him a glutton.

1008. **Glaucetes** (*PA* 2944) is mentioned as a glutton in *Thesm.* 1033 ("the whale") and Plato com. fr. 106 ("the turbot"). He may be identical with Glaucetes of Acharnae, the father of Peisander (*IG* i³ 472.2-3; see on 395); cf. A.G. Woodhead, *AJPh* 75 (1954) 133 with n.7. If so, given that Peisander probably held public office in 422/1 and certainly in 421/0, Glaucetes must have been not less than about sixty years old when *Peace* was produced, and seventy when he was mentioned in *Thesm.*

1009. **Melanthius**: see on 804.

1011. **cry out in grief**: Greek *ototuzein*, a word found elsewhere in Ar. (*Lys.* 520, *Thesm.*1082; cf. *Birds* 1043) but derived from the exclusively tragic exclamation *ototoi* (e.g. Aesch. *Ag.* 1257; Eur. *Or.* 1389) and so appropriate to the tragic dramatist Melanthius.

1012. **Medea**: probably a play of that name composed by Melanthius himself; see A. Dihle, *RhM* 119 (1976) 146-8. Snell in *TrGF*, however, following a conjecture made on quite inadequate grounds by Fritzsche, prints 1013-4 (omitting "amid the beet") as *Morsimus* fr. 1.

1014. **who was confined**: Greek *lokheuomenas*, which in the tragic original no doubt bore its usual meaning "who was in travail", but in relation to the lost eel is apparently to be understood in the unattested but logically possible sense "who lies concealed as though in ambush".

1014. **amid the beet**: eels were often served wrapped up in beet: cf. *Ach.* 894, Eubulus fr. 35, 37.

1017. **professional**: lit. "cook-like": when one was entertaining, it was usual to hire a cook, who would bring a live animal with him and perform its sacrifice himself: cf. Men. *Dysk.* 393ff, *Perik.* 996.

1020. **"nor is her altar bloodied"**: the language is tragic, possibly modelled on Eur. *Andr.* 260 "slay me, bloody the altar of the goddess". The slave is not here, as might be supposed, reminding Trygaeus of some existing cult regulation, for in 421 no Athenian cult of Peace existed; an altar to Peace was first established in 375/4, and animals were sacrificed at it from the start (Isocr. 15.109-110; Nepos, *Timotheus* 2.2; Philochorus, *FGrH* 328 F 151; see Jacoby on the Philochorus fragment and L. Deubner, *Attische Feste* [Berlin, 1932] 37-38). Rather he is *conjecturing* that Peace is the sort of goddess who will find bloodshed of any kind abhorrent.

181

1021.	**the thigh-bones**: regularly these were wrapped in fat and burnt on the altar (e.g. *Odyssey* 3.456-461).

1022.	**that way our sponsor doesn't lose his sheep**: "the sheep, a live stage-property, lives to be eaten another day, and a cheaper property, old thighbones, is substituted" (Dover 57). There may have been religious as well as economic motives for the avoidance of performing the sacrifice on stage (there is a similar avoidance in *Birds* 1056-7); see Arnott, *Greek Scenic Conventions* 53-55. The word translated "sponsor" is *khorēgos*, the wealthy citizen who bore most of the expenses of a dramatic production.

1023.	**it is up to you to remain outside**: that the original text of 1023 contained words which bore this meaning is beyond reasonable doubt; of the remainder of the line (amounting to five or six syllables) there remains only a single two-syllable word, and that hopelessly corrupt. This damage to the text, however, has not created any evident gap in grammar or sense — only in metre — and in the translation I have simply ignored it and translated only what is reasonably certain.

1024.	**put faggots on**: where does the firewood come from? Trygaeus cannot bring it out of the house now, since he is to "remain outside"; nor can the slave, since the wood has to be arranged on the fire before the slave returns with the thigh-bones; nor is it likely that the wood was brought out during 939-955, since there is no mention of it in the text there and it would have required an extra round trip by someone. Possibly at 942 Trygaeus found not only an altar standing ready for him but also wood standing ready piled at the foot of it. Not all this wood is used for the fire; some of it is still available at 1119ff to be used for giving a beating to the obnoxious Hierocles.

1025.	**everything that is requisite**: namely (i) the thigh-bones, wrapped in fat, with pieces of raw flesh placed on top of them; (ii) the sheep's rump (*os sacrum*) and tail (cf. 1054); (iii) the meal-offering (see on 1040); (iv) a libation of wine (1059).

1026.	**like a real diviner**: like one who knows how to ensure that when the offering is placed on the fire it will blaze up and consume the offering quickly, demonstrating that the sacrifice is acceptable to the gods. Evidently an expert diviner (*mantis*) was expected not only to know what phenomena at sacrifices augured well or badly, but also how to carry out the ritual in such a way as to make sure (the gods willing) that the auguries would be good.

1031.	**that's crushed Stilbides**: professional diviners like Stilbides will (it is suggested) lose much of their prestige, now it has been shown that a layman like Trygaeus can arrange an altar-fire as well as any of them. Cf. Pl. *Crat.* 409a where it is said that Anaxagoras will be "crushed" (the same verb *piezei* is used) by the production of evidence showing that he does not deserve the credit of having originated the theory that the moon's light is borrowed from the sun. Stilbides was a noted diviner, who accompanied Nicias on the Sicilian expedition; he died in 413, not long before the lunar eclipse that fatally delayed the Athenian withdrawal from Syracuse, on which occasion his advice was badly missed (Plut. *Nic.* 23.7). Already in 422 he had been mentioned by Eupolis (fr. 211) as one of the outstanding members of his profession.

1036.	**the holy city**: so in *Knights* 582-5 Attica is called "the most sacred of all lands".

1039-41.	On the speaker-assignments see J.C.B. Lowe, *Hermes* 95 (1967) 63-64. The decisive point is that the words "take the thighs" must be spoken by the person who has brought the thigh-bones out, namely the slave (cf. 1021).

1039.	**that's done**: he means that the sheep has been duly slaughtered, skinned and cut up.

1040.	the offals: Greek *splankhna*, the liver, kidneys, heart, etc., of a sacrificial animal. These were roasted over the altar fire and partaken of by all present (see e.g. *Odyssey* 3.9, 3.40, 3.461), a share also being given to the god (*Wealth* 1130; Athenion fr. 1.18 Kock = K-A).
1040.	the meal-offering: a paste made of barley meal, oil and wine, which was scattered over the offerings on the altar (cf. *Odyssey* 14.429 and Porphyry, *On Abstinence* 2.6.2 [quoting Theophrastus]).
1044.	crowned with laurel: and therefore probably a seer or diviner, since the laurel was an emblem of Apollo, the god of prophecy and divination. The slave is told to roast the offals well in order that this religious expert may not be able to find fault with this aspect of the sacrificial procedure.
1046.	Hierocles (*PA* 7473) was a well-known expert on oracles. In 446/5, after the crushing of the Euboean revolt, he had been made head of a committee for carrying out certain sacrifices which an oracle had commanded to be made (*IG* i³ 40.64-67), and it is plausible that at this time he was given an allotment of land in the new cleruchy of Oreus (see next note). Eupolis (fr. 212) calls him "most excellent king of oracle-chanters".
1047.	Oreus was a settlement of Athenian cleruchs, established in 446/5 on land confiscated from the expelled inhabitants of Hestiaea in northern Euboea (Thuc. 1.114.3; Theopompus, *FGrH* 115 F 387; Plut. *Per.* 23.4; D.S. 12.22.2; *IG* i³ 41).
1049.	he's going to make some objection to the peace agreement: how does Trygaeus know this? L. Canfora, *Annali della Facoltà di Lettere e Filosofia* (*Bari*) 15 (1972) 63-64, links this passage with the oracles referred to by Thuc. 5.26.3-4, which declared that the war was destined to last "thrice nine years": in the opinion of those who peddled such oracles, to end the war before this period had elapsed was to flout the will of the gods. Note that Hierocles three times says (1073, 1075, 1079) that it is not *yet* proper for peace to be made.
1053.	get away from the rump: i.e. be careful not to touch the rump, which must be left undisturbed so that it can be properly inspected for good or bad auguries.
1054-5.	the tail is doing nicely: i.e. so far as the tail is concerned, the indications are that the sacrifice has been accepted by the goddess.
1055.	O beloved Lady Peace: apparently an exclamation of delight and gratitude at this evidence of the favour of a deity who has shunned the Greeks for so many years.
1056.	separate the first share and then give it to me: it was common at sacrificial feasts to set aside for the god the first share (*aparkhē, apargmata, argmata*) not only of the offals but also of the meat (cf. *Odyssey* 14.434-6, 446). At one time this portion was burnt on the altar, but later it was often treated as a perquisite of the priest or diviner who officiated at the sacrifice (cf. *Inschr. Priene* 174.8-10; Artemidorus, *Oneirocritica* 3.3 Pack). Hierocles considers himself entitled to this privilege even though he has come to the sacrifice uninvited.
1059.	Where's a table?: this question is usually either continued to Trygaeus or given to Hierocles. But Trygaeus, who brought the table out (1032), would know where it was (and would say "the table" not "a table"); while Hierocles has as yet nothing in his possession that might need to be put on a table. It is the slave who needs a table at this moment, in order to cut up the offals as he has been told to do; he has apparently not yet noticed that a table has already been provided by Trygaeus (he was not present when Trygaeus announced his intention of fetching a table, nor when the table was actually brought out).

1060. **the tongue is cut separately**: the custom was for the victim's tongue to be set aside until the end of the meal, when it was either cut up and burnt on the altar, to the accompaniment of a libation (*Odyssey* 3.332-341; Athenaeus 1.16b-c; cf. *IG* i³ 255.B8-9), or given to the officiating priest or herald (schol. *Wealth* 1110; *Inschr. Priene* 174.9, 364.4; *IG* xii [7] 237.15-20). Hierocles, determined to secure the tongue for himself, does not want it to get mixed up with the offals which will be distributed to all present. Cf. Men. *Kolax* F 1.4-5 where a cook tells his slave to steal the tongue while he (the cook) is praying and making libation.

1062. **to Peace**: Hierocles at last has the information for which he asked at 1052, and at once he begins to spout a string of oracles all of which assert, as Trygaeus had foreseen (1049), that the war ought not to have been ended.

1063-1114. **Metre**: dactylic hexameters, the usual metre of oracles. The same metre is used in other "oracle-mongering" scenes (*Knights* 1015-95, *Birds* 967-985), but the present passage differs from these in that not only the actual oracles but also all the dialogue about them is couched in hexameters.

1065. **fierce-eyed monkeys**: the poetic adjective *kharopos* "fierce-eyed" is usually applied to such animals as lions (Hes. *Thg.* 321) or dogs (*h.Hom.Herm.* 194), and Trygaeus finds its use to describe monkeys laughably incongruous. The Spartans are called "monkeys" because they were allegedly deceitful tricksters (cf. *Ach.* 907, *Knights* 887, and for the Spartans' reputation see on 623).

1067. **tremulous**: Greek *trērōnes*, another epic adjective misapplied, for in Homer *trērōn* is used only of doves (e.g. *Iliad* 5.778, 22.140).

1067. **boobies**: Greek *kepphoi*, an unknown sea-bird, traditionally identified as the stormy petrel, and a byword for imbecility (cf. *Wealth* 912, Hesychius κ2242).

1068-9. **I only wish . . . that your lungs were as hot as this is**: Trygaeus is wishing for Hierocles to have inflammation of the lungs — one of the most common fatal diseases (cf. Hippocr. *Acute Diseases* 5). It is not certain that Trygaeus has been tasting the offals (though 1074 rather supports the view that he has); he *may* have only touched them, or seen the steam rising from them. In any case, any "tasting" will have been simulated, since the actor is masked.

1070. **Bacis**: an ecstatic prophet of Eleon in Boeotia, to whom were ascribed many predictions dealing chiefly, so far as our evidence goes, with wars and the fate of cities and peoples; the implication of our passage that his inspiration was believed to have come from the Nymphs is confirmed by Pausanias 4.27.4, 10.12.11. He was credited with having predicted many of the main events of the Persian War (Hdt. 8.20.2; 8.77; 8.96.2; 9.43), and oracles going under his name seem to have been extremely popular during the Peloponnesian War (cf. *Knights* 123-4, 1003; *Birds* 962-980). Later, like Sibylla (cf. on 1095), he multiplied, so that Aelian *VH* 12.35 (early third century A.D.) says there are three Bacides.

1074. **These have to be sprinkled with the salt**: is Trygaeus pointedly taking no notice of the oracle, or is he deliberately interrupting Hierocles in order to "complete" his sentence with an irrelevant and anticlimactic clause?

1077. **the root-beetle**: Greek *sphondūlē*, an insect, probably a beetle, which ate pungent plant-roots (Thphr. *HP* 9.14.3), was often found indoors (*Hippiatrica Berolinensia* 119 [p. 379.24 Oder-Hoppe]), and used a foul-smelling secretion to help it escape from enemies.

1078. **Acalanthis**: apparently a lofty poetic name for the polecat (cf. 796), derived from a myth which has been discussed by E.K. Borthwick, *CR* 18 (1968) 134-8. The myth told how the endeavour of Hera to prolong the birth-pangs of Alcmena and delay the birth of her child Heracles (cf. *Iliad* 19.96-133) was frustrated by the ruse of a friend or servant of Alcmena named Acalanthis (Libanius *Narr.* 8 Förster) or Galanthis (Ovid *Met.* 9.285-323) or Galinthias (Antoninus Liberalis 29) or Historis (Pausanias 9.11.3) and, in most versions, how she was punished by being turned into a polecat.   Editors have previously taken *akalanthis* as a common noun, but this gives nonsense: *akalanthis* means "gold-finch", and the proverb about hasty parturition resulting in defective offspring (see next note) can obviously never have been applied to a bird.

1078.   **hurries on . . . blind offspring**: alluding to a proverb "the bitch in a hurry brings forth blind offspring" which is also echoed in Archilochus fr. 196a.39-41 West (D) and Aesop *Fab.* 223 Perry. Only here in Greek is it applied to an animal other than the dog. The emendation *kōdīnōn* "and . . . her birth-pangs", in place of the manuscripts' *khē kōdōn* "and the bell" which in its context makes neither sense nor grammar, was proposed by T.L. Agar, *CQ* 12 (1918) 198, and independently by Borthwick (see previous note).

1082.   **rule Greece together**: many Greeks believed in 421 that the Peace of Nicias would indeed result in such a joint Athenian-Spartan dictatorship over Greece; cf. Thuc. 5.29.3-4.

1084.   **dine in the Prytaneum**: the right to take meals at the public expense in the Prytaneum (the building which housed the sacred civic hearth of the Athenian state) was an honour that was normally awarded to winners at the great athletic festivals and sparingly to other persons of exceptional distinction or achievement (e.g. in 425 Cleon received this honour for his victory at Pylos-Sphacteria: see *Knights* 280-3, 709, 766). Hierocles had evidently been honoured in this way at some time for services he had rendered as an expert on oracles and religious matters, perhaps in connection with the Euboean campaign (see on 1046). On the various categories of persons who might be so honoured, see M.J. Osborne, *ZPE* 41 (1981) 153-170.

1085.   **compose . . . after the event has happened**: for this interpretation of a line that has usually been misunderstood, see C. Carey, *CQ* 32 (1982) 466-7, who compares *Birds* 962-5 ("There is an oracle of Bacis that directly refers to Cloudcuckooville." — "Then how come you didn't proclaim that oracle till after I'd founded this city?").

1089.   **Homer's work**: actually the ensuing "oracle" is a patchwork of Homeric formulae (most of them modified in wording) put together on the spur of the moment by Trygaeus himself. 1090 is concocted on the basis of *Iliad* 16.251 and 17.243; 1091 is Trygaeus' free composition; 1092 = *Iliad* 1.464; 1093 combines phrases adapted from *Odyssey* 7.137 and 6.261.

1091.   **installed her with a sacrifice** (sc. of an animal): cf. on 923.

1094.   **a gleaming mug**: the phrase echoes the Homeric "gleaming mixing-bowl" (*Iliad* 3.247), with *krētēr* "mixing-bowl" replaced by *kōthōn* which denotes a drinking-vessel (of uncertain type) that was more suited to the use of travellers, soldiers and sailors than to occasions of festivity (cf. *Knights* 600 and see B.A. Sparkes, *JHS* 95 [1975] 128-9).

1095.   **Sibylla**: an ecstatic prophetess, first mentioned by Heracleitus fr. 92 D-K, whose earliest associations may have been with Erythrae in Ionia. In *Knights* 61 she is alluded to as one alleged source of bogus oracles used by "Paphlagon" (= Cleon). Later she proliferated into a multitude of separate "Sibyls" in various localities, the best known being at Cumae in Italy.

1097-8.   **"No clan, no right . . . of intestine war"**: *Iliad* 9.63-64. The couplet originally refered to those who stir up *civil* war (*epidēmios* "within a community"), declaring that they deserve to be treated as outlaws. Either Trygaeus has misunderstood *epidēmios*, taking it to mean "coming upon a community", or else he means to imply that wars among Greeks are comparable to civil wars (for this attitude cf. *Lys.* 1128-34, Pl. *Rep.* 470c-471b).

1100. **a kite:** it would appear that Hierocles intends this bird, famous as a swift and daring robber (cf. *Birds* 892, 1622-5; Pl. *Phd.* 82a), to represent the Spartans, as did the monkeys, fox-cubs, etc., of his earlier utterances; but the kite was thought to be particularly fond of snatching the offals at sacrifices (cf. Semonides fr. 12; Pausanias 5.14.1), and Trygaeus understands the "oracle" as a warning that Hierocles is about to do some offal-snatching himself.

1103. **do the job myself:** lit. "act as my own bathman", an everyday metaphor for helping oneself instead of waiting to be served. The meaning seems to be that since Trygaeus is evidently determined to perform the whole of the ritual himself without calling on Hierocles' professional services, Hierocles will perform the ritual separately on his own account, likewise without assistance. In order to do so, however, he needs wine and offals, and presently he tries to get some.

1104. **Libation, libation:** as at 433, the ritual call stands outside the metre.

1106-7. **that is not yet pleasing . . . this must first happen:** here Trygaeus begins to cast Hierocles' words back at him (cf. 1074-5).

1109. **give me the tongue:** cf. on 1060.

1109. **you take your tongue away from here:** Trygaeus is angry with Hierocles for having spoken while the libation was being poured.

1110. **Libation:** most recent editors have assigned this call to the slave, who must then be assumed to be about to pour a libation of his own; but the libation on the altar after a sacrifice was normally poured by one person only, the person in charge of the sacrifice (cf. *Iliad* 1.462-3, 11.772-5). Hence I prefer to revert to the older view that the libation announced here is an unauthorized one by Hierocles.

1110. **these:** we cannot tell for certain what is referred to. It is unlikely that blows are meant, since there is no other indication of physical violence until 1119 (cf. B. Marzullo, *Museum Criticum* 5-7 [1970-2] 99); my guess that the reference is to portions of the offals is based on the facts (i) that *splankhna* "offals" is neuter plural, like the pronoun *tautī* used here, and (ii) that when one makes a libation in these circumstances one expects to be given a portion of offals (cf. 1102, 1105). Those who assume that the libation in 1110 is being poured by the slave likewise suppose that Trygaeus here gives the slave such a portion. For Hierocles, however, the offals would not be handed over in friendly fashion: they would be flung at him so hard that he would have little chance of catching anything and might even be startled into dropping his libation-bowl.

1112. **till a wolf shall wed a sheep:** cf. 1076a.

1113. **I beseech you:** lit. "by your knees": for the phrase cf. Eur. *Med.* 709-710, [Dem.] 58.70; for the importance of touching the knees in the act of supplication, see J. Gould, *JHS* 93 (1973) 75-77.

1114. **never will you make the prickly hedgehog smooth:** cf. 1086.

1115-6. **come here and share the offals with us:** the audience have no chance to accept this offer, since Hierocles' attempt to snatch some of the food creates a diversion.

1118. **it's there to be taken:** lit. "it lies in the middle", a phrase often used of prizes for which anyone may compete (cf. Xen. *Anab.* 3.1.21, Dem. 4.5).

1119.	hit Bacis: Hierocles is equated with the prophet whose mouthpiece he claims to be.
1119.	Witness, everyone: Greek *martūromai*, an appeal to anyone present or within earshot to bear witness (when the matter comes to trial) that the utterer was the victim of an assault: in *Ach.* 926, as here, *martūromai* is the last word spoken by an obnoxious character (cf. also *Clouds* 1297, *Wasps* 1436, *Birds* 1031).
1122-3.	strip him: the Greek verb *ekbolbizein* suggests the idea of peeling off the sheepskins as one peels an onion.
1122-3.	those sheepskins: it was a very widespread custom for the skin of a sacrificial victim to be given as a perquisite to the officiating priest: cf. *Thesm.* 758; *IG* i³ 35.11; *SEG* xxi 541.I.50-51; *SIG*³ 1002.3, 1004.30, 1010.5. However, the rule did not apply to all sacrifices, and Hierocles seems here to be accused of demanding and receiving skins to which he had no proper claim in religious law.
1123.	dishonestly: lit. "himself", i.e. on the strength of his own unjustified assertion that they belonged to him (for this use of *autos* "himself" cf. *Iliad* 1.356, 19.89: Agamemnon did not take Briseis from Achilles "personally", for he sent heralds to fetch her, but he did take her "on his own authority", without the consent of the army).
1124-6.	For the division of this passage among the speakers, see B. Marzullo, *Museum Criticum* 5-7 (1970-2) 100.
1125.	what a raven that was: the point is that ravens, like kites (see on 1100), were notorious for stealing sacrificial meats: cf. Aesch. *Supp.* 751-2 with the note of Friis Johansen and Whittle.
1126.	Elymnium: a rocky island off Euboea (Stephanus of Byzantium p. 269.19 Meineke; cf. Soph. fr. 888) on which was a sanctuary called the bridal bower of Zeus and Hera (so the scholia here report, citing Soph. fr. 437). If Hierocles wants to snatch sacrificial meats, let him do so at some sanctuary near his home town of Oreus!
1127-90.	Second parabasis, consisting of: strophe, 1127-39; epirrhema, 1140-58; antistrophe, 1159-71; antepirrhema, 1172-90.
1127-39 = 1159-71.	Metre: mainly cretic, with iambic elements in the first few lines; the closing section (1136-9 = 1168-71) is trochaic, a faster, livelier rhythm which leads easily into the trochaic epirrhema.
1129.	cheese and onions: typical soldiers' far (cf. 368, 529).
1136-7.	toasting some chickpea and roasting acorn: chickpeas and sweet acorns were among the desserts (*tragēmata*) commonly eaten after a meal to accompany the drinking: cf. *Eccl.* 45, Xenophanes fr. 22.3 D-K, Pl. *Rep.* 372c.
1138.	Thratta ("Thracian girl") was a common name for a female slave: cf. *Ach.* 273, *Wasps* 828, *Thesm.* 279-293, Pl. *Tht.* 174a-c, *IG* i³ 421.34, 35, 40.
1140-58 = 1172-90.	Metre: trochaic tetrameters, ending in a brief *pnīgos*. No other trochaic epirrhema in a parabasis ends thus.
1141.	the god: Zeus.
1142-58.	The division of this imaginary dialogue between speakers can be determined from the following considerations. (1) There will be only three men at the party — the chorus-leader himself (Comarchides), his neighbour, and Charinades (1155); no one else is mentioned, and with three men present each will have a whole bird (1149) and a helping of hare (1153). (2) Since Charinades has still to be invited, there are only two speakers in this dialogue. (3) The words "And from my house" (1149) show that there is a change of speaker at that point. (4) The foods mentioned in 1144-5 are everyday fare, while those

mentioned in 1149-50 are luxuries; hence it is probably the neighbour, not Comarchides, who is imagined as speaking 1149ff, since while it is always pleasant to eat and drink instead of working in the fields, it is even more so when this is done mainly at someone else's expense. Since we know that the neighbour is also the speaker of 1142, it follows that 1143-8 are imagined to be spoken by Comarchides.

1142.   **Comarchides**: an appropriate name for the leader of a comic chorus, being derived from *kōmos* "band of revellers" (cf. *kōm-ōidiā* "comedy") and *arkhos* "ruler, chief"; see F. Heberlein, *Pluthygieia: Zur Gegenwelt bei Aristophanes* (Frankfurt, 1980) 100 n.108. In *Wasps* 230 an ordinary member of the chorus bears the name Comias.

1144.   **quarts**: the Greek *khoinix* was actually rather less than a quart or rather more than a litre.

1144.   **cowpeas**: Greek *phasēloi*, a type of pulse most plausibly identifiable with a variety of, or a species similar to, the cowpea or black-eyed bean (*Vigna sinensis*).

1146.   **Syra** ("Syrian girl") is attested as a slave-name at Athens in third-century comedy (Philemon fr. 125; Apollodorus of Carystus fr. 8) and in *IG* ii^2 12687.

1146.   **Manes**: a common Phrygian name (cf. *IG* i^2 1084.2) much used for male slaves of Phrygian origin (*Birds* 1311; *Lys.* 908, 1211; *IG* ii^2 12034; cf. Strabo 7.3.12).

1147.   **work on the vines**: this is one of two interpretations of Greek *oinarizein* offered in the scholia. The other, "strip off surplus leaves", is to be rejected, since this was done in summer to help the grapes ripen (cf. Theocr. 7.134; Columella 11.2.61), whereas the reference to the completion of sowing (1140) indicates that the imaginary time of the dialogue is in the winter half of the year. At that time the most important work to be done on the vines was pruning (Hes. *Works* 570; Columella 4.23).

1149.   **the thrush**: for thrush as a delicacy cf. on 531.

1149.   **the two chaffinches**: chaffinch is paired with thrush in culinary contexts in Ar. fr. 387.7 Kock = 402.7 K-A and Eubulus fr. 150.5.

1150.   **beestings**: the first milk after birth, mentioned as a delicacy in *Wasps* 710 (alongside hare) and in Cratinus fr. 142 Kock = 149 K-A.

1150.   **hare**: cf. 1196, 1312; *Ach.* 878, 1006, 1110-2; *Knights* 1192-9; *Wasps* 709.

1153.   **give one to my father**: the neighbour's father, it seems, will stay at home, being too old to go to the party.

1154.   **some myrtle-branches, the ones with berries on**: the berries will be removed and eaten (cf. Pherecrates fr. 148; Phoenicides fr. 2; Pl. *Rep.* 372c) and the branches then either plaited into wreaths (cf. Eur. *Alc.* 759) or held by the symposiasts when they sing (cf. *Clouds* 1365; Ar. fr. 430 Kock = 444 K-A).

1154.   **from Aeschinades' place**: since the manuscripts' reading *ex Aiskhīnadou* cannot be proved corrupt, I retain it, but it is under grave suspicion. The second syllable of the same name ought to have a short vowel and not, as metre here demands, a long one; and it is surprising that Ar. should have chosen to use two such similar names as Aeschinades and Charinades in the same metrical place in successive lines. Van Leeuwen's conjecture, "six (myrtle-branches) from Aeschines", is very tempting: with six branches, as he notes, each man at the party would have one to hold in his hand and one to make into a wreath (see previous note).

1155.   **will someone call**: the change from second to third person is without significance, and does not imply that more than one slave is to go on the "errand". The neighbour, who is calling into his house from outside, is not addressing one of his slaves in particular, but whichever of them may happen to be available.

1155.   **Charinades** is also the name of one of the old jurors in *Wasps* 232.

1159.   **the cicada:** lit. "the chirper"; there is a reminiscence of Hes. *Works* 582ff "When . . . the chirping cicada sits on a tree and pours out his clear-toned song . . . . then let there be the shade of a rock, and Bibline wine, and milk cakes, and the last milk of goats, and the meat of a heifer . . . and of newborn kids."

1162.   **Lemnian vines:** a variety of which little is heard elsewhere, but mentioned in the fourth century by Androtion, *FGrH* 324 F 80.

1168.   **"Beloved Seasons":** possibly the opening words of a traditional expression of thanksgiving to the Seasons, goddesses of the annual cycle of nature, for bringing round again the time of fruitfulness: cf. Theocr. 15.102-5 and (for the association between the worship of the Seasons and the growth of crops and fruits) Philochorus, *FGrH* 328 F 5 and 173.

1169.   **pound some thyme and mix a drink:** a beverage made with thyme was often taken together with figs, as an aid to their digestion: cf. Athenaeus 3.79e, quoting the medical writer Phylotimus.

1172.   **taxiarch:** see on 444.

1173.   **scarlet cloak:** Greek *phoinikis* (cf. on 303).

1174.   **Sardian colour:** as the name *phoinīkis* indicates, the dye of the cloak will have been the famous dark-red dye made in Phoenicia from the murex shell; but this dye was widely exported for use in the manufacture of luxurious garments, and many such garments came to Greece from (or by way of) Sardis, the old capital of Lydia (cf. *Wasps* 1136-49), so that by the 420s the term "Sardian colour" was in common use (it is applied to blood in *Ach.* 112).

1176.   **Cyzicene colour:** the pale colour of electrum, the alloy of gold and silver used in the coins of Cyzicus (a city on the Asian shore of the Sea of Marmara) which circulated widely throughout the Greek world. There may also be a suggestion, by means of a pun on *khezein* "defaecate", that the taxiarch soils himself in his terror (see on 241).

1177.   **a tawny horsecock:** the horsecock *(hippalektruōn)* was a mythical beast with the front end of a horse, the rear end of a cock, and wings; it appears often in Athenian art of the sixth and early fifth centuries. See H. Lechat, *Revue des Universités du Midi* 2 (1896) 121-130 = *Au musée de l'Acropole d' Athènes* (Lyon, 1903) 453-464; D. von Bothmer, *Bulletin of the Metropolitan Museum of Art* 11 (1952-3) 132-6; J. Boardman, *Athenian Black-figure Vases* (London, 1974) pl. 150. These pictorial representations are unlikely to have been known to Ar., and for him the horsecock was probably no more than a name which he knew from a reference in Aeschylus' *Myrmidons* (fr. 134N = 212f M) to a "tawny horsecock" painted as an emblem on a ship. The phrase caught his fancy, and he uses it again in *Birds* 800 (likewise of a strutting military officer) and *Frogs* 930-4. The adjective *xouthos* is here translated "tawny" merely for convenience; it is doubtful whether the fifth-century poets who used the word (mainly in describing birds and bird-like creatures) could have assigned any definite meaning to it (see M.S. Silk, *CQ* 33 [1983] 317-9).

1178.   **like a net-watcher:** when hares were hunted, it was usual to set up nets to trap the hare as she tried to escape the hounds. A man was posted to keep watch on the nets, and he had to stay by them continuously while hunter and hounds were away finding and chasing the hare. See Xen. *Cyneg.* 6.11-26. The text has been suspected of corruption, because the first vowel of *līnoptōmenos* "net-watching" (from *linon* "flax, net") would normally be expected to be short, not long as for metrical reasons it must be here; however, a long vowel seems to be found in other compounds of *linon* in Soph. fr. 44 and Antiphanes fr. 49.

1180.   **enter ... on the lists:** the lists are of men called up to serve on forthcoming military expeditions. In *Knights* 1369-71 it is similarly complained that these lists are altered after they have been compiled, through corruption or favouritism.

1182.   **the man:** the Greek has merely a pronoun, as if our attention were already focused on a typical citizen going about his business unaware that he had been called up to go on campaign next day.

1182.   **provisions:** the "three days' rations" of 312.

1183.   **in front of the statue of Pandion:** Pandion, a legendary king of Athens, was the eponymous hero of the tribe Pandionis. His statue, together with those of the eponyms of the other nine tribes, stood in the western part of the Agora, and around this monument public notices of many kinds were displayed: notices relating particularly to a given tribe or its members would naturally be placed next to the statue of that tribe's eponym. See *Agora* iii 85-90, xiv 38-41, and T.L. Shear, *Hesperia* 39 (1970) 145-222.

1185.   **a curdling look:** lit. "a fig-juice look": the acid latex of the fig-tree was used for curdling milk (cf. *Iliad* 5.902-3). Ar. is fond of calling a mordant, irate facial expression "an X look" where X is the name of some acrid herb or fluid: cf. *Ach.* 254, *Knights* 631, *Wasps* 455, *Frogs* 603, *Eccl.* 292.

1186.   **these men ... throwing their shields away:** lit. "these shield-droppers to (in the eyes of) gods and men", where *rhīpsaspides* "shield-droppers" is a surprise substitute for *ekhthroi* "(persons) hateful". Throwing away one's shield was the classic sign of cowardice: cf. 446, 678, 1298-1301.

1189-90. **acting like lions at home but like foxes in battle:** i.e. seeming courageous only so long as they do not have to prove their courage in action. The expression was proverbial; in the early fourth century it seems to have been applied especially to Spartan soldiers and officials who when abroad displayed none of the traditional Spartan virtues (the scholia here have one variant of the saying, Plut. *Comparison of Lysander and Sulla* 3.2 has another).

1192.   **what a crowd's come to dinner:** Trygaeus' house is so full of guests that he has had to come outside to give instructions to his slave. We need not assume that the guests have been seen by the audience entering the house: Trygaeus' exclamation pictures the scene they are to imagine within, without the need to bring on a large number of silent extras.

1193.   **wipe the tables clean with this:** the text gives us no clue to what "this" is, except that it is an item of military equipment (cf. 1194) the Greek word for which is of feminine gender. The scholia suggest a helmet (*perikephalaiā*), whose crests could be used for sweeping the table; but the normal Aristophanic word for helmet is *kranos*, which is neuter. Several editors have suggested that the object is a soldier's cloak (*khlamus*); but the *khlamus* was by no means exclusively a military garment (see Stone 169). There is much to be said for the suggestion put forward, but not adopted, by van Leeuwen that the reference is to the headband (*tainiā*?) which Athenian soldiers tied round their heads before putting on their helmets: cf. (I. von Müller and) A. Bauer, *Die griechische Privat- und Kriegsaltertümer* (Munich, 1893) 350 and figs. 27, 28; A.M. Snodgrass, *Arms and Armour of the Greeks* (London, 1967) pl. 45. The headband would have to be fairly thick, and one could imagine its being used as a scrubbing cloth.

1197.   **I'm stewing thrushes:** there is no other sign that Trygaeus is doing his cooking on stage (as

190

Dicaeopolis does in *Ach.* 1003ff and Peisetaerus in *Birds* 1579ff), so presumably he
means "I am busy at present; I want to go back inside and finish stewing the thrushes".

1200. **a mite:** Greek *kollubos*, a very small coin; its value at Athens is not known, nor has it been
identified numismatically, but on the analogy of inscriptional evidence from other areas
it is probable that there were between 16 and 32 *kolluboi* to an obol (between 96 and
192 to a drachma). For the evidence see M.N. Tod, *Numismatic Chronicle* (6th series)
5 (1945) 108-116, 6 (1946) 47-62.

1201. **for fifty drachmas:** the text has often been suspected because (1) the first syllable of *drakhmē*
"drachma" has exceptionally to be scanned long, (2) the price is too high, (3) it is out
of proportion to the price of jars mentioned in 1202. But (1) the scansion has parallels
(*Wasps* 691; *Wealth* 1019; Men. *Epitr.* 335; Men. fr. 951.5); (2) the whole point is that
there is a fantastic boom in sales of agricultural equipment, as formerly in sales of military equipment (for which equally absurd prices are quoted later: 1224, 1241, 1251);
(3) pottery was needed for so many purposes, and was so liable to breakages, that it is
not surprising to find it selling very much more cheaply than metal implements.

1201. **jars:** or "buckets"; Greek *kados* "is . . . a fairly general word that takes its specific meaning
from the context" (B.A. Sparkes, *JHS* 95 [1975] 127-8).

1204. **please also accept this:** the third gift is referred to in the Greek by a neuter plural pronoun,
which could denote anything. I accept the suggestion of van Leeuwen that it consists of
food, and that this is the food which is offered to the chorus in 1305ff; similarly, the
"gear" which the chorus are told in 1318 to take home to the countryside may be represented on stage by the sickles and jars brought in the present scene. This accounts for the
otherwise curious fact that Trygaeus asks for the gifts to be left outside, when it would
have been easier and quicker for the visitors, who are already carrying them, to bring
them in.

1210. **ARMS-DEALER:** Greek *kapēlos* denotes a retail dealer, a man who sells goods which he
has not made but bought from others. The manuscripts divide the part here assigned to
the arms-dealer into five different speaking roles (a crest-maker, a cuirass-maker, a trum-
pet-maker, a helmet-maker and a spear-maker); but only three individuals are mentioned
in the actual text — the retail dealer (1209), a spear-maker (1213, 1260), and a helmet-
maker (1255; he is "this man" in 1213) — and it is almost certain that the second and
third of these are non-speaking parts: even in the passage about helmets (1250ff) it cannot be the helmet-maker who is speaking, since the speaker says he *bought* the helmets.

1211. **ill with a crest complaint:** the Greek verb used, *lophān*, is comically derived from *lophos*
"crest" on the model of many verbs referring to diseases, e.g. *lithān* "suffer from a cal-
culus" from *lithos* "stone", *splēniān* "have an enlarged spleen", *podagrān* "have gout".

1215. **I'm ashamed to name it:** Trygaeus is still pretending to play the bargaining game which he
began in 1214, the object of which, on both sides, is to avoid being the first to name a
price. Here he declines to name his offer on the ground that the seller might think it
ridiculously low. In reality, however, he has no intention of buying the crests at all, and
in a moment he will in fact be making an offer which *is* ridiculously low and which he
knows to be so.

1216. **collar:** Greek *sphēkōma*, lit. "wasping", probably a metal band holding the hairs of the
crest together and pinching them like the waist of a wasp.

[1218]. The manuscripts have an additional line at the end of Trygaeus' speech: "so that I can wipe

the table clean with this". Not only would this be a dull repetition of 1193, but the singular *toutōi* "with this" could not refer to a *pair* of crests which have been described in
the dual number in 1214 and 1217. Probably the line was in origin a variant form of
1193, accidentally inserted in the text in the wrong place, and later adjusted to fit its
context grammatically as far as possible.

1222.   **rubbish:** lit. "nothing".

1224-5.   **this rounded cuirass:** lit. "this concave container (in the form) of a cuirass", a tragic turn
of phrase (cf. Aesch. *Seven* 495-6, Eur. *Supp.* 1202) which here rubs shoulders incon-
gruously with the salesman's patter of "a beautiful fit" and the prosaic reference to the
article's cost price.

1224-5.   **a beautiful fit:** the Greek phrase, to which there is no exact parallel, might alternatively be
rendered "beautifully adorned with decorations", but in purchasing a cuirass there was
nothing more important than to make sure that it fitted well: cf. Xen. *Mem.* 3.10.9-15,
On Horsemanship 12.1, and on the type of cuirass apparently referred to here (a metal
one, shaped to the contours of the body) see Snodgrass, *Arms and Armour* 92. The
dealer has, of course, no right to assert that the cuirass is a good fit before it has been
tried on; but, desperate to make a sale, he is fitting the customer by eye, like a ready-
made tailor.

1224-5.   **ten minas:** one mina equalled 100 drachmas.

1228.   **it'll be very convenient to crap in:** M.I. Davies, *AJA* 84 (1980) 203, notes that the upturned
metal cuirass would somewhat resemble the shape of "the Greek child's potty".

1230.   **three stones:** Greeks used stones to wipe their bottoms (cf. *Wealth* 817-8), and according
to a proverb (quoted by the scholia) three rough stones or four smooth ones should be
enough for this purpose.

1232.   **the oarport:** the armhole is so termed in order to prepare the way for the joke in 1234
(see next note).

1234.   **leaving an oar of my ship unmanned:** lit. "stealing a hole of my ship". The basic pay of
naval oarsmen was supplied by the state, but its actual distribution to the men on each
ship was evidently the responsibility of the trierarch (the wealthy citizen appointed to
command the ship and be responsible for its maintenance). A trierarch might thus attempt to defraud the state by undermanning his ship and keeping the surplus money for
himself, and the present passage is evidence that official inspections were held to ensure
that this was not being done. As such an inspection the oarsmen, or at least those of the
lower tier (*thalamītai*, cf. *thalamiā* "oarport" 1232), would be ordered to extend "both
hands at once" through their respective oarports, enabling the inspectors to ascertain by
a quick visual check that the full complement was on board. The joke here is based almost entirely on the *phrase* "both hands at once", since Trygaeus' *action* is not the same
as that of the oarsman at an inspection — Trygaeus is putting his two hands through *different* "oarports". See J. Taillardat, *RPh* 38 (1964) 42-44.

1236-7.   **do you think . . . a thousand drachmas?:** two meanings are present simultaneously in this
question: (1) "my bottom is worth more than 1000 drachmas (=10 minas) to me" (and
therefore I am prepared to pay that amount to make sure that it is comfortable); (2) "I
would not become a homosexual prostitute at any price".

1242.   **this hole:** the broad end of the trumpet.

1243.   **the top end:** the mouthpiece; so too "this end" in 1247.

1244.   **one of the knock-off cottabus targets:** the game of cottabus (cf. 343) had two main varieties; the trumpet, it is suggested, could be made into a target for the variety called *kataktos*. In this form of the game the target consisted of a vertical rod, with a disc or basin half-way up and another balanced on the top; the object of the game was to dislodge the upper disc so that it fell and hit the lower one. The term *kataktos* may refer to the "bringing down" of the upper disc, or to the fact that some targets of this general type were telescopic, consisting of a thin rod within a larger one, so that the height at which the players had to aim could be varied. See Antiphanes fr. 55; Eubulus fr. 16; H.W. Hayley, *HSCP* 5 (1894) 73-82; B.A. Sparkes, *Archaeology* 13 (1960) 202-7.

1246-9. **Pour in the lead . . . out in the country**: the trumpet is to become the beam of a balance, with the scale-pan (and its contents) at one end being balanced by the weight of the lead at the other. Such a balance could be held in the hand, and would weigh out varying amounts according to where along its length it was held.

1250. **"Inexpiable curse, how thou didst ruin me"**: either a quotation from an unknown tragedy, or an imitation of tragic style: the speaker ascribes his misfortunes to an evil spirit or curse (*daimōn*), called into being by the crimes of some ancestor, which nothing he can do will purge or placate.

1254. **laxative**: Greek *surmaiā*, a drink used by Egyptians as a purgative and emetic (cf. *Thesm.* 857; Hdt. 2.77.2); according to the Alexandrian scholar Didymus, it was a mixture of salt water and radish juice.

1256. **this man**: the helmet-maker.

1258. **if he learns**: RV have "if you learn", which would have to be addressed to the helmet-maker himself, and would be the sole evidence in the actual text for his having a speaking part; but in 1259 they have a third-person verb like the other manuscripts, and it is therefore likely that "if you learn" here is an error (or a deliberate alteration) by a scribe who assumed (wrongly, as 1255 and 1256 show) that the helmet-maker was Trygaeus' interlocutor at this point.

1258. **to make handles like these**: an inverted helmet can be used as a bowl (cf. 1254), but bowls with handles would be more useful and fetch a better price than those without.

1262. **if they could be sawn in half**: the reference is to the long wooden shafts of the spears.

1266-7. **for a piss . . . in order to practise the openings**: the passage has often been suspected of being corrupt because two different reasons are given for the boys' coming out. It is, however, sound: the boys could have relieved themselves in the house had they wished, using a chamber-pot (*amis*: cf. *Wasps* 807, *Frogs* 544); instead they have come outside for the purpose, because they want to practise their songs.

1267. **what they're going to sing**: for the practice of boys singing or reciting epic or epic-style poetry after dinner cf. *Eccl.* 678-680.

1270-83, 1286-9, 1292-3. Metre: dactylic hexameters.

1270. **"But now let us begin of younger warriors –"**: the opening words of the cyclic epic *Epigonoi* (fr. 1 Allen), ascribed by some to Homer (Hdt. 4.32), by others to Antimachus of Teos (so the scholia here), which told the story of the successful attack on Thebes by the sons of the seven champions who had fallen before the city in the time of Eteocles and Polyneices. The lines orginally ended *Mousai* "O Muses"; here Trygaeus interrupts with the similar-sounding *pausai* "stop!"

1270-1. **stop singing of warriors**: in the Greek, Trygaeus' objection is to the word *hoploteroi* "younger", which suggests the unwelcome idea of *hopla* "arms, weapons".

193

1273-4. **"And when ... their centre-bossed shields"**: a slight misquotation of *Iliad* 4.446-9 ("And when, coming together, they reached the same spot, | they dashed together their bucklers, together came spears and the strengths of men | clad in bronze cuirasses; and their centre-bossed shields | came close to one another"). The altered version of the first line is one that appears several times elsewhere in the *Iliad* (e.g. 3.15). The telescoping of the quotation makes more evident the tautology that already existed in the original, the "bucklers" (*rhīnoi*) and the "centre-bossed shields" (*aspides omphaloessai*) being one and the same.

1276. **"And then together ... cries of triumph"**: *Iliad* 4.450.

1280-1. **"Thus they feasted ... most pleasant to taste"**: neither these lines nor the phrases composing them are found in surviving epic poetry in the form they have here (though see on 1282-3); it may be that Trygaeus is improvising in epic style, to give the boy an idea of the kind of subject-matter he prefers.

1281. **to taste**: R's reading *pásasthai* is greatly preferable to the variants *másasthai* "to seek, to desire" and *masâsthai* "to chew" (the latter a verb not found in epic).

1282-3. **"Thus they feasted ... sated with war"**: this couplet appears, in a slightly different form, in the *Contest of Homer and Hesiod* (107-8 Allen), which may be of sixth-century origin (see N.J. Richardson, *CQ* 31 [1981] 1-3).

1285. **how they ate after being sated**: Trygaeus' omission of "with war" humorously alters the meaning of the couplet from the *Contest*, as if the heroes had continued eating after being sated *with food*.

1286. **they fortified themselves**: Greek *thorēssonto*, by which the boy means "they put on their armour" but which can also (though not in epic) mean "they got drunk", whence Trygaeus' comment. There is a similar play on the two senses of this verb in *Ach.* 1134-5.

1287. **"And poured out ... unquenchable rose up"**: a modification of *Iliad* 16.267 ("walls" being substituted for "ships").

1290. **the son of Lamachus**: cf. on 304. In real life Lamachus appears to have had a son named Tydeus, after one of the Seven against Thebes; it may or may not be coincidental that the boy's first words in the present scene (1270) came from an epic about the sons of the Seven. See H.B. Mattingly, *op.cit.* (on 835 above) 238, and (for another possible allusion to this Tydeus) *Ach.* 965.

1293. **some lummock who wants ... not having one**: lit. "some man who is *boulomakhos* (wanting a fight) and *klausimakhos* (lamenting a fight)", playing twice on Lamachus' name. It is likely that *klausimakhos* is also intended to suggest that Lamachus is *klausomenos* "one who will howl, one who is destined to suffer" (cf. 1277, *Ach.* 1131).

1295. **Cleonymus**: see on 446.

1298-1301. **Metre**: the boy recites an elegiac couplet from Archilochus (see next note); Trygaeus interrupts with a hexameter; the boy then begins the next couplet, only for his hexameter to be interrupted and completed by Trygaeus.

1298-9. **"Some Saian now glories ... beside a bush"**: the opening of an elegiac poem by Archilochus (fr. 5), the seventh-century poet of Paros; the theme was imitated by Alcaeus (fr. 428) and Anacreon (fr. 36[b]) and later by Horace (*Carm.* 2.7.9-14). The Saioi were a Thracian tribe: Archilochus spent much of his life on the northern Aegean island of Thasos, where the Greek colonists were often at war with the Thracians of the mainland opposite. See H.D. Rankin, *Archilochus of Paros* (Park Ridge, N.J., 1977) 10-35.

1300. **my little cockerel**: Greek *posthōn*, from *posthē* "(small) penis".

1301.	"But I saved my life": the continuation of Archilochus' poem; the rest of the couplet, as quoted by various other authors, ran: "What do I care about that shield? Let it go hang! I can get another just as good."
1305-10 =	1311-5. Metre: iambic (two tetrameters, a dimeter, then two more tetrameters).
1306.	not let your oars trail idly: the allusion is to the practice of lashing oars to their tholepins, or to the side of the ship, when not in use: cf. *Odyssey* 8.37; Cicero, *In Verrem* 2.5.135; Ovid, *Met.* 11.475. The meaning is "not waste time, set to work at once".
1314.	you can find flat-cakes wandering about unclaimed: an echo of the notion, frequent in Old Comedy, of a Utopian world in which food comes to man without effort, sometimes literally asking to be eaten: cf. Crates fr. 14 Kock = 16 K-A; Telecleides fr. 1; Pherecrates fr. 108, 130; Metagenes fr.6; Nicophon fr. 13 Kock = 20 Edmonds.
1315.	The natural inference from the text is that the chorus now proceed to eat the food, presumably lifting up their masks to do so: cf. my discussion in *BICS* 31 (1984). Another possibility, however, is that when about to begin eating they are interrupted by the re-entry of Trygaeus, and eventually take the food away with them, to be consumed at a second feast when they arrive home in the countryside (cf. 1359).
1316-28.	Metre: four anapaestic tetrameters, followed by an anapaestic *pnīgos*.
1316.	let all speak fair: cf. on 96.
1317.	cheer us: or, with V^2, "dance in our honour".
1319.	getting rid of Hyperbolus: see on 681 and 921.
1328.	the glittering steel: i.e. weapons of war; the phrase is an epic one (e.g. *Iliad* 4.485).
1329-end.	On the text of this passage, and its division among voices, see H.J. Newiger, *RhM* 108 (1965) 241-254; B. Marzullo, *Museum Criticum* 5-7 (1970-2) 102-114; K.J. Dover, *ICS* 2 (1977) 158-162; Zimmermann 186-8. Newiger has shown that the brief and enigmatic fragments of metrical scholia which survive in V do not justify the positing of numerous lacunae in an attempt to "restore" a regular strophic structure, as was done by van Herwerden and Platnauer. In the assignment of lines, as between Trygaeus and the chorus, I agree with G. Mastromarco, *Commedie di Aristofane* i (Turin, 1983) 104-5; but I have also attempted to distinguish among different (groups of) voices within the chorus itself. There is also much inconsistency among editors as regards the numbering of the lines in this passage; I have followed the numbering employed by Coulon.
1329-59.	Metre: telesilleans and reiziana (cf. on 856-867).
1332.	Hymen, Hymenaeus, O!: the traditional wedding-chant (cf. *Birds* 1736, 1742, 1754; Eur. *Tro.* 314; Theocr. 18.58); from the time of Pindar (fr. 139.6), if not earlier, it was understood as an invocation of a wedding-god Hymen or Hymenaeus.
1339.	we'll gather her vintage: this easily-understood sexual metaphor (cf. Henderson 167) plays on the names of the bride (see on 523) and of the groom (see on 62); the pretence that the chorus, having got possession of the bride, mean to carry her off for a mass rape is typical of the heavy jocularity associated with weddings both ancient and modern (cf. 1351-2; Sappho fr. 110a, 111; Catullus 61.119-143).
1348.	cultivating your figs: to be taken in both an agricultural and a sexual sense, for the fig and the fig-tree were common metaphorical expressions for the female and male genitals respectively: cf. *Ach.* 996; *Eccl.* 708; Henderson 117-8, 135; V. Buchheit, *RhM* 103 (1960) 200-229.
351.	long and thick: cf. *Ach.* 787, *Lys.* 23-24, *Eccl.* 1048.
353.	you'll say that all right: i.e. you will felicitate us even more enthusiastically.

1358.   **if you follow along with me** is probably to be taken in two senses: (1) if you come now
to my home in the country (where another feast will be held); (2) if you make peace as
I have done.

1359.   **you'll have flat-cakes to eat**: and thus the play has come full circle, "from the dung cakes
of the opening line to the wedding cakes of the last" (C.H. Whitman, *Aristophanes and
the Comic Hero* [Cambridge, Mass., 1964] 110).